Corporations in the Moral Community

Corporations in the Moral Community

Peter A. French
Jeffrey Nesteruk
David T. Risser
with
John M. Abbarno

Harcourt Brace Jovanovich College Publishers

Fort Worth   Philadelphia   San Diego   New York   Orlando   Austin   San Antonio
Toronto   Montreal   London   Sydney   Tokyo

Publisher	Ted Buchholz
Acquisitions Editor	Jo-Anne Weaver
Senior Project Editor	Charlie Dierker/Steve Welch
Production Manager	Tad Gaither/Milt Sick
Art & Design Supervisor	John Ritland
Cover Design	Pat Sloan
Text Design	Circa 86, Inc.

Library of Congress Cataloging-in-Publication Data

French, Peter A.
    Corporations in the moral community / Peter A. French, Jeffrey
Nesteruk, David Risser with John Abbarno.
      p.   cm.
    Includes bibliographical references and index.
    ISBN 0-03-030782-1
    1. Social responsibility of business.   I. Nesteruk, Jeffrey.
II. Risser, David.   III. Title.
HD60.F75   1992
658.4'08—dc20   91-32044
                                                 CIP

ISBN: 0-03-030782-1

Address for Editorial Correspondence
Harcourt Brace Jovanovich College Publishers, 301 Commerce Street, Suite 3700, Fort
Worth, TX 76102

Address for Orders
Harcourt Brace Jovanovich College Publishers, 6277 Sea Harbor Drive, Orlando, FL 32887
1-800-782-4479, or 1-800-433-0001 (in Florida)

Printed in the United States of America

2 3 4 5   016   9 8 7 6 5 4 3 2 1

Contents

Preface   vii

Chapter 1   Ethics and Life at Liberty Oil   1

Chapter 2   How Corporations Qualify for Membership
in the Moral Community   12

Chapter 3   Management   25

Chapter 4   Employees   50

Chapter 5   Directors and Shareholders   64

Chapter 6   Political Perspectives, Economic Justice,
and Legal Aspects of Corporations   80

Chapter 7   Corporations in a Global Community   110

Appendix Relevant Documents   123

Index   173

Preface

The theory that the corporation itself is a moral actor is given serious consideration or treatment in only a few of the currently available business ethics texts. In those books, the focus is almost exclusively on the moral problems of individual human agents, such as managers and engineers, and to the extent that the corporation itself is given attention, it is often just the setting in which individual moral problems arise. Great social problems, however, not only are typically provoked by corporate actions, many of them can only be solved on the corporate level. Some have recently argued, Roger Scruton for example, that corporate entities are necessary if we are to effectively address the great problems confronting the world. In this book, we explore the concept that corporations should be treated as full-fledged members of the moral community. We start with an argument that corporations are moral persons, then build outward in various directions to generate a middle-level theory that should show how ethical analyses can be applied to particular corporate cases. The concept of corporate moral personhood bridges the gap between the practical demands of specific cases and more theoretical concerns.

The book begins with a fictional story involving both corporate and individual actors. The story becomes a point of reference in later chapters to highlight theoretical issues and to provide a context for the discussion of particular moral problems.

A corporation embodies a complex set of relationships around a structure for making decisions and is engaged in relationships with other groups and individuals. It is important to appreciate these relationships in order to understand corporate life from the moral point of view. Attention may be fruitfully focused on the corporation as a system of internal relationships and then expanded to include the corporation's relationships to other members of society, both individual and collective. Rather than attempt to achieve some objective or neutral perspective, we examine corporate behavior from a series of vantage points both within the organization itself and throughout society. Through the examination of these different perspectives, we expand the understanding of the place of corporations in the moral community.

A number of topics arise as we try to expose the place of corporations in the moral community. We arranged these topics so that we first examine the theoretical underpinnings of the idea that corporations are moral entities, then connect that discussion with topics of practical import. We start with the manager's view of corporate legal liability. That is a perspective with which readers should be able to identify, particularly if they plan business careers. We then look at issues specifically involving employees, directors, and shareholders. In the last two chapters, we study the legal and political roles of corporations and the place of corporations in the global community.

We are grateful to those scholars who reviewed the finished manuscript for this book and provided helpful comments: Judith Andre, Old Dominion University; Jan Edward Garrett, Western Kentucky University; Tony McAdams, University of Northern Iowa; Michael Palmer, Evangel College; Dean Spader, University of South Dakota; Paul Thompson, Texas A&M University; and Joan Whitman Hoff, Lock Haven University.

We also wish to express our heartfelt thanks to Virginia Redford, who produced the manuscript and coordinated our efforts.

About the Authors

Peter A. French

Peter A. French is Lennox Distinguished Professor of the Humanities and Professor of Philosophy at Trinity University in San Antonio, Texas. Dr. French has a national reputation in ethical and legal theory and in collective and corporate responsibility and criminal liability. He is the author of fifteen books including *Responsibility Matters*, *The Spectrum of Responsibility*, *Collective and Corporate Responsibility*, *Corrigible Corporations and Unruly Laws*, and *The Scope of Morality*. Dr. French is the senior editor of *Midwest Studies in Philosophy*, editor of the *Journal of Social Philosophy*, and was general editor of the *Issues in Contemporary Ethics* series. He has published numerous articles in the major philosophical journals, many of which have been anthologized.

Jeffrey Nesteruk

Jeffrey Nesteruk is an Assistant Professor of Business Policy and Environment at Rider College in Lawrenceville, New Jersey. He is a graduate of the University of Pennsylvania Law School. Professor Nesteruk has published a number of articles and book reviews in various legal journals such as the *Columbia Business Law Review*, *University of Cincinnati Law Review*, and *DePaul Law Review*. He is coauthor of *An Introduction to Law and the American Legal System*.

David T. Risser

David T. Risser is an Assistant Professor in the Political Science Department at Millersville University in Millersville, Pennsylvania. He teaches primarily in the areas of political theory and American politics. He holds a Ph.D. from Temple University in political science and publishes on collective agency, political responsibility, and democratic theory. Dr. Risser's most recent article appeared in *Business and Professional Ethics Journal*.

John M. Abbarno

John M. Abbarno is an Associate Professor of Philosophy at D'Youville College in Buffalo, New York. His doctoral degree in philosophy is from Southern Illinois University at Carbondale. He has written and published several articles on ethical theories and issues in applied ethics. Professor Abbarno is the president of the American Society of Value Inquiry.

Corporations in the Moral Community

Ethics and Life at Liberty Oil

R obert Krebs eased his Mercedes into his personal parking place at Liberty Oil Company's home office in Houston. It was only 9:30 in the morning, but the temperature was already above 90 degrees. It would be even hotter in the board room. The lead story in the morning news was from California. One of Liberty's tankers ran aground off Carmel. The ship broke up, and thousands of barrels of oil polluted Monterey Bay.

Krebs rode up in the elevator with Shirley Lewis, Liberty's director of public relations. An awkward silence lasted for two floors, then Lewis spoke.

"It's pretty bad news, isn't it?"

"Sounds like it."

"We met at the garden party last month. I'm Shirley Lewis, public relations . . . you're here for a special board meeting, aren't you?"

He nodded. "I expect you people are going to have to do a lot of spin control after this."

"We're on it. Currently, of course, we're basically just saying 'no comment' or 'we're sending a team there to evaluate the situation.'"

"That won't fly for long."

The doors opened on the fifth floor, and Lewis left the elevator for her office. She passed Harry Mayer in the hall. As a member of the corporate legal team, acquisitions of leases and other property matters are Mayer's specialty, but the oil spill was on his mind, as well.

"Shirley, do you guys know any more about the spill than was on the news?"

"It's worse than has been reported so far."

"How could that be? They say that even the inlets and small bays in the Pebble Beach area are devastated."

"That's true, but what *I* meant is that several of the ship's officers were high as kites."

"Drugs?" he asked.

"And booze," she replied.

"What are we doing about it?"

"That's for the board to decide this morning. Krebs was just on the elevator, going up to the tenth floor."

"Are the captain and the crew in custody?" Mayer continued.

"No, the police haven't got them."

"Do you know where they are?"

"Sort of."

"What's that supposed to mean?"

"It means that I'm not authorized to say anything about where they are," Lewis responded.

"You're kidding. We've got them hidden away somewhere?"

"Two were killed, did you know?"

"There was nothing about that on the news."

"Are they likely to bring you in on this, Harry?"

"No way. Acquisitions, leases, they're my thing. But this could mess up the deal we've got working in Ireland for a refinery and storage plant. That's been rough enough. We've got a referendum to defeat over there. All we need is this sort of thing. My boss, old Nevels, will take care of this spill business himself. He'll be at the board meeting. The other top guys are working on a way to head off the move Bartles Oil is making on us."

"I didn't know the merger was still in the works."

"It's hardly a merger. 'Hostile takeover' is more like it. It's hard to say whether the oil spill will hurt or help our position. I know we want to make ourselves look as unattractive as possible, economically, that is."

"That might protect management, Harry, but what about the ordinary employees? You know that layoffs and cutbacks could be a part of the way they build the picture to keep the raiders away."

"Since when has upper management cared about that? This is America. . . ."

"You're getting pretty cynical, Harry. I don't want to hear that gospel-of-greed stuff again."

The two continued to chat until Lewis's secretary called her to the phone.

Mayer headed down the hall to Charles Osborne's office. Osborne is a researcher assigned to the Irish project. Their conversation, like most of those in the building throughout the morning, opened with a discussion of the oil spill. Mayer, however, rapidly moved the discussion to the Irish election.

"Our negotiator is meeting with the city council of Waterville in Ireland tomorrow. He needs instructions."

"We're sure the harbor and the topology of the area are going to work?" It wasn't really a question, just Mayer's way of asking for further assurance.

"They're terrific—one of the best harbors in Western Ireland. You've seen my reports on the siting of the refinery and the storage tanks."

"The Irish environmentalists are going to devil us with this California business. We've got to make a big push if we're going to defeat the referendum. What do you think will do the trick?"

"Bribery," Osborne said facetiously.

"Sure, a few pints in the hands of half the folks in Kerry. Be serious."

"I am, in a way," Osborne continued. "We offer them economic improvement—you know—jobs. The Irish are desperate for jobs."

"But will they go for jobs against the environmental risks?" Mayer asked. "Damn, I wish this spill hadn't occurred just now. Still, we'll clean it up, and the Irish will act on their own interests."

"What makes you think they'll see their interests in financial terms? That's pretty country, you know."

"Oh, I'm sure there'll be enough of them who won't turn down the opportunity to get better-paying jobs."

"Well, if they find out that there really aren't that many jobs for them in the plant and that we're planning to move all the key personnel from Galveston, we're not going to win many votes," Osborne speculated.

"That's another thing. Are we really going to close Galveston? That's going to sting the economy there and it's already struggling."

"We've heard only rumors, but they're all over the building. The OSHA regs and the EPA controls are costing us a fortune in Galveston. At least in Ireland, governmental intervention will be minimal."

Mayer and Osborne continued to discuss the pluses and minuses of the Irish project, while five floors above them Krebs was engaged in the emergency board meeting that was as hot as he'd predicted.

Most of the board members accepted the president's contention that the captain and crew of the tanker should be held solely and fully responsible for the spill. It was agreed that stories would be released to the press to that effect, and that Liberty voluntarily would pay all costs of the cleanup, while admitting no corporate responsibility for the disaster.

Krebs was worried. "Will the press swallow that?"

"Why not?" was the board members' unison response.

"What was the captain's prior record?" Krebs asked.

He was told that no previous shipping accidents had been blamed on the captain. His record in that regard was clean.

"Yes, okay," Krebs continued, "but what's this you hinted about drugs and alcohol?"

"There are a few problems in that regard," Chief Counsel John (Jack) Nevels answered. He went on to explain that the captain's driver's license in Texas had been suspended twice for DWI arrests, and that he had been arrested three times, twice in California, on drunk and disorderly charges.

"What's the evidence on the drugs?" another board member asked.

"We didn't run urine tests on them, but there's a lot of material evidence that cocaine and marijuana were used on the ship. That can help us," Nevels responded.

"How?" asked Krebs.

"Our company rules forbid that stuff on the tankers. We can argue that we had nothing to do with the spill. It was an individual, not a corporate, matter. The guys on the ship were operating well outside their corporate positions."

He went on to explain that Union Carbide had used a similar defense with regard to the Bhopal tragedy, Exxon had tried it in the *Exxon Valdez* spill in Alaska, and that McDonnell-Douglas defended itself against negligence claims in a Paris air crash by showing that failure to confirm that repairs had been made on the plane was the fault of sloppy inspectors, not of company procedures and policies.

Krebs was not satisfied. He wondered if the company weren't seriously exposed even if the public *could* be persuaded that the primary responsibility for the disaster belonged to the captain and crew. "It was *our* ship doing *our* business," he said.

"That's why we'll agree to cover cleanup costs," said Nevels.

"And I suppose they can be written off."

"Taxes are the least of our problems," Nevels continued.

One of the other members interrupted. "Are you sure we want to pay for the cleanup? We might be better off to see what we can get in court. How can we control costs? Every fisherman on the coast will make a claim against us. The State of California will demand reparations, and before you know it, we'll be paying out hundreds of millions of dollars. We could be paying to clean the same rock ten times over. What's the point of laying the blame on the ship's officers, if we're going to pick up the tab anyway?"

The board member was told that it was important to the corporate image to dissociate the company from the cause of the spill. Paying for the cleanup also could have many positive features. Liberty should be seen as environmentally conscious, prepared to make right what its irresponsible employees damaged.

"God save us from ads with before-and-after pictures of sea otters!" uttered another board member.

"But are we not responsible?" asked Krebs. "Won't they say that we should have ensured that our ships were under competent hands, not run by drunks and drug addicts? It is *our* oil."

Nevels shook his head. "That's for a court to determine, if California prefers charges against us. For now we can give them the ship's officers."

"Don't they have them already?"

Nevels explained that Liberty's fast-thinking port director in Monterey had rounded up the captain and other officers and, using one of the company planes, had flown them to Mexico.

"We secreted them out of the country?" Krebs asked incredulously. "Isn't there something illegal in doing that?"

"They hadn't been charged with anything," one board member stated.

"But now they will be," Krebs added.

"It's possible," Nevels responded.

"Pretty likely, I'd say," Krebs retorted.

Other members raised questions about ways to distance the company from the incident and the limits of legal liability. One, Larry Putnam, refocused the discussion.

"Look, there's more to this than some oil on Monterey Bay that's killing a bunch of fish, birds, and otters. What about Bartles Oil? We could plunge on Wall Street when the stockholders realize that cleanup costs are going to take a big bite out of profits. Bartles Oil is lurking in those financial waters like a barracuda, ready to buy up as many of our shares as possible, positioning itself for another shot at us. What are we doing to fight that off?"

Company President Horace Quinn acknowledged the threat, but assured the board that Director of Product Marketing, Vice President Mary Rogers, and her team, having spent much of the evening analyzing the gasoline market, were confident that it would support a significant increase in pump prices, blamed in part, of course, on the wreck of the ship and the disruption that would occasion in the regular flow of oil.

Krebs exploded. "I don't believe it! We crack up a tanker because of a drunken captain and a drug-happy crew, and now we're going to get the consumers to pay for it so we can go on without hurting profitability."

Nevels smiled cynically, "The savings-and-loan industry's pulled it off. Why can't we?"

"Come on, the other oil companies aren't going to raise prices because we are. They'll reap the profits from higher volume, and there's bound to be anti-Liberty sentiment among those stirred up by the bleeding-heart environmentalists," Krebs countered.

Quinn interjected that he had good reason to believe that all the oil companies were looking for a reason to raise pump prices, so they would probably follow suit. Krebs was not convinced, but most of the other members were.

The meeting continued for some time, but after giving her report, Vice President Rogers left at noon to return to her office. She had a scheduled luncheon meeting with her brother Martin, a stockbroker in the Houston office of a major Wall Street firm. Their luncheons were monthly affairs, preserving family ties. They seldom talked business and when they did, the discussion was never specific. Rogers had no knowledge of her brother's clients or accounts.

During lunch, Martin asked his sister how Liberty was responding to the news of the big spill. Rogers, so carried away by the events of the last 24 hours that she didn't realize she was getting very specific, rattled on about the plan to lay the blame on the ship's officers, to offer to pay for the cleanup, while raising prices at the pump. She explained that Liberty was especially concerned about the Bartles Oil takeover bid and the possible loss of the referendum in Ireland, where the company was deeply committed to the building of a major refinery and storage unit. Her brother finally interrupted to ask if she wanted him to sell her shares in Liberty.

"Oh, I couldn't do that," she replied, then thought about it for a minute. "You really think I should? Could I make some money before it plunges?"

He assured her that he thought so. She could make a sizable profit if she sold now, before all these matters affected the market. Once he could be sure that Bartles Oil was buying and the price would rise again, he'd buy her back in. She could then sell it long to Bartles. She figured to make a killing going down and up. It was all a matter of timing—timing and knowledge.

It sounded good to her, but how would he know when to make the right moves? Her brother smiled and assured her that that would be no problem because he had connections with the man in New York who handled the Bartles Oil account. Convinced that she could hardly lose and that she stood to gain a great deal, she told her brother to sell her Liberty stock. He rushed back to his office and did so, then called his contact in New York, and told him everything he'd learned from his sister about the Liberty board meeting.

Rogers returned to her office where a message was waiting, asking (or ordering) her to President Quinn's office. With trepidation, she rode the elevator up to the tenth floor. She waited for five or 10 minutes while Quinn finished a telephone call to California.

"Mary, I want to thank you especially for the work you and your team put in on those analyses. That presentation really sold the board on the price increase. There'll be some big rewards in this for you."

"Thank you, Mr. Quinn. Of course, the others on the team deserve credit, too."

"I suppose that's right, but you're the one who brought it together. I'm proud of you."

Rogers was getting nervous about the praise being heaped on her, as she knew well that three other members of her staff had done most of the work. She'd organized them, that was true enough; but she kept a long-standing date, went to a concert, and only then returned to assemble the materials for the final presentation.

Gingerly she asked, "Was there much more discussion of the marketing issue?"

"Well, some, but most of the talk was about ways to keep Congress on our side in all this mess. I'm confident that the Texas contingent will back us."

"Back us how?"

"In California they're already calling for investigations of our shipping procedures, and you can bet that when the prices go up, the consumer-protection crowd will be screaming for congressional hearings. We'll need our friends on the Hill then."

"Senator Grafton's always been a free-market supporter."

"He'd better be. He's gotten his share of support from us over the years."

"Well, all the Texas legislators know how crucial we and the other oil companies are to the economy down here."

"That's the other reason I wanted to see you. You've heard the stories about our closing the Galveston plant when we build the refinery in Ireland?"

Rogers acknowledged that she had and wondered why that was relevant. Quinn explained that the Texas senators and representatives would be furious if the Galveston plant closed. A statement would be released from his office the next day, denying the rumors about the closing.

"Modernizing that plant to meet all the regulations would be expensive. That would eat up the profits from the higher pump prices," Rogers noted.

"That's what we'll tell Congress in order to get support for the price adjustment. Oh, there'll be some posturing, but you've got to let them do that. It's their votes that matter."

"So the plant closing is off?"

"I didn't say that. I said we'll release a statement denying the rumor, and that denial is what I want you to spread around."

"Oh, I see," Rogers said sheepishly.

"Still, that's not what's crucial here. I recall we've got, shall we say, a spy in the marketing section of one of our competitors."

"Bill Schwegel at Superior Oil," she said.

"I don't care what his name is. Does he report in to you this week?"

Rogers acknowledged that he did. Quinn told her to leak the higher prices plan to Superior through Schwegel, and then find out if Superior would follow suit or keep their prices at current levels and thereby weaken Liberty's position in the market.

Rogers returned to her office and jotted down a note to talk to the PR staff about the price-increase story. Her door was open. Charles Osborne passed and waved. He had just come from Bob Talcott's office where they'd ordered in sandwiches for lunch. Talcott, a friend of Osborne, worked in the transportation division. He spent most of his time on supervision of maintenance contracts for the company's tankers. Osborne had invited himself up for lunch to try to learn some of the inside scoop on the Monterey Bay disaster. Talcott was his usual gregarious self. He explained that the maintenance records on the tanker would stand up to any scrutiny. The president's office had called for copies, and Talcott had personally checked them. All regular service had been performed, and all federal regulations had been met or surpassed.

Osborne asked if there were anything about the ship that might be a target of some reporter's attempt to uncover more than just problems with the officers and crew. Talcott first spoke with confidence.

Everything on the ship had been first-class, he assured him. Then he shook his head.

"Well, there is something they may get on to. It was a single-hulled ship. It should have been three-hulled. Most tankers working for the other oil companies are three-hulled. All of Bartles Oil's ships are. The Japanese use nothing but three-hulled jobs. If it had had three hulls, it wouldn't have broken up. There would have been some loss, of course, but not as much as what occurred."

"Do you mean we're in violation of safety standards?" Osborne asked.

"Oh, hell no. We're okay. Somehow or other we got Congress to weaken the hull strength requirements," replied Mayer. "They'll do anything, if you contribute . . . well, you know. At any rate, that's Congress' fault, not ours."

Osborne worried about the fact that Liberty's fleet of oil tankers was below the industry standard and significantly beneath the state of the art, even though they satisfied governmental regulations. Back at Mayer's office, he asked Mayer what he thought about it, but Mayer shrugged it off.

"That's no big deal, but suppose the Irish environmentalists latch on to the fact that our ships are more vulnerable than most of the others? They're going to talk about a potential break-up in Ballenskelligs Bay. Think of pictures of dead birds and gooey, oil-covered otters on posters all over Ireland."

"We'll have to keep a lid on this, won't we?" Osborne asked. "You know, Harry," Osborne continued, "if Bartles Oil takes us over, they'll scrap or sell off our fleet. They use only three-hulled tankers. This sort of thing wouldn't happen with Bartles."

"You sound like you're pulling for the takeover," said Mayer.

"No, I didn't say that. What I mean is that . . . you know. . . . We should at least bring our ships up to the standards of the industry, not the artificial ones set by Congress."

"Charlie, we're the third most profitable oil company in America. We're in the top dozen corporations in *Fortune*, year-in, year-out. You and I get paid damn good salaries to do our jobs for Liberty. Leave the other stuff to the president and the board. You're a geological researcher for the acquisitions department. That has nothing to do with the number of hulls on a tanker. Just do your job well. That's all the law and ethics require of you."

Osborne acknowledged that Mayer was probably right, but he continued to worry about the fact that Bartles Oil's ships were obviously safer than Liberty's. Perhaps the takeover wouldn't be that bad for the company, he thought.   Certainly the shareholders would realize a sharp rise in the value of their stock.   There might be employment cutbacks, but Liberty itself was going to close Galveston, and there could be other closings on the drawing board.   Management would probably be replaced, but they'd arrange golden parachutes to ease their departures.   Maybe Liberty had run its course.   Everything has its time.   The disaster in California might be the sign of the end of the company, thought Osborne.

If Liberty did survive, it would have to rebuild its position.   He'd heard through the grapevine that there were plans to merge with a big retail store chain, if Bartles were beaten back.   That merger would diversify the company and prepare it for possible shifts in the dependency on oil in the next decades.   His job for now was relatively secure.   Still, it bothered him that his company was less than what he regarded as honorable in many of its recent activities.

After the board meeting, Krebs, as was his custom, wandered around the building, "to get a feel for what was happening," as he liked to say.   He ran into Nevels, who was leaving to attend a charity auction.   The event raised money for the Houston public television station.   Nevels also did pro bono work for the station.

Krebs asked Nevels if he had a few minutes.   Nevels, of course, made the time for a member of the board.

"Jack, we've been with this company for a long time," Krebs began.   Nevels knew what was coming.   He hated the "good-old-days" approach.   In the first place, he didn't want to be reminded that he'd been around for a long time, and secondly, for some years he'd divorced himself from corporate decision-making.   He thought of himself as just a legal facilitator.   He didn't plot strategy, didn't tell management what to do, and always tried to avoid making moral judgments about company business affairs.

"I don't like what's happening on this oil spill business.   We're in deep stuff, aren't we?   I still think we've got to make a clean breast of it all, give them some of the executives, and get back to business."

"Give whom to whom?" Nevels asked.

Krebs suggested that a few high-ranking executives might be "let go," and blamed for the California spill.   He hadn't any particular ones in mind.   Nevels only nodded, but Krebs persisted, so Nevels finally offered the opinion that there *could* be corporate criminal liability involved that would not be exhausted by laying the blame on the tanker's officers, its crew, and a few executives.   "The courts have been moving in that direction."

Krebs shook his head. They walked out together to their cars. "It's a different world, Jack. Whatever happened to the old-fashioned pursuit of profit and the simple values?"

"The simple values? They're still around. The business world just got too complex for them. The community in which we do business is now the whole damn world, and everyone's got an idea about what we ought to be doing and how and when. Half of the people are spying on the other half, trying to catch them in some infraction or other, if only to embarrass them. We're targets, successful corporations. The press wants us, government is after us, and so are consumer advocates and other corporations. You name it. It's a moral jungle."

"How then do we and Liberty Oil survive . . . and thrive in that community?" asked Krebs. "You're corporate counsel. What's the law of the jungle?"

How Corporations Qualify for Membership in the Moral Community

L iberty Oil is in deep trouble on a number of counts. Some are legal, some financial, some political, but most are moral or have strong ethical over-tones. How should we understand moral judgments made about Liberty? Consider these examples that might appear in the press:

(a) Liberty Oil is responsible for polluting Monterey Bay.

(b) Liberty Oil should not have used single-hulled tankers, despite the federal regulations.

(c) Liberty ought not to close its Galveston plant.

(d) Liberty is to blame for the rise in pump prices.

(e) Liberty's support of public television is exemplary corporate citizenship.

In all of these examples, the name of the corporation appears, and no reference is explicitly made to individual human beings. It looks as if Liberty Oil is being treated as a member of the moral community, as a subject of moral evaluation. Does that make sense? Should Liberty Oil (and other corporations) be included in the class of moral persons, the class of entities to whom moral principles, rules, and judgments apply? Or, are statements like (a)–(e) in need of translation before they can be understood from the moral point of view? Are all apparent moral judgments about Liberty Oil actually moral judgments about individual human beings?

It is natural to say such things about Liberty Oil. We regularly say similar things about other corporate entities. ("Allied Chemical is responsible for polluting the James River"); governmental bodies ("The Congress should not have given itself a raise"); sports teams ("The Dodgers ought not to have moved from Brooklyn to Los Angeles"); and groups of people ("The people on the plane deserve praise for the way they responded to the crash landing"). In all of these cases we use a name (or a collective noun) to refer to an entity that includes human beings, though we do not specifically identify who those people are. Sometimes, of course, we refer to the entity just as a convenient way of talking about individual people, those who are members of the entity. Think of the people on the airplane. When we say that they deserve praise for their behavior in the crisis, we mean that each of the passengers did something worthy of some degree of praise. At the very least, none of them lost control and so disrupted the others that orders were not followed, and so on. If we say that the people on the corner should have helped the elderly woman (when she was being harassed by a few punks), we are saying that none of them did so. Furthermore, we are saying that each ought to have gone to the woman's aid, that each had a moral obligation to do so. The group all but disappears when we try to explain what we were saying about it.

Some group cases are not so easily reduced to their membership. If the action(s) or the task(s) in question cannot be done by an individual but requires concerted effort, we might blame the group for the failure to do it, but only blame the individuals for their failure to do some portion of the task. For example, if 10 people were needed to move a boulder that blocks an escape for miners trapped in a shaft collapse and 10 bystanders failed to make the effort, we should blame that group for the fact that the boulder wasn't moved. Since no one individual could have moved the boulder, however, we could hardly hold each of them responsible for not moving it. On the other hand, we could hold each of them responsible for not organizing the rest into a viable unit to move the boulder. Some of the group, however, may lack organizational skills. On discovering that, we might focus the blame only on those capable of succeeding in getting the others to do the task. Suppose one such person in the group, rather than trying to organize the others, tries to move the boulder without help. All he manages to do is severely strain his back. Should his effort get him off the hook? It would seem not. He tried to do what he could not in any case do and omitted to do what he might have accomplished: organizing the group to move the stone. Those who try to singly do the right thing in circumstances where only a collective effort stands a chance of succeeding, hardly deserve credit.

Reduction of statements about groups to statements about the individuals that comprise them is usually adequate for social organizations or collectives that develop and function in ways analogous to the solar system. The solar system behaves in certain ways, but its behavior can be fully explained by applying scientific laws to its components, the planets, moons, sun, and so on. Understanding the behavior of the solar system involves reduction of the system to the behavior of its parts. Human organizations, however, are not all constructed in such a way. Many collectives act in ways that are not fully explainable by reducing the action to the behavior of members. "Congress should not have given itself a raise," may refer to such a collective. Many things said about sports teams also do not easily reduce.

Suppose it is said that Liberty Oil raised its pump prices by 15 cents. That would not be taken to mean that everyone who works for Liberty raised the prices. They're Liberty's prices, not Mary Rogers' prices or Horace Quinn's prices. Of course, for Liberty to raise its prices, a number of people associated with Liberty must do certain things. Still, it is Liberty that raises the prices at the pump.

There isn't much of a problem with understanding actions of corporate entities as requiring, but not being reducible to, the actions of its managers and employees. Problems arise with statements such as (a)–(e). If Liberty is praised for supporting public television, who is being praised? If Liberty ought not to close the Galveston plant, who is being admonished? When Liberty is held responsible for polluting the bay, who is being held responsible?

Corporations have been (and are) understood in many different ways, from different perspectives. In the history of law, for example, the personhood of corporations has been variously interpreted as fictional (the result of legislative enactments and other creative acts of states), and as actual, entities existing within the social world that are *acknowledged* but not *created* in law. On some accounts the personhood of a corporation is a matter of legislation. On others it is a matter of fact acknowledged by law. In tort and contract law, corporations are typically treated as full-fledged persons. Rulings and sentences are made for or against them, and no attempt is made to reduce those judgments to ones about the individual human beings who work for them. In a number of recent and well-publicized criminal cases, corporations in and of themselves have been charged with crimes and tried as persons.

In the field of economics, theorists that focus on the individual rational decision-maker tend to see corporations as little more than convenient mechanisms for individual profit-maximization. Such economists usually treat corporations as legal fictions that allow the pooling of investments and the limiting of individual liabilities. They are seen as legal tools to achieve the economic ends of individuals. Regardless of whether or not legal or economic theorists treat corporations as fictional entities, however, neither law nor economics is very helpful in telling us how to interpret moral judgments like (a)–(e). If we say that Liberty acted immorally, do we necessarily mean that all the people, or some of them, who work for Liberty did immoral things? Might we instead mean that there is something morally wrong with the corporation itself?

To answer these questions, we should first establish the basic conditions of membership in the moral community. There are two types of entities in the moral community: those we might call "regular members," and those that are protected or granted standing and rights but who are not accorded full membership status, because of a lack of capacity. The latter category, often called "moral patients," would include young children, the mentally impaired, animals, even trees and other parts of the natural environment. Although they can have claims against the regular membership, moral-patient entities are not held accountable for things they do. Full-fledged members of the moral community, or "moral agents," *can* be held responsible, blamed, or praised for their actions. What is the crucial capacity difference between these types of entities?

It has been relatively standard since, at least, the time of Aristotle to say that for something to be responsible for what it does it must have acted voluntarily: that is, it must have acted intentionally. It must be an intentional actor in the social world. If corporations are moral persons, then they must be intentional actors in a way that cannot be eliminated by reducing what they do to the actions of individual human beings.

The non-eliminative condition is important, for though it may be said that a rioting mob was to blame for destroying the shops on Main Street, such an ascription of responsibility can usually be distributed to those who comprised the mob. That is another way of saying that the mob is not a moral entity in and of itself. It is, for moral purposes, merely an aggregate of persons, each of which may or may not be held responsible for the damage on Main Street. An important reason for not holding the mob as an entity responsible is that a mob has no established way of making decisions, of determining its courses of action, setting goals, assigning tasks, and so on. The people in the mob could each be on Main Street for purely personal reasons. Something happens, and the destruction ensues. No organization, just a mob! If you were a member of it, then you were probably responsible for some of the damage. Morally, you could share in the responsibility for all of it. The mob itself, however, does not bear the moral blame. It goes out of existence when its members cease behaving in a riotous fashion and disperse.

Importantly for moral purposes, corporations are not like mobs in a variety of ways. In the first place, a corporation like Liberty Oil will usually remain the same entity even though it may have an almost constantly changing membership. The list of its stockholders, executives, board members, and employees is typically in a state of flux. Stock is bought and sold, employees are fired, hired, die, resign, and so on. Yet Liberty Oil goes on, and it makes sense to talk of Liberty Oil as the same corporation regardless of such changes in personnel.

Imagine that two lists have been compiled. One is the Liberty Oil list of executives and employees for noon on Friday, October 26, 1990. The other is the list for 4:00 P.M. on the same day. The names on both lists are identical except that "Mary Rogers" appears on the first list and not on the second. Mary's insider trading activities have come to light, and she has been fired. Should we say that the name "Liberty Oil Corporation" does not at 4:00 P.M. denote the same thing that it did at noon on that day? Do we have two different corporations? Surely not. "Liberty Oil" refers to the same corporation whether or not Mary Rogers works for the company. The identity of a corporation is not dependent on particular persons being in particular positions in the corporation. Being a discrete and persisting entity certainly, however, does not make Liberty Oil a member of the moral community. It will, in and for itself, have to be able to act intentionally to be a full-fledged member.

If Liberty Oil is an intentional actor, then some of the things that happen, some events, must be describable in a way that makes true sentences that say that what Liberty Oil did was intended by it. To say that some entity intended to act in a certain way is to describe its movements as upshots of reasons it had for their occurring. That means that if the world could only be described in terms of the physical movements of various objects, like ricocheting billiard balls, there would be no intentional actors, no moral persons, and so, no moral community.

Imagine a simple piece of behavior: the movement of a pen across paper. We can describe that behavior as the mere physical movement of a human hand or as certain muscular movements. It can also be described as someone, Horace Quinn, signing the order to close Liberty's Galveston plant. Actions appear only when the movement described is intended, that is, done to bring about some state of affairs or done to satisfy certain expectations or desires, and so on. As long as there is one true description of an event that says it was intended by someone, the event is an action *of that person*. For example, if I dump out a glass of iced tea, believing it to be a cola and wanting to dump out the cola, then it is true that I *intentionally* dumped out the contents of the glass. That is one of my actions. Because it is also true that dumping out the contents of the glass is dumping out the iced tea, *that* is also one of my *actions*, though not my *intention*. I never intended to dump out iced tea.

Horace Quinn's signing of the plant closing order normally would be what he intended, though we could imagine a situation in which he signed the order thinking he was signing something else: a memorandum to Mary Rogers about the pump price increase. His intention at that time was to sign the pump price memorandum. He intended to sign the plant closing order later. Still, he affixed his signature intentionally, and signing the paper was signing the plant closing order, so signing the order was one of his actions. In this case, however, much more is involved than in the example of my dumping out the iced tea. Quinn's signing the plant closing order can be further described as Liberty Oil's closing its Galveston plant.

In effect, the same event can be described in a number of different and non-equivalent ways. Simply, though a number of different descriptions may be true of the same event, they cannot be substituted without a significant change in meaning. At various levels of description the same event may be identified as an intentional action, and at each such level there must be an intentional actor performing it. The important question for us is: Does the physical action of Quinn's hand that leads to stating that Liberty Oil closed its Galveston plant reveal a *corporate* person acting, and not merely a *biological* person acting?

It is obvious that a corporation's doing something involves or includes human beings doing things and that the human beings who occupy various positions in a corporation usually can be described as having reasons for *their* behavior. Quinn had reasons for signing the plant closing order, even if he mistook that order for an interoffice memo. There are also corporate reasons for closing the Galveston plant, but for Liberty to do so, its president has to sign the order. Corporations, and not just the people who work in them, can be said to have reasons for doing what they do. We might even imagine situations in which Quinn or any number of others in corporate positions have no personal reasons, one way or the other, for taking a corporate action. Some of their physical movements and actions, however, will be necessary for Liberty to act on its corporate reasons.

Every corporation has an established way in which it makes decisions and converts them into actions. We call this the corporation's internal decision structure (CID Structure). Such a structure has two elements crucial to our understanding of how corporations act: (1) an organizational flow chart that delineates stations and levels within the organization; and (2) rules that tell us how to recognize decisions that are corporate ones and not simply decisions of the humans who occupy positions in the flow chart. These rules are typically embedded in "corporate policy." The CID Structure is the organization of personnel for the exercise of the corporation's power with respect to its ventures, and as such, its primary function is to draw various levels and positions within the corporation into decision-making, ratification, and action processes. When operative and properly activated, the CID Structure subordinates and synthesizes the intentions and acts of various human beings and mechanisms into a corporate decision. When viewed in another way, the CID Structure licenses the descriptive transformation of events, seen under another aspect as the acts of human beings (those who occupy various stations on the organizational chart), into corporate acts by exposing the corporate character of those events. A functioning CID Structure *incorporates* acts of human persons.

To see how this works, think of the CID Structure of a corporation as containing two sorts of rules: organizational rules and policy/procedure rules. These rules make descriptions of events possible that would not be possible if those rules did not exist. These rules play a role similar to the role rules play in our descriptions of sporting events. A person may catch an ovoid ball and run across a number of painted lines on a field, but without the rules of football the activity is not describable as catching a forward pass and scoring a touchdown. In football there are also two types of rules: those that define positions—the boundaries of the field, what makes one line the goal line as opposed to another yard marker, and those that allow certain activities and outlaw others—rules that permit throwing the ball, forbid holding or interfering with the pass, catcher, etc.

The organizational chart of a corporation distinguishes "players" and clarifies their rank and the interwoven lines of responsibility within the corporation. The organizational chart of Liberty Oil tells us, for example, that anyone holding the title Executive Vice President for Finance Administration stands in a superior position to anyone holding the title Director of Internal

Audit and to anyone holding the title Treasurer. These "players" report to the Executive Vice President. He ratifies their actions, and so on. In effect, the organizational chart maps the interdependent and dependent relationships, line and staff, that are involved in determinations of corporate decisions and actions. The organizational chart provides what is called the grammar of corporate decision-making. The policy/procedure rules provide its logic. Policy/procedure rules are what we call recognition rules because they provide conclusive and affirmative grounds for describing a decision or an act as having been made or performed for corporate reasons in the corporately approved way. Recognition rules in a CID Structure address either procedure or policy matters. Some of the procedural rules are embedded in the organizational chart. For example, by looking at the chart, we can see that decisions are to be reached collectively at certain levels, and that they are to be ratified at higher levels or within inner circles. A corporate decision is recognized, at least internally, however, not only by the procedure of its making, but by the policy that it reflects.

Every corporation creates a general set of policies (as well as an image) that must inform its decisions if they are to be properly described as being decisions of the corporation. Such policy statements are necessary for the attribution of intentionality to corporations. When a corporate act is an implementation of corporate policy, then it is proper to describe it as done for corporate reasons or for corporate purposes—as an intentional corporate act. Corporate reasons and purposes will often be quite different from those that motivate the individual human beings who occupy positions in the corporation to do the things they do.

We can describe events in terms of the physical movements of human beings and in terms of the reasons those persons have for their actions. Moreover, using a CID Structure of a particular company, we can describe those same events as corporate actions done for corporate reasons. When we are able to do so, we have intentional corporate action and grounds for including corporations among the subjects of moral judgments, and so as members of the moral community.

It is a basic principle of moral fairness that a person ought not to be held responsible for untoward events that in their first instance were merely incidental to his or her intentional actions, unless the person was negligent. In many of the recent, widely publicized corporate cases (the Air New Zealand crash on Mt. Erebus, the Ford Pinto case, the *Exxon Valdez* and other pollution cases, etc.), it is very difficult to demonstrate that individual employees or executives had intentions or acted in ways that would normally be regarded as morally relevant with respect to the untoward event. Nonetheless, through a tangled process of corporate decision-making, a series of motives, goals, policies, concerns, etc., did form into what may reasonably be called a corporate intention or corporate negligence regarding the matter. In fact, this process was a central feature of these situations. Treating corporations as morally responsible persons, then, is consistent with the social facts and it does not violate our standard principles of moral fairness.

Holding corporations responsible for something does not, in itself, shield those who work for the corporation from responsibility in the matter. For example, suppose Quinn took a bribe from an Irish economic development group to close the Galveston plant and move the operations to Ireland. He will stand before moral judgment personally, even though it is Liberty Oil that will move its operations to Ireland and close the Galveston plant. The fact that the context for the bribe is a corporate action explains in part how Quinn was able to work the bribe, but it does not alleviate his personal moral responsibility.

Imagine Quinn in the decision process with regard to closing the Galveston plant. He has before him an Everest of reports and studies prepared by lower-echelon managers and team leaders. Some of the materials are factual reports, some contingency plans, position papers from various departments, financial analyses, legal opinions, etc.—all processed through Liberty Oil's CID Structure. Whatever personal reasons any individual executive or management team member may have had for writing a report or making a certain recommendation were diluted by subordination of their input to peer-group and superior review and reformation well before they reach Quinn. Quinn decides to sign the order and does so. Liberty Oil's CID Structure authorizes redescribing Quinn's actions as Liberty's closing the plant, but so far that doesn't say that Liberty acted intentionally in closing the plant. Liberty's CID Structure, as already suggested, also provides the grounds in its statements of corporate policy for an attribution of corporate intentionality in this case. Insofar as closing the plant is an implementation of corporate policy, as developed by the board, then Liberty Oil has closed (or ordered the closing) of its Galveston plant for corporate reasons, for example, to increase profits, increase productivity, cut expenses, and so on. Hence, Quinn's signing the paper can be redescribed as Liberty Oil closing its plant for corporate reasons. Because those reasons exist whether or not Quinn took a bribe, the act is a corporate one.

The way a corporation typically has of achieving its goals is through the actions of its personnel, such as Quinn, who fill various stations and roles in the company. However, that does not change the fact that corporate goals, desires, interests, etc., may be radically different from those of the persons in such roles. Sometimes corporate actions can be accomplished without direct actions by humans. For example, computers may perform a number of corporate actions while humans in the company are unaware of what is actually happening.

Corporations have reasons for doing things because they have interests in realizing their established corporate goals regardless of the transient self-interest of directors, managers, etc. If there is a difference between corporate goals and desires and those of human beings, it is probably because the corporate ones are relatively more stable and not very wide-ranging. That is only because corporations can do relatively fewer things than human beings, being confined in action predominantly to a limited socio-economic sphere. The attribution of corporate intentionality is opaque with respect to other possible descriptions of the event in question. It is, of course, in a corporation's interest that its component membership view the corporate purposes as instrumental in the achievement of their own goals. (Financial reward is the most common way in which this is achieved.)

Isn't it the case, however, that a corporation's policies really just reflect the current goals of its directors? In many cases, of course, that will be true. In many other cases, however, it is neither necessarily nor practically true for most large corporations. Usually, of course, the original incorporators will have organized to further their individual interests and/or to meet goals which they shared. Even in a corporation's infancy, however, the melding of disparate interests and purposes gives rise to a corporate long-range point of view that can be distinct from the intents, purposes, and interests of the collection of incorporators viewed individually. Also, corporate basic purposes and policies, as already mentioned, tend to be relatively stable when compared to those of individuals and not couched in the kind of language that would be appropriate to individual purposes. Furthermore, as histories of corporations show, when policies are amended or altered, typically it is peripheral issues that are involved. Radical policy alteration constitutes a new corporation.

Corporate intent, undeniably, is dependent upon policies and purposes that are an artifact of the socio-psychology of a group of human beings, the original incorporators. Corporate intent may appear to be a tarnished, illegitimate offspring of human intent, but such an assumption reveals an anthropocentric bias. If we concentrate on the possible descriptions of events and acknowledge that describing some entity as an agent only requires that we can describe it as having done something for its own reasons, then we don't need to reduce statements about corporate actions to ones about the actions, reasons, or interests of individual humans. Corporate policies will provide the reasons and other intentional elements needed to view the event as a corporate action. Still, the action also must be procedurally correct for it to be corporate.

In some corporations—perhaps Liberty Oil is one—procedural rules in the CID Structure may be minimal. Among department managers there may exist an understanding that superiors are to be kept informed of decisions at lower levels and that superiors can veto inferior-level decisions. The notions of "within one's authority" and "exceeding one's authority" then will be defined in daily operations. Importantly, the CID Structure must do a normative job. An action is not that of Liberty Oil just because President Quinn says that it is. No corporate president has that authority. Otherwise, anything Quinn did to enrich himself from the corporate funds or in using corporate employees, for example, to clean his house, by his merely saying so, would be an action of Liberty Oil. Such a shield, from the point of view of morality, would be entirely too thick. If, on the other hand, an act of Quinn, such as signing the closing order, is in accord with the established procedures of Liberty Oil, then the corporation is the actor, and its CID Structure reveals it as such.

The recognition of procedures is relatively easier than identifying policy in a corporation, even though some procedures may be the result of common practice rather than official sanction. Recognizing corporate policy is made problematic by the fact that formal documents, like charters, do not exhaust its sources. Most charters are rather vague about the goals, interests, and purposes of a corporation. They may say only that the corporation is formed to engage in business for any lawful purpose. Does that mean that corporations can never break the law? Surely not. In fact, the doctrine that corporations can only act within the strict boundaries set by their charters has been superseded in law by an implied powers doctrine, giving rise to what is known as the business judgment rule. This rule tells us that corporations may pursue legitimate corporate ends through legitimate corporate enterprises. As long as their personnel work within the limits of those pursuits, as established by procedurally appropriate corporate decisions and corporate history, their acts will be understood as corporate actions. What is a legitimate end or endeavor? The use of "legitimate" has more to do with being in accord with general expectations and standards and with being reasonable in the circumstances, than with actual legal constraints. Hence, at Liberty Oil, the policy of closing old, expensive-to-operate plants in the United States and opening new ones where labor is cheaper, is a legitimate corporate endeavor.

Whether or not Liberty Oil, from the moral point of view, ought to close the Galveston plant has nothing to do with the legitimacy of its doing so. The business judgment rule depends for its sense on an understanding of what is reasonable within the standards of business for the corporate enterprise, given the history, type of enterprise, and policies of that corporation. In effect, recognizing corporate policy involves understanding the business in which the corporation is engaged. It is not just a matter of learning some rules or slogans or broad-based claims that may be preserved in its charter. Corporate personnel must grasp the customs, goals, and expectations of the corporation, appreciate the corporate history and culture to ensure that their business actions and decisions are corporate. Formal documents will be of some help to them and to those who seek to determine whether particular actions are corporate, but they usually tell only a part of the story.

A corporation's policies are generally embedded in rather broad principles that describe what the corporation believes to be its purposes and how it intends to operate. Policies contain the *what* and the *how* of life in that corporation. G. C. Buzby wrote:

> In order to be effective as guides to innumerable day-to-day decisions and actions, policies must be stated in broad terms, yet they must be sufficiently precise and clear to have real meanings for the people involved. . . . Policies must also be formulated with a long-range point of view in order to achieve the advantages that derive from consistency of purpose and to avoid the disadvantages that inevitably result from decisions based on shortsightedness and expediency. . . . The moment a policy is sidestepped or violated, it is no longer the policy of that company.[1]

Corporate policies, as Buzby saw, must be accepted as authoritative by those who work in the corporation. In fact, the policies of a corporation seem to be inviolate. In that regard they are unlike policies adopted by individual humans. You could adopt a policy of honesty, but you may occasionally violate that policy by lying. When you lie, it is still you lying. If employees act in ways that violate corporate policy, however, their acts would no longer be those of the corporation, assuming that Buzby is right. There are, however, some problems with this analysis of policies.

Imagine that Jack Nevels, the head of the legal department at Liberty Oil, is well aware of a clearly written policy in the corporation against the use of corporate funds to support Houston charities. Because he was well-known and respected in town, Nevels was asked to become involved in the local public television station's corporate membership campaign. He accepted, and after numerous meetings with executives of other Houston companies, Nevels felt compelled by the others to make a sizable pledge in the name of Liberty Oil. Is Nevels' act an act of Liberty Oil Corporation?

Our first inclination may be to say that it is not, but that is too hasty. What we need to know before we can authoritatively exclude it from the acts of Liberty Oil is the reaction Liberty board made when Nevels' pledge in the name of Liberty became known in corporate headquarters. Suppose President Quinn takes the matter to the board. After all, Nevels is a senior executive in the company. The board discusses the matter and decides that the pledge might have considerable value in public relations in Houston, even though stated policy is that only national charities will be funded. The good will to be gained, especially with the Galveston plant closing forthcoming, could be valuable. The board decides to honor the pledge. By doing so, Liberty Oil identifies itself with a policy different from its written one, thereby revealing that the true policy of Liberty on these matters is not really the written one. If they had decided not to honor the pledge and to fire Nevels for overstepping his authority, they would have been making clear that his actions, despite appearances, were not those of the corporation. Written policy would still govern at Liberty.

Whether or not a policy is actually in place in a corporation is dependent not on just what is "on the record," but on how those in power to act for the corporation respond to apparent violations of stated policy. We should say that every corporation has a set of policies, and some are more central or fixed than others. The central policies seldom, if ever, change, but other policies are not so firmly fixed. Discovering which policies are central and which are more peripheral at Liberty would involve one in a careful study of the way Liberty acts over time. Its written documents might turn out to be no more than "window-dressing." Policies in a corporation are then somewhat more flexible than Buzby suggests.

One further aspect of a CID Structure is crucial to our treating corporations as full-fledged members of the moral community. A corporation must be capable of making non-programmed decisions. It must be more than merely mechanical. The reason for this condition is that regular members of the moral community must be capable of responding to criticism, altering offensive behavior, reacting to unanticipated outcomes, and so on. Most corporations do evidence non-programmed decision-making. Consider new product development. Although adherence to procedure is usually required, the process cannot really be routinized. There are generally too many variables. So, to make major product-development decisions, businesses will have to make allowances in their CID Structures for non-programmable elements. A corporation that is incapable of innovation is unlikely to realize its vital economic interests.

Members of the moral community should have the structural capacity to innovate and respond to situations, as well as have interests in and reasons for what they do. Insofar as most corporations can develop new products, initiate mergers, relocate plants, select new board members, and acquire properties, they demonstrate the required non-programmed decision capacity. We have already shown how they can be understood as intentional actors in their own right and not as mere aggregates of human actors.

If we return to the moral judgments about Liberty noted earlier, we can now read them as making claims on and about Liberty Oil Corporation in and of itself; claims, however, that do entail that actions by Liberty personnel occurred or might occur. In other words, they reveal that there are at least two levels of moral judgments that might be made in corporate cases. When it is said, as in (a), that Liberty is responsible for polluting Monterey Bay, does that imply that the captain of the Liberty tanker is responsible for the pollution? Or does it imply that some appropriate managerial team at Liberty is responsible for the transportation system that resulted in the spill? Suppose, with respect to the latter, that everyone in the transportation division conscientiously acted on corporate policies, especially those concerned with profitability. Would it make sense to say that the transportation division's management or the individual managers are responsible for the spill? If certain conditions prevailed, it would make sense to say that the managers, or some of them, were responsible. For example, suppose they had received reports that the single-hulled tankers were dangerous or that the officers of their tankers were often drunk when they left port. Still, they chose to ignore the reports and to operate as usual. Perhaps they decided that Liberty's interest in getting its crude oil to its refineries overrode all other issues. Besides, they might have said to each other, they had not yet experienced an accident in those waters.

Sorting out corporate and individual responsibility quickly becomes very complicated in cases of this sort. The simplest thing to do is to dump everything, from the moral point of view, on Quinn. As we have seen, that will not be fair in many cases, however. Alternate ways of conceiving of the issues of moral responsibility in corporate cases should be seriously explored. In the rest of this book, some of the complications and implications of treating corporations themselves as members of the moral community are addressed.

Notes

1. Buzby, G.C. "Policies—A Guide to What a Company Stands For." *Management Record* 24:5, March 1962.

Sources for Additional Reading:

Curtler, Hugh. *Shame, Responsibility, and the Corporation.* New York: Haven Publications, 1986.

Donaldson, Thomas. *Corporations and Morality.* Englewood Cliffs, NJ: Prentice-Hall, 1982.

Donley, John. "Corporate Moral Agency: The Case for Anthropological Bigotry." *Action and Responsibility: Bowling Green Studies in Applied Philosophy*, Vol. II, 1980.

French, Peter A. *Collective and Corporate Responsibility.* New York: Columbia University Press, 1984. See especially Chapters 3, 4, 12.

Goodpaster, Kenneth. "Morality and Organizations." *Proceedings of the Second National Conference on Business Ethics*, Michael Hoffman, ed. Lanham, MD: University Press of America, 1979.

Ladd, John. "Morality and the Ideal of Rationality in Formal Organizations." *The Monist* 54, 1970.

Management

anagers must be decision-makers.[1] Before they can guide, lead, cajole, and inspire, managers need to have decided upon the proper course of action. Some decisions involve a major corporate choice, such as those confronting Robert Krebs as he struggles with how Liberty Oil should respond to the California oil spill. Others are of a more personal nature. For example, should Mary Rogers be more forthcoming with President Quinn regarding the credit due her staff? Whatever their scope, these decisions are part of a manager's job. These decisions must be confronted, pondered, and resolved, often in the face of considerable ambiguity and uncertainty.

Information is crucial. In the business world, this means a general knowledge of areas such as finance, marketing, organizational behavior, and business strategy. It also includes an understanding of the particular set of people and circumstances which relate to the problem at hand. Robert Krebs's custom of wandering around the company after board meetings "to get a feel for what was happening" is one informal way of such specific fact-gathering. Managers must synthesize and apply these various sources of information in the decisions that confront them. Failure to tap a vital source of information increases the risks inherent in any business decision. In the modern business environment, such risks range from individual career setbacks to loss of the company's market share to irreversible damage to our natural environment.

Such information by itself is incomplete, however. With only his general business knowledge and an awareness of the specific facts of the oil spill, Robert Krebs would still lack an adequate basis for the decisions he must make. Effective business decision-making also requires an appreciation and awareness of the *normative realm* of decision-making. By normative realm, we mean the norms, values, and philosophic beliefs that express the aspirations we have for ourselves and others. Such norms, values, and beliefs permeate the day-to-day choices of managers in fundamental, though sometimes hidden, ways. Understanding this complex dynamic between normative considerations and personal choices is essential to informed and responsible decision-making.

The forms such normative considerations take may vary. They are present in the legal framework within which managers make business decisions. They are found in the ethical views of individuals and the corporate cultures of companies. Furthermore, such normative considerations may exist in the many unspoken assumptions which managers make about fellow employees, organizations, and the nature of the business environment.

A good place to begin to explore the normative side of business decision-making is in the law. For many, the law represents the most concrete and familiar expression of our norms, values, and philosophic beliefs. Furthermore, the law is unavoidable. Backed by the power of the state, its prescriptions are an integral part of the modern business world.

This chapter begins by providing a broad overview of three legal developments that set boundaries on management's decision-making. The first is management's consolidation of power over the internal corporate decision-making process. The second is the government's increased regulation of managerial choices in the public interest. In discussing this second development, particular attention is given to the problem of how to punish those who engage in illegal conduct. The third development is the investor's market demand for profit. The chapter then proceeds to show how underlying this legal framework are three often-conflicting ways in which management may view its role and function. The manager may see himself or herself as (1) an autonomous professional, (2) a public trustee, or (3) an agent for the shareholders. The conflicts among these roles form the basis for many of the ethical dilemmas confronted by corporate managers. The chapter concludes by putting forth an alternative view of the corporation—the corporation as moral agent—and suggesting that such an alternative view entails re-examining the ethical issues facing management today.

Our purpose is to understand the larger significance of the doctrines of corporate law. Focusing not on specific rules relating to corporate transactions, but rather on the general overarching trends that have come to shape the law in this area, we will bring into view the basic legal tensions faced by today's business executive. Through our study of the law's historical development, we hope to uncover the fundamental norms applicable to management.

MANAGEMENT'S CONSOLIDATION OF POWER

Popular thinking about corporations usually contains a somewhat hazy legal image of the corporation. At the core of this image is what has been called the received legal model of the corporation.

There does exist a more or less standardized model of formal corporate decision-making which may be called the received legal model—whose outlines are well-known. Under this model, the board of directors manages the corporation's business and makes business policy: the officers act as agents of the board and execute its decisions; and the shareholders elect the board and decide on "major corporate actions," or "fundamental," "extraordinary," or "organic" changes . . . . [2]

A striking feature of this received legal model is the particular image of the corporation that it presents. The image is one in which shareholders as individuals control the corporation. As owners of the corporation, they set broad policy through their representatives on the board of directors. They are thus presented as an effective electorate in a "shareholder democracy."

Like all models, this one helps us to understand the world around us in a selective way, emphasizing certain aspects and denying others. We are concerned here with bringing to light what is denied by the received legal model of the corporation.

A central trend in the development of modern corporate law is the recognition of a shift in the internal control of the corporation from the shareholders to management. While the shareholders are still the nominal legal owners of the corporation, for the most part they fail to exercise the control over the business enterprise which we would associate with traditional ownership.

This separation of ownership from control has its roots in the widely scattered nature of stock ownership typical of the largest, publicly held corporations. This wide dispersal of stock means that individual shareholders are less likely to amass the percentage of stock necessary to control the membership of the board of directors. Unable to determine the outcome of board elections, large numbers of shareholders no longer participate directly in internal corporate governance.

More than 50 years ago, the myth of a shareholder democracy was dislodged by Berle and Means in *The Modern Corporation and Private Property*. Their first observation concerned the implications of the wide dispersal of corporate ownership:

As the ownership of corporate wealth has become more widely dispersed, ownership of that wealth and control over it have come to lie less and less in the same hands. Under the corporate system, control over industrial wealth can be and is being exercised with a minimum of ownership interest. Conceivably it can be exercised without any such interest. [3]

The essential point made by Berle and Means is that in large corporations with their multitudes of stockholders, the functions of ownership and control have been divorced from each other. Thus those in control are no longer the owners, and the owners are no longer in control. Later writers continued this theme.

> The trend, pointed out by Berle and Means, and long since consolidated, is for corporations to be under management control, with stockholders having no real voice in choosing the board of directors. For most stockholders control is confined to a choice between voting for or against proxies chosen by management. . . . [4]

In discussing this increase in management's control, we wish to emphasize two significant corporate law developments which require some elaboration. Their significance lies in the manner in which they have broadened and changed the arena of discretion allowed to management by the law.

The first development in modern corporate law has to do with the character of the restrictions on management's decision-making. The law has moved from a rigid *ultra vires* conception of management responsibility to the more flexible notion of the business judgment rule. Under the older *ultra vires* concept, management's discretion was strictly circumscribed by a rigid adherence to the corporation's charter of incorporation. The corporation's charter provided specific rules that prohibited particular conduct, such as entering a new line of business. Now, with the advent and wide adoption of the business judgment rule, the discretion of management is much broader, restricted instead by the generalized duties of loyalty, good faith, and due care.

In substituting generalized duties for specific rules, the law expressed society's recognition that running a business often requires difficult decisions based on imperfect information. Managers must make judgments that are not readily reducible to some set formula. What the business judgment rule says is that unless corporate leaders violate basic duties such as their duty of loyalty to the corporation, the courts will not second-guess their business judgments and impose legal liability. On the other hand, if corporate directors and officers were to be disloyal to the corporation, acting for their own benefit while harming the enterprise, the courts would seek a legal remedy. Indeed, with the rise in corporate takeovers, the courts have increased the obligations of those in the corporate hierarchy under the business judgment rule.

The second legal development concerns the goals that inform the decision-making of management. Formerly, the dominant notion was the idea that management's fiduciary duty ran solely to the interest of the shareholders. This has been largely replaced by the view that management is a fiduciary of the corporation as a whole, and as such should respond to a broader constituency including employees, customers, and the public at large. Recent state statutes explicitly allow directors and officers to consider the effects of corporate action on groups other than shareholders.

Both legal developments contribute to the creation of a certain measure of autonomy for management, but such autonomy is a mixed blessing. Today's executive must often make difficult ethical decisions without the benefit of clear and unambiguous rules. Furthermore, the particular character of management's autonomy has itself complicated the choices to be made. The more flexible framework of the business judgment rule coupled with the more inclusive fiduciary duty to the corporation itself broadens the ends or goals which management must evaluate in its decision-making. As an individual is confronted with competing ends or goals in making his or her moral choices, so management often faces conflicting demands in its decisions regarding corporate direction.

From the ethical point of view, management has moved from simple rule-following to the assumption of morally significant roles. Appreciating what this richer notion of responsible action means requires looking at how rules and roles function differently as prescriptions.

On the surface, the law seems largely rule-oriented. When clients ask lawyers for the law in a particular area, they typically expect and hope for a rule to guide their behavior; but roles as well as rules can be used to guide our conduct.

Consider, for instance, what it means to be a "good father." In reflecting upon this, we could probably come up with some particular rules which we could agree would have to be followed by a man in order for us to consider him to be a good father. We might agree, for example, that if they are financially able, good fathers should provide their children with the basics of food, clothing, and shelter. Most of us would also agree that being a good father means more than meeting such minimal standards. Depending on the particular circumstances, it may mean coaching a Little League team, driving to a junior high school dance, or devising a punishment for the underage use of alcohol. It is apparent that what we expect of a good father cannot be reduced to a set of specific rules. Rather, the core of fatherhood has more to do with assuming a general orientation than performing particular actions. It means adopting a basic comportment of love and concern toward one's children, and responding to developing situations out of such love and concern. When a man assumes such an orientation, he is doing more than following rules. He is assuming a role, the role of good father. Such an orientation is as legitimate a guide to fatherhood as any particular set of rules.

Systems of ethics that adopt shame as their central notion provide a useful illustration. The possibility of shame often operates to control our behavior. Most of us, unless handicapped, would not park in a handicapped parking space, even if the chance of legal action were slight. This is because we would be ashamed of taking such an action. When ethical systems emphasize shame as a means of controlling conduct, the predominant standard is one of roles.

> In a shame-based morality, evaluation of behavior is not made against rules. . . . Moral worth is measured against role or type models. Do you remember how your mother or grandmother ingrained this type of morality in you?

> "Act like a human being, only a pig would do that," or "your brother or sister would never behave like that." To feel shameful a person must come to regard one's behavior as having fallen below or short of what is

expected of or associated with the role, station, or type to which one belongs. The feeling of shame is the feeling of inadequacy or inferiority.[5]

Roles tend to require more of us than rules. While we live *by* rules, we live *up* to roles. It is important to remember that the rules of law are often minimal standards. They define basic boundaries of conduct at a minimally acceptable level. Roles, however, call for exemplary behavior. Their prescriptions represent an ideal or model we must strive for.

A further distinction may be drawn between rules and roles. This distinction relates to what is required of one who breaches the relevant set of standards. In the breaking of a legal rule, the infraction is seen as similar to a debt. Such debts must be repaid in order to restore the status quo which existed before the breach. Thus, if a person driving negligently hits and damages another's car, the law will require that person to pay the cost of repairs. A person who has fallen short of his or her role, however, cannot be rid of shame by repaying a debt. What is required is something more profound than restoring the status quo. What is required is a basic reformation of self.

> Importantly, shame cannot be purged by repayment. Shame is not translatable to debt. It is not a matter of paying a fine and restoring the *status quo*. To regain one's sense of worth, to reclaim one's desired identity, the shameful person must act in positive, creative, and even heroic ways so that he or she may again feel and be seen as worthy. Often the shameful persons must go well beyond what is ordinarily required to again value themselves.[6]

This notion of roles is helpful in comprehending the complex set of demands and expectations that confront individual managers in today's business environment. Modern business leaders realize that legal rules are only part of the story. As a professional with some autonomy, today's corporate manager has assumed a morally significant role. What is currently weighing on Robert Krebs's mind is more than the possibility of legal liability. He is struggling with what is demanded of him by his professional role. And he's confused: "It's a different world, Jack. Whatever happened to the old-fashioned pursuit of profit and the simple values?" A first step toward sorting out Krebs's confusion is a look at other fundamental legal developments in order to appreciate the additional roles imposed on corporate management.

LEGAL DUTIES AND THE PUBLIC INTEREST

Along with management's consolidation of power over the corporation's internal decision-making process, there has been a second and countervailing legal trend. The government has increasingly placed legal duties upon management in order to protect the public interest.

During the 1960s and 1970s, there emerged a substantial body of federal law aimed at social goals. In areas such as environmental protection, employment discrimination, employee health and safety, and product liability, legislatures and courts redefined in important ways the scope and character of our social policy. Such social legislation inevitably impacts the decision-making of management. Beyond traditional involvement with private law concepts such as contracts and torts, management must today concern itself with public regulatory intrusions.

Public regulation has produced a number of new and complex duties for corporate management. These new legal duties for managers often come in the form of specific requirements in statutes or regulations, such as those contained in the environmental laws. Charles Osborne's expression of concern over whether Liberty's single-hulled ship met government regulations illustrates the sort of concern that has become part of the corporate manager's world. The aim of the environmental laws is to protect the public's interest in such resources as clean air and water. Their existence reflects society's judgment that business decision-making must incorporate additional levels of responsibility.

PUNISHING CORPORATIONS THAT VIOLATE THE PUBLIC INTEREST

A central issue running through the environmental statutes and other statutes promoting social goals is the question of punishment. This reflects the special status of the law in the normative realm. Group norms, personal values, and individual beliefs cannot draw directly upon the coercive power of the state. The prescriptions of the law, however, are backed by the tremendous enforcement powers of local, state, and national governments. This special relationship between the law and governmental power requires that we consider how the law responds to breaches of legally required duties. The effectiveness of much social regulation may depend on the law's approach to the question of punishment.

In Chapter 6 we will consider corporate punishment more specifically and suggest some new forms of corporate punishment and control. For now, it is necessary only to gain an appreciation of some of the basic issues raised by individual and corporate punishment.

By and large, the law's punishments of corporations come into play only after the fact of harm, and they then exercise deterrence through some external threat to the corporation's profits. Rarely does the law intrude into the corporation's internal decision-making process other than to provide for the disclosure of specified information.

This approach to a corporation's breach of its legal duties is rooted in the "black box" theory of corporate punishment.[7] The idea is that the law should treat the corporation as an impenetrable "black box" and not seek to probe or alter directly the internal process of corporate decisions. Rather, in this view, the way to promote socially desirable corporate behavior is to change the corporation's external environment. A common approach by which the law alters the external environment of the corporation is through the threat of monetary fines. For example, if a particular violation of the environmental laws carries with it the possibility of a $100,000 fine per day of violation, this fine changes the context in which corporate decisions are made. Along with the demands of the market, social considerations embodied in the environmental statute become a factor in corporate choices. In theory at least, this legally altered environment leads to a change in corporate decision-making. The threat to corporate profits posed by the monetary fine encourages a corporate choice consistent with social goals such as clean air and water. It does so only indirectly, however, not requiring specific changes in the process of internal decision-making, but only promoting a particular end-result.

Some legal theorists have challenged this black-box theory of corporate punishment, calling for major legal intrusions into corporate internal decision structures. Their proposals aim at altering the decision-making process itself in order to promote socially responsible decisions. A major advantage of this more interventionist[8] approach is the possibility that the law may act in a preventive and not merely in an after-the-fact fashion. Thus, the law may be used to avoid the pollution of a river rather than merely to provide financial compensation to those injured by the river's contamination.

A major proponent of this interventionist approach is Christopher Stone. In his work, he proposes two situations where the law's intervention should affect directors and high-level managers. He refers to them as the *demonstrated delinquency situation* and the *generic industry problem*. A demonstrated delinquency situation is one in which a particular company has repeatedly broken the law. The generic industry problem refers to industries that involve matters of great public concern.

Stone does emphasize that caution is warranted in applying interventionist measures. To begin with, he notes that imposing additional duties or concerns on those highest in the corporate hierarchy will inevitably detract from the time and attention they can give to their principal missions. Secondly, he points out that not all problems are best dealt with at the higher levels of the corporate hierarchy. Such is the case, for example, with the protection of workers from unsuspected hazards in the workplace. More than needing a seat in the corporate board room, workers need participation on lower-level health and safety committees in order to most effectively address this problem.

The sort of intervention Stone proposes involves either requiring additional duties of existing positions or mandating the creation of new positions within the corporate bureaucracy. In a demonstrated delinquency situation, the company's repeated violations of the law show that conventional legal controls are inadequate. In such cases Stone believes:

> As a last resort, a court or other agency, as part of a probation order
> and subject to a hearing, might either impose special compliance chores

on some designated high-level officer, or even mandate the appointment of a "special public director" to monitor the company's compliance efforts. Such a thing is not unheard of. In the past 15 years or so, a number of securities law cases have been settled on terms requiring the defendant company to establish special committees of the board with designated tasks (compliance committees, litigation committees), to hire investigative counsel, and even, in some cases, to add to the board a new director subject to the approval of the Securities and Exchange Commission and court. Such dispositions are generally unfamiliar outside the securities area, where they function to advance, or at least their rationale is to advance, traditional investor interests.

On the other hand, a few cases have been settled on terms aimed at providing comparable relief for noninvestors. The government's case against the American Telephone & Telegraph Company, alleging employment discrimination against women, blacks, and other minorities, was ultimately settled with a consent decree that added new offices to the management structure (compliance officers in each operating company) and grafted additional tasks onto existing managers. For example, the Vice-President of Personnel was required to review and take action on specified information regarding the firm's hiring and advancement of minorities.[9]

Stone believes that in these cases of repeated offenses there is reason to think that the interventionist measure will be effective. Because of the company's repeated violations of the law, the company's personnel will be more likely to recognize that a problem exists and regard the law's intervention as legitimate. This recognition will diminish their natural tendency to attempt to subvert or co-opt those responsible for implementing the interventionist measure.

The generic industry problem involves a quite different situation. Certain industries by the very nature of their activities involve matters of great public concern. Stone mentions, for instance, industries which "produce waste whose hazards will hang as a sword over future generations."[10] In such cases, companies within the industry may not have violated any law. In fact, the problem may exist because regulations that adequately deal with the problem are not in force. Still, at times there may be reasons for intervention. Stone writes:

> In these circumstances, it may be preferable for the agencies involved to defer promulgating sweeping substantive rules until they have developed more information; but as a quid pro quo for temporizing, and to provide the public assurances that something positive is being done, the government might be warranted to impose high-level interventions specially designed to support its lawmaking efforts. For example, each company in the industry might be required to establish an executive committee assigned to gather in-house data, assess the hazard, and relay findings to

the appropriate authorities. In fact, there is already a gesture in this direction in the regulations of the Nuclear Regulatory Commission. . . . Each company in the industry is not only required to adopt procedures whereby "responsible officers" are informed of serious problems, but those officers are also obligated, under penalty of law, to relay certain information regarding hazards to the NRC.[11]

Stone stresses the need to avoid vague mandates such as advancing "the public interest." With both the demonstrated delinquency situation and the generic industry problem, the emphasis should be on the appointment of qualified individuals who have specific goals and well-defined relationships.

Finally, I want to emphasize that in none of these situations (of either the demonstrated delinquency or generic industry variety) would anyone be assigned to advance "the public interest." Anyone working under so foggy a mandate can barely know where to begin. Instead, wherever the powers, qualifications, duties, etc., of an executive were to be affected, the details would be specially tailored to fit the particular exigency at hand. Take for example a company with a history of repeated toxic waste violations. A court that responded by appointing a special director as part of a probation order would be expected to designate not some well-meaning generalist, but a sanitary engineer or epidemiologist. Such an appointee, by virtue of having recognized relevant expertise, gains credibility throughout the firm. Moreover, the terms of the probation order would be expected to focus the appointee's efforts, spelling out, for example: (1) the problem for his or her concentration; (2) the resources the company would have to make available, in terms of records, staff, and budget constraints; (3) the character of the appointee's linkage to outside bureaus, e.g., the requirements of divulsion and privilege in communications with the court itself, the Environmental Protection Agency, and various state pollution bureaus.[12]

This legal approach, Stone argues, serves the goals of both deterrence and rehabilitation. He points out that such threats to a corporation's autonomy may be taken more seriously by corporate management than even large monetary fines. Furthermore, such a restructuring of the corporate hierarchy signals a serious commitment to corporate reform. This could be an encouragement to those individuals within the organization who wish to make the company a better one.

PUNISHING INDIVIDUALS WHO VIOLATE THE PUBLIC INTEREST

We have been focusing mostly on the punishment of corporations regarded as entities in themselves. In many cases, however, the possibility of imposing *personal* liability on individual managers exists. This area of the law has been of growing interest to legislatures, courts, and prosecutors. In some instances, such liability may extend beyond civil penalties to criminal sanctions, such as punitive fines and imprisonment.

Remember how the issue of individual responsibility was a key part of the discussion during Liberty's board meeting. Liberty Oil's president contended that the captain and crew of the tanker should be held solely and fully responsible. The plan was to release stories to the press, blaming the captain and crew while admitting no corporate responsibility for the disaster.

Imagine being present at the meeting of Liberty's board. How should the directors and other officers have reacted to this plan? Robert Krebs was clearly skeptical. "Will the press swallow that?" he asks. And moments later, he says, "It was *our* ship doing *our* business." Did those in the board room have any obligations to the tanker's captain and crew? Was there anything that those in the board room failed to consider?

It should be noted from the outset that corporate and individual liability are *not* mutually exclusive legal strategies. The law might call for both the imprisonment of a high-level manager and the imposition of a monetary fine on the corporation in a particular case. It may well be that the best approach lies in an effective combination of both tactics.

Arriving at such an effective combination requires a full understanding of the strengths and weaknesses of both approaches. Therefore, it is important to examine each of the positions.

Holding the corporation responsible for the violation of various pieces of social legislation, such as the environmental statutes, has a number of consequences. To begin with, the huge financial resources of the larger corporations give such corporations the ability to pay significant monetary damages. While the millions of dollars necessary to clean up the spill of a major oil tanker may be well beyond the resources of an individual corporate manager, such resources are available from the corporation.

Forcing corporations to pay large fines has other ramifications, as well. Given the proper market conditions, the costs of judgments against the corporation may be passed on to consumers in the form of higher prices. Furthermore, since such judgments may be covered by insurance, the actions of insurance companies come into play. Premiums may be raised, thus spreading the costs of a single company's wrongdoing throughout the industry. The position of the company's shareholders and employees should also be considered. Often most shareholders and employees have neither participated in nor have knowledge of the particular illegal acts. Thus, questions of fairness are raised if these shareholders and employees suffer penalties. The payment of large financial fines by the corporation can reduce the value of individual shares of stock and lower the capital available for company expansion and job creation.

On the other hand, in some cases, imposition of personal liability on individual managers may have a greater deterrence value than corporate liability.

The threat of a jail sentence may well deter a corporate manager, more so than a corporate fine which can be passed on to consumers. Beyond the actual threat, the social stigma of imprisonment may have an impact. While financial fines may in some business quarters be accepted as a routine cost of doing business, the shame of serving time may still have considerable effect.

One problem with focusing on the individual responsible for the illegal action is that such an ascription of responsibility may in some cases be impossible. This can merely be a problem of information gathering, but it may also be something more. Decision-making in the corporate setting often involves the coordination within a particular decision-making structure of thousands of individual actions. This raises the possibility that no single individual is responsible for what occurred, but rather responsibility lies with the decision-making structure and thus with the corporation itself. For example, consider Liberty Oil's decision to use single-hulled ships rather than those with three hulls. Such a decision may more properly be considered a corporate decision rather than the decision of any particular individual. It certainly has a different character than, say, the captain of the tanker's choice to be drinking when the tanker ran aground in Monterey Bay.

GOING BEYOND PUNISHMENT: THE CONCEPT OF SOCIAL RESPONSIBILITY

An understanding of the law's special connection with the punitive powers of the government should be coupled with attention to the law's broader, normative significance. The law has an impact beyond the conduct which it prohibits. While it forbids certain kinds of behavior, the law also permits and encourages other activities. It is important to acknowledge this dimension of the law, for it suggests the reciprocal nature of the law's interaction with emerging ethical concerns. Our collective beliefs and individual values certainly contribute to the formation of the law, and the law also influences the development of such beliefs and values.

There are a number of such emerging ethical concerns in the corporate area. For instance, intertwined with and complementing the legal strategies we have discussed is the concept of management's social responsibility. While the concept is controversial and not susceptible to easy definition, it is nonetheless having a significant impact on the formation and application of corporate law. For example, as we have already noted, some states have enacted statutes that allow corporate directors and officers to take account of the broad effects of corporate actions on such groups as employees, customers, and local communities.

Just how the notion of social responsibility relates to legal prescriptions is a subject of considerable debate. Some view management's social responsibility as entailing nothing more than obeying the law. If this is so, the notion would not require separate mention in addition to our discussion of social legislation, but we wish to consider the concept of management's social responsibility in a more expanded sense. The concept, in our view, conveys the possibility of *voluntary* managerial actions beyond the requirements of the law.

This understanding of management's social responsibility brings into play more than the law's prohibitive function. One role for the law regarding this expanded sense of social responsibility is to provide a permissive framework. Thus, the state corporate statutes just mentioned, which allow consideration of the broad effects of corporate action, are permissive and not mandatory in nature. There is also an intermediate possibility for the law. In between the permissive and mandatory standards of the law are those areas where the law encourages but does not demand certain actions. An example of this would be the law's granting the corporation tax deductions for charitable contributions.

Christopher Stone has been one of the leading voices in the corporate social responsibility debate. He augments his proposals for interventionist legal strategies with some important reflections on the nature and scope of business' social obligations. In the passage below, Professor Stone begins by noting the common arguments against social responsibility for business:

> First, the opponent of "corporate social responsibility" will point out that the discretion of the firm's managers to divert funds to noneconomic uses is limited by the pressures of competition. If the managers ignore these constraints in any nontrivial way, the company, it will be said, cannot survive.
>
> Second, the managers have obligations to others to consider—investors, creditors, employees—obligations which have a moral as well as a legal basis. If competition in the industry is imperfect enough that the managers are retaining discretionary funds, the shareholders, it will be said, have a prior claim on them. For that matter, why should a risk be transferred from the firm's neighbors to its lenders?
>
> Third, there is the presumptive capacity of the market to allocate resources correctly. And the opponents of social responsibility need not stand upon any exaggerated virtues of "the market system" per se. If a disapproved course of conduct emerges profitable under prevailing market constraints, then, as we have observed, society can "correct" the company's course by superimposing legal constraints—if need be, through some of the nonconventional interventionist techniques examined above. The law-corrected profit signal can thus be portrayed as presumptively the most accurate proxy for the social welfare.
>
> From this last point, one could argue, finally, that any deviation by the managers involves an unwarranted arrogation of political power. . . .[13]

Granting the general strength of these arguments, Stone contends that there still remains a need for voluntary action by management in the social responsibility area. He points out that these arguments against corporate social responsibility prove too much. In their usual form, most could be used as arguments against any sort of unselfish behavior by natural persons. In our society and in others, however, individuals are encouraged in many ways to act not only in accord with the law but in harmony with various ethical codes and social mores. Most of us, after all, would not push to the front of a supermarket line even in the absence of legal liability. Such codes and conventions serve a valuable purpose. They make our lives more harmonious and pleasant without incurring the costs involved with legal intervention.

Just as we wish individuals to internalize a sense of ethics, Stone argues, so we should want corporations to be guided by more than minimal legal compliance. Having the decisions of corporate managers guided by a genuine sense of social responsibility would in some ways be superior to a legislative approach.

> We know that it is futile to expect lawmakers to anticipate and sensibly provide for all forms of socially undesirable behavior as the society evolves. We know, too, that to order and control society through law entails various sacrifices, and that beyond some margin, the incremental benefit of enforcing social desiderata by law exceeds those marginal costs. Indeed, it is possible that by relying on law as a control device, and therefore laying down a relatively precise "bright line" standard of impermissible conduct, we may tempt actors to press their conduct to the outer bounds of what they can get away with. As a consequence, reliance on clear legal rules may induce more unwanted activity than if we trust in the looser and less authoritative prohibitions of moral codes.[14]

THE MARKET DEMANDS OF INVESTORS

A third significant development in corporate law is the new perception of the relation of the individual shareholder to the corporate enterprise. Although, as previously noted, such shareholders are largely excluded from the internal decision-making process of the corporation, they continue to exert an influence of a different kind. This influence stems from their market demands as investors. Such an influence was a significant factor during the corporate mergers and acquisitions that prevailed in the 1980s.

Mergers and acquisitions are not always friendly. Many involve hostile takeovers of the sort which concerns the directors and officers at Liberty Oil. A hostile takeover is a merger or acquisition that occurs without the approval of the targeted company's board of directors. Thus, there is a danger that the present members of the corporate hierarchy at Liberty could lose control of the company. This can occur because of the willingness of an outside group seeking control of the target company to pay a higher price for the company's stock than is available elsewhere. By paying a premium price and acquiring the corporation's shares, Bartles Oil may be able to secure the votes necessary to elect its own slate of candidates to Liberty's board. Once it has inserted its own members on the board of directors, Bartles Oil will have effective control of Liberty.

Thus, the perspectives of Liberty's shareholders are a key part of any possible takeover scenario. In dealing with the Bartles's threat, corporate managers at Liberty must be sensitive to the current relationship of Liberty's shareholders to the company.

With the wide dispersion of stock ownership, the relationship between management and shareholders has become more abstract and formalized. This "distancing" between management and individual shareholders depersonalizes the shareholder's relation to the corporation. The shareholder becomes less an individual human being and more an occupier of a relatively narrow, formalized position, that of investor. The scope of his or her interaction with the corporation shifts from a range of critical perspectives to a single demand: profit.

What has also changed is the shareholders' forum for exercising influence. As investors, they no longer look primarily to the corporate internal process but rather to the market as the instrument for effectuating their choices. Their legal right to vote has been replaced by the economic choice to buy or sell the corporation's stock. What began as direct participation in the internal decision-making process of the corporation has become an external, indirect control mediated through the stock market.

Corporate management ignores the market demand of investors for profit at its own peril. With the everpresent possibility of a hostile takeover, managers must continually consider the effects of their decisions on the value of the corporation's stock. Failure to maximize shareholder value invites others to buy the corporation's stock at a premium and thereby gain control of the corporation. Thus, it is not surprising that the threat of a takeover by Bartles Oil is on the minds of Liberty's corporate hierarchy as they struggle with the recent oil spill.

It is also true that others besides management and the shareholders have a stake in the outcome of Bartles's takeover attempt. Lower-level employees should also be concerned. As Charles Osborne is aware, upper-level managers can sometimes negotiate golden parachutes for themselves, thus lessening the impact of a job loss, but ordinary employees are in a more vulnerable position. Bartles Oil is likely to wish to restructure Liberty in some way so as to make it a more efficient company. This may entail the loss of a great many lower-level positions. Moreover, ordinary employees may have little influence over the directors, officers, and shareholders who are making decisions regarding these matters. Director of Public Relations Shirley Lewis's expression of concern for these employees is understandable.

Along with involving the interest of the employees, corporate takeovers also have bearing on issues of concern to the wider community. For example, it appears that Bartles Oil uses ships which are more environmentally safe than those used by Liberty. As Charles Osborne tells Harry Mayer, "Harry, if Bartles Oil takes us over, they'll scrap or sell off our fleet. They use only three-hulled tankers. This sort of thing wouldn't happen with Bartles." To what degree should such public concerns influence the outcome of Bartles's takeover attempt?

Another important aspect of the investor's market demand for profit is present in the trend toward individuals owning stock not directly but rather indirectly through entities such as pension plans. Pension plans hold a tremendous amount of stock in American companies and do not necessarily act in the ways that characterized individual investors of the past.

It is, therefore, essential to recognize that investors include not only individuals but also institutions. Because of their expertise, resources, and control of large blocks of stock, the institutional shareholders are a central part of modern corporate developments.

Indeed, it has been argued that we have entered a new stage of corporate governance, the stage of "finance corporatism."[15] This new stage is dominated by institutional investors and professional investment managers. A mark of this new era was the wave of corporate takeovers in the 1980s. Institutional investors managing their capital so as to maximize short-term performance provided the means for a number of highly leveraged corporate takeovers. Such takeovers raise tremendous issues for shareholders, employees, customers, suppliers, communities, and the general economy. Most dramatically, the actions of institutional investors appear to have contributed to the October 1987 stock market crash.

ETHICAL DILEMMAS AND CORPORATE MANAGERS

We have discussed three overarching legal trends affecting modern corporate law. They are: the consolidation of management's power over the internal corporate decision-making process; the government's increased regulation of managerial choices in the public interest; and the shareholder's market demand for profit. Each of these three trends implies something about the proper role for managers. Underlying the trends are three different views which management may take with respect to its role and function.

(1) The consolidation of management's power over the corporate internal decision-making process leads managers to see themselves as autonomous professionals. Granted a certain degree of discretion by the law, managers may act according to their professional judgment and purposes.

(2) Government's regulation of managerial choices in the public interest leads management to view itself as a public trustee. With the emergence of a substantial body of federal law aimed at social goals,

managers must accept a broadened range of responsibilities which foster the public good.

(3) The shareholder's market demand for profit leads management to see its role as an agent for the shareholders. Faced with the possibility of hostile takeovers, management needs to maximize the value of the corporation's shares.

Clearly, these three different views of management's role are in tension with each other. The conflicts generated by these differing role obligations are the basis of many of the particular ethical dilemmas faced by corporate managers. For example, does management's desire for a greater market share justify the marketing of a less nutritious food product? Or, what should a manager do if short-term profit demands by shareholders call for actions that conflict with the manager's view of the corporation's long-term needs?

A growing number of corporate executives have recognized the ethical dilemmas which are presented by their positions and have begun to speak out on these issues. Consider, for example, the following excerpt from a presentation by William D. Smithburg, chairman and chief executive officer (CEO) of the Quaker Oats Company. He begins by acknowledging the growing interest in ethics. Then, he proceeds to discuss his approach toward particular ethical dilemmas. Throughout his remarks, there is evidence of the three views of management's role which we have discussed. In reading the passage below, look for the conflicts among the manager's roles as autonomous professional, public trustee, and agent for the shareholders. In particular, you should note the way in which Chairman Smithburg attempts to resolve such conflicts and accommodate various perspectives. Does he succeed?

"Ethics," in general, has become a "hot" theme, thanks to studies published by the Conference Board, the Business Roundtable, and others. I'd like to discuss a specific issue—how we treat employees when we raise performance standards and how we handle plant closings and staff reductions.

All of us in America today live and work in an environment of rapid economic change and escalating performance demands.

The news about plant closings, takeovers, leveraged buyouts, increased foreign and domestic competition, and the short-term focus of investors must raise questions about how we treat our employees, and all our constituencies. Obviously, we must answer to shareholders—many of them institutions. I also have responsibilities to our 31,000 employees—many of whom are also shareholders—to the communities in which they work, and to the trade customers and the consumers who buy our products.

As managers, our job is to balance the responsibilities to all these constituencies and treat them all fairly. We also have to balance the long-term and short-term interests of these groups. And in today's environment, we can't afford to lose the long-term focus. Sometimes I'm concerned that investors lose sight of the longer-term in their fascination with short-term gratification. Our country's standard of living and its economic success were not built by short-term gratification.

Some people ask why businesses have to raise performance standards, reduce work forces, or close plants. But the economic facts indicate that these steps are usually necessary and can't be ignored. A business that doesn't become a low-cost producer in today's environment won't be around for long. You'll lose market position and all aspects of your business will suffer, or someone will buy you out and either make the operation more efficient or break it up.

The approach I suggest for dealing with tough decisions affecting employees may not be the optimal one, but it's the standard we strive for at Quaker. To start, we try to be guided by a belief in the worth and dignity of individuals, and we try to recognize the contributions they've made to the company by providing them with a "safety net" when tough actions need to be taken.

What about cases of cutbacks and raised performance standards? First, we have the responsibility to communicate clearly and consistently with employees on a timely basis. We should start communicating with them as soon as we know what we're going to do, or what we'll need from them. Second, we have to give employees the skills needed to do the job or to help them get on with their lives. That means providing the training to meet higher performance standards or, in cases of cutbacks, providing severance packages and assistance that truly help people make the transition to a new life. This assistance has to go beyond money. It should at least: help employees deal effectively with the psychological impact of job loss, and prepare them effectively for the job search, preferably in their own community. Where communities are significantly affected, we have to assist them to make the transition as well.

The reputation of our company and the trust put in Quaker's brands are ultimately at stake in how we treat our employees, especially in these tough situations. And we believe that the trust consumers put in our brands is an invaluable asset.

In summary, I think the demands on management to make tough decisions will only intensify in the years ahead. The pressure we face today will increase as a common Western European market, more developing countries, China, and even the Soviet Union all join Japan as stiff competitors with us. Moreover, demand from our investors will not diminish, and their time frames will get even shorter. In this environment, business has no choice but consistent excellent performance. But, at the same time, we cannot forget that all our constituencies deserve fair and equal treatment. The law may not demand that, but our consciences should. To steal a line from our own advertising: "It's the right thing to do."

Taking this approach requires the vision and willingness to balance both the short and long term as we lead our organizations. In trying to manage this way, strong corporate values are a great help for steering you through the tough decisions. And I'm grateful to the founders of Quaker and their successors for establishing and maintaining a strong sense of fundamental fairness and trust at the company.[16]

THE QUESTION OF CORPORATE MORAL AGENCY

The underlying assumption of most people is that corporations are a kind of property, entities acted upon but not themselves actors. This basic notion of the corporation as property is present in each of the three different views of management's role which we have discussed. The perspectives differ only in that they disagree as to the *use* to which such property should be put. An autonomous management emphasizes the primacy of professional discretion in guiding the corporation. The notion of managers as public trustees requires the resources of the corporation to be used in a manner consistent with the public good. Management serving the shareholders' desire for profit brings to the fore the corporation's function as an investment vehicle and the demands of the market.

As we saw in the previous chapter, the corporation may be viewed itself as a moral agent, an actor on the social scene which may be held responsible for many of its actions just as individual humans are held responsible for much of what they do. Thinking of the corporation in this way raises a number of further questions. Is the corporation a moral agent in the sense that a person is or in some different sense? Does it have moral duties? Moral rights? Should it be treated equally with human beings under the law, or does its organizational character call for different treatment? These questions and many more related to them will be explored throughout this book.

For now we will focus on the impact of corporate moral agency on corporate management. If, as we have argued, the corporation is a moral agent, the ethical dilemmas of management require redefinition. We have just seen how each view of management's role is related to a different perspective on the corporation. Earlier, we noted how conflicting role obligations lie at the heart of many of the ethical dilemmas facing corporate executives today. Thus, rethinking our concept of the corporation may provide a new and helpful way of looking at the ethical problems of corporate managers.

THE ETHICAL DILEMMAS OF MANAGERS RECONSIDERED

Viewing the corporation as a moral agent spotlights the importance of the internal decision-making structure of the corporation. The CID Structure is the "character" of the corporation. As is true of the character and actions of an individual, there is a causal relationship between the character of the corporation and the actions which it takes. This doesn't mean that one kind of CID Structure will *necessarily* produce a particular action. It only means that the CID Structure will tend to foster or promote certain kinds of decisions. For example, a company whose CID Structure grants sufficient power and input into the decision-making process to the engineers who review the safety of its products is more likely to produce safe products than a company whose CID Structure is defective in this regard.

The importance of the corporation's CID Structure adds a new dimension to the ethical responsibilities of individual managers. A central responsibility of corporate managers is to maintain a decision-making structure which tends to promote ethical corporate actions.

This new orientation does not replace the more traditional responsibilities presented by other perspectives on the corporation. Individual managers still have a duty to exercise professional judgment, consider the public interest, and meet the investor's demand for profit. What this new orientation does is provide a focus for meeting these concerns.

We believe that there are two main aspects to individual managers' duty to maintain an ethically sound, internal decision-making structure. The first has to do with the choices made regarding the basic structure of the company's decision-making process. This structure designates an interrelated set of roles or positions to be occupied by individual decision-makers. It also consists of policies and procedures that determine how and why corporate decisions are made. Those high in the corporate hierarchy have the ethical responsibility to critically examine this structure. They must consider the structure not simply from the standpoints of efficiency and organizational effectiveness. They must also ask whether the structure meets ethical scrutiny. To pass ethical muster, a CID Structure must promote corporate decision-making that is ethical in its process and its outcomes. Such attention to the CID Structure can make a significant difference. Consider, for instance, how a high-level corporate committee charged with monitoring Liberty Oil's environmental policies might have reacted to the proposal that Liberty use ships that were below industry standards. If such a committee had been part of Liberty's internal decision-making structure, would Liberty be facing its current crisis?

Beyond this larger responsibility for developing morally effective decision-making procedures, there is a second important aspect to corporate management's focus on its CID Structure. This second aspect stems from the realization that no organizational structure is fool-proof. Indeed, experience has shown some corporate decision-making structures to be faulty in critical areas. Thus, doing the right thing may sometimes conflict with the assigned duties of one's role and established policies or procedures. No longer is the ethical responsibility of an individual manager exhausted by the performance of the duties assigned by his or her role in the corporation. Individual managers now have a duty to consider their assignments in light of the possibility that the structure itself is faulty. This can lead to some difficult issues of individual choice, such as those involved in whistle-blowing.

THE IMPORTANCE OF INDIVIDUAL RESPONSIBILITY

It is crucial when examining the corporate enterprise to remember the importance of individual moral responsibility. The notion of corporate responsibility leaves the moral responsibilities of individual managers intact. What the concept of corporate moral agency does is enlarge the universe of responsibility. This additional layer of responsibility is a helpful notion in understanding the moral complexities of the modern business world. Combined with a deep appreciation of individual moral responsibility, it opens new possibilities for fostering an ethical business community.

In our earlier discussion, we spoke interchangeably of corporate social responsibility and the social responsibility of corporate managers. Having introduced the idea of corporate moral agency, we can now see that these are two different notions. The action of an individual manager may express a personal sense of social responsibility. For instance, John Nevels, head of Liberty's legal department, does pro bono work for the Houston public television station. It is his way of expressing a commitment to the community. This work and this commitment arise not from a corporate decision but an individual choice. Yet Liberty as a corporation is not thereby freed from its corporate social responsibilities. Indeed, Liberty Oil acts in a socially responsible fashion when it honors Nevels's corporate pledge to support the same Houston station. Such corporate action in no way diminishes Nevels's own responsibilities or obscures his actions.

What the notion of corporate moral agency does is make comprehensible and legitimate Liberty Oil's acts of corporate social responsibility. Only when we acknowledge that there is a level of collective responsibility which accompanies individual duties can we begin to sort out such responsibility and duties in a clear fashion. Such clarity can be an important step forward for both ethics and the law.

Scholars who are antagonistic to the notion of corporate social responsibility are eager to deny the corporation's status as a responsible agent.

> Those who argue that corporations have a social responsibility . . . assume that corporations are capable of having social or moral obligations. This is a fundamental error. A corporation . . . is nothing more than a legal fiction that serves as a nexus for a mass of contracts which various individuals have voluntarily entered into for their mutual bene-

fit. Since it is a legal fiction, a corporation is incapable of having social or moral obligations much in the same way that inanimate objects are incapable of having these obligations.[17]

What such scholars overlook is that these "legal fictions" have an unavoidable reality. Corporations influence the way we work, think, play, and relate to each other. Such a "mass of contracts" can do good or evil. We should not pretend otherwise.

THE RIGHTS OF CORPORATIONS

We have argued that corporations are moral agents in the sense of being capable of having responsibilities and bearing blame, but are corporations full-fledged moral agents in the sense of functioning as moral persons and having moral rights? The question of corporate rights introduces additional complexities. For instance, we have stressed how the concept of corporate responsibility in no way diminishes the duties which individuals may have, but corporate rights are a different story. Granting rights to corporations would give such entities claims against natural persons. Such corporate entitlements thus have the potential of limiting or restricting the freedoms of individuals. As individuals intimately involved with corporations, corporate managers must consider the issue of corporate rights.

One area in which the rights of corporations have received increased attention is the political arena. There is a growing involvement of corporations in the political process. Often, there is a political dimension to decisions made by corporate management. It is this political dimension that is currently worrying Harry Mayer, a member of Liberty Oil's corporate legal team. The team has been working to defeat a referendum in Ireland. On the ballot is a proposal that would prohibit the building of Liberty's refinery and storage plant. Mayer is concerned that the oil pollution caused by the break-up of Liberty's tanker will turn public sentiment against the company. A number of Irish citizens have already raised concerns regarding the environmental risks of the new plant.

Corporate involvement in the political process has become an issue in our legislatures and courts. Consider a landmark U.S. Supreme Court case, *First National Bank of Boston* v. *Bellotti*.[18] In *Bellotti*, the Court considered whether the political speech of corporations deserved First Amendment protection. Clearly, the First Amendment protects the free speech rights of individuals. Should corporations have similar constitutional protections? Should the law give to the corporate entity the same free-speech rights it grants to natural persons? This issue of corporate First Amendment rights obviously connects with the involvement of corporations in our political process.

The *Bellotti* case arose from a Massachusetts referendum in November 1976. On the ballot was a proposed state constitutional amendment. The amendment would have permitted the Massachusetts State Legislature to impose a graduated income tax on individuals. A Massachusetts statute prohibited business corporations from making contributions or expenditures "for the purpose of . . . influencing or affecting the vote on any question submitted to the voters other than one materially affecting any of the property, business, or assets of the corporation." The statute also stated that "[N]o question submitted to the voters solely concerning the taxation of the income, property, or transactions of individuals shall be deemed materially to affect the property, business, or assets of the corporation." Because this Massachusetts statute limited the ability of business corporations to participate in the referendum, it evoked controversy both inside and outside the business community. The stage was set for a constitutional challenge. Two national banking associations and three business corporations wishing to spend money to publicize their opposition to the proposed state constitutional amendment brought suit claiming that the statute violated their First Amendment rights.

The Court considered the values underlying the protection of free speech. It emphasized the "significant societal interests" served by the First Amendment. Society is served by the First Amendment in that it has an interest in the dissemination of information and ideas. Corporate speech, like the speech of natural persons, clearly promotes the societal interest in information. Said the Court: "The inherent worth of the speech in terms of its capacity for informing the public does not depend upon the identity of the source whether corporation, association, union, or individual."

The State of Massachusetts put forth important arguments. It claimed its regulation of corporate speech was justified by two state interests. The first interest was that of "sustaining the active role of the individual citizen in the electoral process and thereby preventing the diminution of the citizen's confidence in government." The idea here is that because of their vast financial resources and organizational power, corporations have the potential of corrupting the political process. The second interest advanced by Massachusetts was the state's interest in "protecting the rights of shareholders whose views differed from those expressed by management on behalf of the corporation." Here the concern expressed is that shareholders might be forced to pay for the furtherance of social or political views with which they disagree. After all, the funds used to publicize the corporate position would have to come from the corporate treasury.

Without yet revealing the court's decision, we would like to point to a curious aspect of the Court's reasoning. The Court's analysis focused on corporate speech but not on the corporate speaker. It considered whether the *speech* of corporations served society's values, but this seems mistaken as a matter of logical priority. Before deciding whether corporate speech promotes certain values, what corporate speech is must be clarified, and this requires an understanding of the nature of the corporation, including its moral status. The Court seems to have approached the matter backwards, and in Chapter 6, we will examine the issue of corporate rights more closely.

In the preceding discussion, we have tried to show that treating corporations as moral agents affects many of the assumptions that we make about the role of managers in the modern corporation. In the next chapter, we will examine how corporate moral agency affects the conventional view of the relationship between corporations and their employees. As we move through this issue and others, we will continue to emphasize how the concept of corporate moral agency can provide a new and useful perspective on many of the important questions in business ethics.

Notes

1. This chapter uses and at times modifies copyrighted material from the following sources:

   Nesteruk, Jeffrey. "Bellotti and the Question of Corporate Moral Agency." *Columbia Business Law Review* 3, (1988): 683.

   Risser, David T. Dissertation. *Corporate Collective Responsibility*. Ann Arbor: UMI, 1985.

2. Eisenberg, Melvin. *The Structure of the Corporation*. Boston: Little Brown, 1976. 1.

3. Berle, Adolf A. Jr., and Gardiner C. Means. *The Modern Corporation and Private Property*. Buffalo, NY: Hein, 1932, rev. ed. 1968. 69.

4. Nadel, Mark. *Corporations and Political Accountability*. Lexington, MA: D. C. Heath and Company, 1976. 204.

5. French, Peter A. "Publicity and the Control of Corporate Conduct." *Corrigible Corporations and Unruly Law*. B. Fisse and Peter French, eds. San Antonio: Trinity University Press, 1985. 162.

6. *Ibid.*, 20-21.

7. Stone, Christopher. "Corporate Regulation: The Place of Social Responsibility." *Corrigible Corporations and Unruly Law*. B. Fisse, Peter French, eds. San Antonio: Trinity University Press, 1985. 18.

8. Stone uses this term. *Id.*, 14.

9. *Ibid.*, 20-21.

10. *Ibid.*, 21.

11. *Ibid.*, 21-22.

12. *Ibid.*, 22.

13. *Ibid.*, 24.

14. *Ibid.*, 25-26.

15. Lipton, Martin. "Corporate Governance in the Age of Finance Corporatism." *University of Pennsylvania Law Review* 136, 1987: 1.

16. Smithburg, William. Address made at The Center for Ethics and Corporate Policy's Third Annual Benefit Breakfast, 16 Nov. 1988.

17. Fischel, Daniel. "The Corporate Governance Movement." *Vanderbilt Law Review* 35, (1982): 1259, 1273.

18. *First National Bank of Boston* v. *Bellotti*, 435 U.S. at 765 (1978).

Employees

In the examination of management in the last chapter we emphasized the importance of understanding the nature of the corporation as an organization. We also saw that one's view of management's proper role depends in large measure on one's concept of the corporation, and we pointed out how differing concepts lie at the roots of many of the ethical dilemmas faced by business executives. In presenting our picture of corporations and their activities we have stressed the importance of understanding them as moral agents.

Now we turn to a consideration of corporate employees and will look at the implications that corporate moral agency has for resolving some of the issues encountered in this area. Corporate employees are drawn from all segments of American society and form a group which is as diverse as the general population. At Liberty Oil, employees often find themselves in vulnerable and morally questionable positions while performing their corporate duties. In a complex marketplace that is frequently uncertain and increasingly internationalized, an employee's relationship to a corporation is the most significant link connecting him to the economy. The decisions that corporations make have significant effects on the lives and the communities of their employees, who often feel that they are subject to events and changes beyond their control. What kinds of responsibilities do corporate agents have to the members of this important constituency: their employees?

The corporation is a moral agent. It also provides or creates the environment or the context in which many individual moral agents make choices and take actions. The environments which corporations create are not neutral, and they condition many of the choices open to employees as they do their work and pursue their careers. The corporate environment can significantly affect the quality of individual moral decision-making for the better or for the worse.

A corporation is an organizational environment in which individual agents make significant decisions. Corporations must have some responsibility for the kinds of environments they develop and maintain. They have a responsibility to monitor these environments and, if necessary, to alter them. The corporation is the context in which employees perform their labor, interact with others, and make some of their most important moral choices. They also often derive a large measure of their sense of self-worth and even personal identity from their corporate positions. Therefore, care for this environment lies at the center of a corporation's responsibilities to its employees.

As we examine the relationship of corporations to their employees we will continue to pay close attention to the environments which they create. We will look at some of the approaches corporations are now taking to promote more ethical work environments and at some common ethical dilemmas confronted by employees.

THE CORPORATE ENVIRONMENT

Individuals act differently in organizational settings from the way they act outside such contexts. As one scholar notes, "[O]rganizations plainly exert great influence upon the behavior of many, if not most, of their human components."[1] This influence can take many forms. In a typical business corporation, for instance, there are many rewards and punishments at the corporation's disposal, and employees who perform as desired can look forward to raises and promotions; those who do not are subject to dismissal. As we saw in Chapter 2, if a corporation were not able to guarantee that employees in the various positions in its CID Structure were performing their roles as prescribed, it would be unable to make decisions or take actions as a single agent.

The rewards and punishments at a corporation's disposal operate to ensure that the behavior of employees contributes to the overall goals of the firm. For example, a corporation seeking to encourage greater productivity might tie an employee's wages to her output and reward the more productive employees with larger paychecks.

Beyond explicit rewards and punishments of this sort, there are also more subtle forces at work. Raises, promotions, and dismissals are external devices that channel the choices and the actions of employees toward corporate goals. The environments in which we work do more than influence our choices externally, they affect the very formation of our preferences as well, by influencing the development and character of these preferences. The corporate environment can affect not only what we do, but what we want.

Because corporations exercise this power over their employees' choices, they represent a critical aspect in the morality of individual decision-making. By fostering a particular environment, characterized by its own corporate culture and set of social relationships, a corporation is a decisive factor in an employee's moral outlook both on and off the job. "In the welter of practical affairs in the corporate world," notes one observer, "morality does not emerge from some set of internally held convictions or principles, but rather from the ongoing albeit changing relationships with some person, some coterie, some social network, some clique that matters to a person."[2]

Moral values can undergo a transformation in the corporate environment. The values and expectations that operate in other areas of the employee's life may lose much of their influence in the corporate work setting. One former executive put it bluntly. "What is right in the corporation is not what is right in a man's house or his church. *What is right in the corporation is what the guy above you wants from you.* That's what morality is in the corporation."[3] Given the influence and pervasiveness of the corporate environment, it is crucial for corporations to be attentive to the quality of the environments they foster, and any failure to exercise care in this regard may be a breach of their moral responsibilities.

Let us look back for a moment at the conversation between President Quinn and Vice President Mary Rogers. Rogers, you will recall, felt uneasy about the praise she received from Quinn for the market analysis of a price increase because she had attended a concert while three of her staff members had done most of the work. Imagine you are one of Rogers's staff members. Standing outside the door, you happen to overhear the conversation in President Quinn's office. Angered by Rogers's silence regarding the contribution of her staff, you report what happened to the other two staff members. What might you now do?

Often, in situations such as this, there are few options open to employees. The most obvious option is to bring the matter up with Rogers herself, but this may be unwise depending on your relationship with her. If she is hostile to being approached in this way by subordinates, the discussion may only cause friction which could disadvantage you at some later time. As your boss, she will have plenty of opportunities to hinder your career without this being known to you. Or, she may simply tell you that you misunderstood her conversation with Quinn. In such a case, it may be impossible or imprudent for you to challenge her. In all likelihood, President Quinn would not look favorably upon you were you to go "over Rogers's head" and raise the matter with him.

At first glance, the difficult position in which you find yourself seems to be the result of morally questionable behavior by Rogers. If she had been more forthright with Quinn, you would not feel slighted. Looking more carefully, we see there is a corporate dimension to this situation. The corporation has not provided its employees with a mechanism or set of procedures by which they can safely and effectively voice their grievances. Liberty Oil might have created the position of ombudsman for such matters or it might have made possible more direct communication between employees and someone in the hierarchy beyond immediate superiors. Is Liberty Oil morally responsible for this state of affairs? Has it been negligent in not providing some organizational mechanism for resolving situations of this sort?

Consider another case. Imagine that a manager of a large warehouse for a supermarket chain has a specific budget to be used to remedy infractions resulting from health and safety inspections by local authorities. In a series of cost-cutting moves, corporate headquarters has been decreasing the amount of this budget so that the manager believes he can no longer run a safe operation. He reports the situation to headquarters, but his concerns are ignored. Finally, he tells his immediate supervisor that he may inform the authorities of the unsafe warehouse. His supervisor tells him that unless he drops the entire issue, he will be demoted or dismissed entirely. This is a particularly difficult situation because if the manager does what he believes to be morally right, he will pay a very high price—demotion or dismissal. What responsibility does the corporation have for the moral dilemma this employee finds himself in?

ETHICS AND ORGANIZATIONAL STRUCTURES

Corporate leaders have long recognized the influence of the organizations they manage on individuals and have traditionally used this influence primarily to increase profits. In recent years, corporate leaders have more actively discussed organizational structures which are designed to further other goals in addition to promoting profit. William D. Smithburg, the chairman and CEO of Quaker Oats, noted that corporate ethics is a "'hot' theme" and obviously, for a corporation to pursue its responsibilities seriously, requires more than speeches or public relations campaigns. It requires specific organizational changes designed to encourage ethical behavior among the members of a corporation, and there is a growing interest in organizational structures which help to create more ethical corporate environments. Organizational attempts to pursue this goal can include changes in the CID Structure and are most often associated with explicit programs.

Corporate codes and credos, ethics conferences and workshops, and ethical audits are examples of the kinds of programs that can alter the norms and expectations that prevail in a company. Organizational actions taken under the auspices of such programs can even serve to enhance a firm's profits. For instance, one precept of a company code might prohibit waste and require the prudent use of company resources. One is also likely to find principles in such codes that borrow heavily from common morality. For example, the code of a company might require truth and accuracy in communications with others and may be supported by such a noneconomic principle as the Golden Rule: one ought not to lie because one does not wish to be deceived.

Patrick E. Murphy has examined three kinds of formal organizational changes which are helpful in creating ethical corporate climates: corporate credos, ethics programs, and ethical codes.[4] He begins by characterizing the ethics problems in organizations in a particular way. In his view, ethical problems are for the most part the result of too much—not too little—loyalty.

For the most part, ethical problems occur because corporate managers and their subordinates are *too* devoted to the organization. In their loyalty to the company or zest to gain recognition, people sometimes ignore or overstep ethical boundaries. For example, some sales managers believe that the only way to meet ambitious sales goals is have the sales reps "buy" business with lavish entertaining and gift giving. This overzealousness is the key source of ethical problems in most business firms.[5]

Murphy believes that employees are looking for help with the ethical dilemmas which are part of their working lives. Corporations need to develop and nurture structural ways for employees to receive the assistance in decision-making they require. "We know that ethical business practices stem from an ethical corporate culture. Key questions are, How can this culture be created and sustained? What structural approaches encourage ethical decision making?"[6]

CORPORATE CREDOS

Corporate credos are general statements of a firm's beliefs. "A corporate credo," writes Murphy, "delineates a company's ethical responsibility to its shareholders; it is probably the most general approach to managing corporate ethics. The credo is a succinct statement of the values permeating the firm."[7] The credo's general nature is both its strength and its weakness.

According to Murphy, credos work best in companies that have a strong corporate culture. They depend for their effectiveness on organizational settings in which there is open and free-flowing communication. He notes that small companies in particular find a corporate credo satisfactory.

However, there are likely to be problems, asserts Murphy, with the use of credos by a number of corporations. In particular, corporate credos are likely to be inadequate for the ethical problems faced by large, multinational corporations dealing with different societies. General credos are also unsatisfactory for recently merged corporations that must deal with different corporate cultures or for companies that are part of industries exhibiting chronic ethical difficulties.

Given Murphy's analysis, a corporate credo is unlikely to be of much help to a company such as Liberty Oil. With its far-flung operations and international dealings, it lacks the corporate culture necessary to reinforce a general credo. As we watch the individuals at Liberty Oil deal with an environmental crisis in California, there seems little clear commitment to any common values. There is no mention of the "way we do things here." Indeed, the individuals at Liberty Oil often seem at odds over which norms and standards should be the basis of their decisions.

ETHICS PROGRAMS

Ethics programs can involve a wide variety of corporate activities. For example, Murphy mentions an ethics education program. He describes a company in which all new employees attend an orientation session. During this session, they read and sign the company's code of ethics. Employees also view a videotape by the company's chairman, which emphasizes values and ethical standards. For the corporation's vice presidents, there is more in-depth training in making ethical decisions. These vice presidents attend a two-day seminar in which they discuss case studies that present ethical issues common to the company's business. Murphy also spotlights a different kind of ethics program, an "ethics audit." As Murphy describes the process:

> Auditors meet with the manager in charge the evening before to ascertain the most pressing issues. The actual questions come from relevant sections in the corporate code and are adjusted for the audit location. At sales offices, for example, the auditors concentrate on issues such as kickbacks, unusual requests from customers, and special pricing terms; at manufacturing plants, conservation and environmental issues receive more attention.[8]

The entire process provides a means for the gathering and exchange of information which many companies may lack. This gathering and exchange of information sensitizes employees to ethical issues and helps them to respond more knowledgeably to difficult situations they may face.

The ethics programs Murphy mentions might have something to offer Liberty Oil. At the very least, an orientation program involving the discussion of Liberty's ethical norms would give the individuals at Liberty a common basis for approaching the oil spill by one of its tankers. Indeed, an ethics audit may have prevented the spill altogether. If it had been more widely known in the company that the hulls on Liberty's ships were below industry standards, internal opposition to the practice might have developed. After all, employees have a genuine personal stake in the reputation of their corporation. Their own sense of personal worth is, as many writers have maintained, dependent on the social and moral status of the corporation. Few people want to be identified with a corporation that has failed to operate in a socially and morally acceptable fashion, even if it has been profitable. It is important for the corporation to recognize the central role it plays in creating valued membership relationships and positions from which individual humans obtain satisfaction and a sense of personal worth, and the importance of action to maintain responsibly its status in the moral community. Furthermore, employees should be trained to recognize that some of the responsibility for the maintenance of their corporation's moral status and hence, their own worth, rests on their shoulders.

CORPORATE CODES

Corporate codes are codes of conduct. More than general statements of belief, they give guidance to corporate employees regarding their behavior in a number of key areas. These codes commonly deal with such issues as conflict of interests, gift-giving, privacy, and political contributions.[9]

According to Murphy, an effective code must be tailored to the company's functional areas, such as marketing, finance, and personnel, or to a major line of business. He explains the reason for this:

> Functional areas or divisions have differing cultures and needs. A consumer products division, for example, has a relatively distant relationship with customers, because it relies heavily on advertising to sell its products. A division producing industrial products, on the other hand, has fewer customers and uses a personal sales-oriented approach. A code needs to reflect these differences.[10]

Liberty Oil would benefit from a well-drafted ethics code. Consider, for instance, the corporation's political involvement. It regularly lobbies Congress and has become involved in an Irish referendum crucial to its business interests. In such cases, there are often a number of difficult ethical issues, along with the potential for illegal and unethical conduct. An ethics code that detailed permissible conduct in this area would likely be a welcome guide to involved employees. It also might lessen the likelihood that Liberty Oil would suffer public embarrassment or be exposed to legal prosecution.

Within corporate cultures, individual employees make choices that are conditioned and influenced by their environment. Over time, the roles and rules of the hierarchy which comprise the CID Structure can influence the development of an individual's character and moral values in a significant way. The influence of the organizational environment never removes the need for the individual to make decisions or his responsibility for them. If it did, the autonomy and dignity we normally accord individuals would be violated. If employees did not remain responsible for their actions in a corporate context, they would be serving merely as the means to achieving the ends of the corporation. They are not mere means; they are individual moral agents who are ends in themselves with their own goals, values, and responsibilities.

It should be acknowledged that joining a corporation involves a moral choice, because like other organizations, such as religious groups, the military, political parties, and professional associations, corporations embody a set of norms, expectations, and moral values. A person's choice of a job and a company is an ethical decision, because offering one's talents and efforts to a corporation implies, to a significant degree, a personal commitment to the corporation's goals. Since our personal values cannot be separated from the goals of the organizations we represent and work for, the importance of this decision needs to be emphasized. Consider the case of an accountant employed by a defense contractor that produces components for nuclear weapons. Although this employee may never be called upon to do anything that is illegal or unethical in carrying out her day-to-day responsibilities, she may discover, upon reflection, that she is opposed morally to the continued production of nuclear weapons. The psychological conflict resulting from this discovery could have been avoided if she had thoroughly evaluated the corporation in question before accepting a position. Any prospective employee should be concerned not only with whether a firm conducts its business ethically, but also with whether the business it conducts, and particularly the products and services it produces, are consistent with her sincerely held personal moral beliefs, or at least are not fundamentally opposed to them. Making such a determination will require some serious moral reasoning even before a person accepts employment.

Following the initial choice to participate in the collective enterprise of the business, there are those decisions, both large and small, which must be made on the job daily. These decisions may involve issues such as how to treat a co-worker with a drug problem, with whom to share confidences, or what to do upon discovering a legally questionable corporate practice. These daily decisions require employees to struggle with moral conflicts which are often not easily resolved. The way in which they are resolved, though, will not only be significant in the individual moral agent's development, it can also affect the health of the entire organization.

Three important issues that involve the interests of corporate employees and raise significant moral questions are affirmative action, whistle-blowing, and the responsibility of corporations to provide moral work environments. We will discuss each of these.

AFFIRMATIVE ACTION

Title VII of the Civil Rights Act of 1964 makes it illegal for businesses to maintain employment practices that discriminate against any individual on the basis of race, color, religion, sex, or national origin. This act is one of the most significant pieces of civil rights legislation of the entire post-Civil War period, but affirmative action programs have their origin in a federal executive order, not in a law of Congress.

In 1965, President Lyndon Johnson issued an order (Executive Order #11246) which, among other things, required private contractors doing business with the federal government to have acceptable affirmative action programs. Since then, such programs, set up by businesses as a way of promoting hiring and promotion opportunities for women and minorities who have been discriminated against in the past, have proliferated. By promoting the recruitment and advancement of members of these groups, affirmative action is seen as a way of compensating them for past discrimination. Although the use of quotas to achieve affirmative action goals is illegal under Title VII, corporations have developed a variety of approaches. For example, PRIME (Philadelphia Regional Introduction for Minorities in Engineering), a program sponsored jointly by corporations including Dow, DuPont, and Atlantic Richfield, conducts workshops at local high schools and offers internships and visits to the companies to introduce minority students to careers in chemical engineering. General Foods has an affirmative action program in place which provides training and job counseling geared to helping minority members and women already employed by the firm to advance their careers.

Because affirmative action programs identify certain groups as protected categories and extend them preferential treatment, its attempts to redress imbalances in the work force through such measures have been challenged by some as a minority spoils system based upon reverse discrimination.

During the 1980s, the Reagan administration took a conservative approach to affirmative action and generally did not support race-, ethnic-, or sex-conscious goals in the area of employment. It tended to strongly associate affirmative action with the use of a quota in some form and felt the whole idea of affirmative action to be divisive and counterproductive. In the words of one Reagan official:

> I oppose quotas because they create an ethnic spoils system for certain groups to grab more power for their members—at the expense of individuals outside the group. That's contrary to our civil rights laws that guarantee equal protection of civil rights for all Americans, not just for blacks, women, and other minorities. . . . Just as discrimination done in the name of white supremacy was wrong, discrimination done in the name of racial or sexual preference is wrong.[11]

In 1989, in the case of *Richmond* v. *Corson,* the U.S. Supreme Court struck down an affirmative action plan of the City of Richmond that required nonminority city contractors to subcontract at least 30 percent of their contracts to minority businesses. The decision in this case has cast doubt on the constitutionality of at least some forms of affirmative action. In a bitter dissenting opinion, Justice Thurgood Marshall argued that there is "a profound difference separating governmental actions that themselves are racist, and governmental actions seeking to remedy the effects of prior racism."[12] The Bush administration has thus far not spoken with a clear voice on affirmative action policy. Questions concerning its fairness and constitutionality are far from resolved and promise to generate some of the most significant domestic political issues of the 1990s.

In this atmosphere of moral uncertainty, each corporation will have to use its decision-making capabilities to arrive at its own position on whether to adopt affirmative action programs. This will involve assessing its responsibilities to the various groups that have been victims of discrimination, as well as its general obligation to assure equal opportunity for all employees. Corporate obligations regarding equal opportunity are particularly important to consider in light of the responsibilities of corporations as moral agents. Both current and prospective employees are, as stated earlier, ends in themselves with their own goals, values, and responsibilities. Providing equal opportunity in hiring and promotion decisions requires that each person be considered on the basis of individual merit and achievements. Each person expects and deserves such treatment. Affirmative action programs are intended to improve the relative position of particular groups of people in the work force. A person is extended preferential treatment depending on whether he or she is a member of a protected group. In implementing affirmative action, the focus is on the group and on membership in that group, not on the individual. Perhaps corporations can guarantee equal opportunity to each person while also pursuing affirmative action, but in order to do so, they must remain constantly aware of the possible tension between the two goals. The failure of decisions affecting one's interests to be based upon individual merit and achievement is especially damaging when a person is already an employee and has made a contribution to the success of the firm. There are no easy answers to questions of how corporations should fulfill their responsibilities to help in rectifying social wrongs, such as those resulting from racial and sexual discrimination, while at the same time fulfilling their responsibility to provide equal opportunity for each current and prospective employee.

WHISTLE-BLOWING

Moral conflicts arise which must be faced by individual employees in every corporate environment. Most of them are resolved within the structure of the corporation itself. Whistle-blowing involves instances in which a moral conflict confronting an employee is extended beyond the walls of the corporation. A whistle-blower is an employee who takes information out of corporate channels in an attempt to stop, prevent, or expose what he or she perceives to be wrongdoing by the firm.

A recent, well-publicized, whistle-blowing case involved the Sierra Research Division of the LTV Corporation in New York state and one of its employees, Robert Grasty. Grasty was a $65,000-a-year marketing executive who began working for Sierra in 1987. At that time, the firm was competing for a contract from the U.S. Air Force to build an anti-radiation missile decoy system. Grasty, as the firm's marketing manager for advanced technology products, was put in charge of the effort to sell Sierra's proposal to the military. At a meeting in January 1987, he learned that the company had obtained classified Air Force documents containing its acquisition plan for the decoy system.

Over the next two years, Grasty conducted a private internal investigation in which he saved interoffice memos and other documents on the missile project and secretly tape-recorded discussions he had with other Sierra executives.

His persistent questioning of company officials about the missile project and their relationships to the Pentagon led to his firing in 1989. Immediately after his dismissal, he contacted the FBI office in Buffalo, New York, which started its own investigation lasting over a year and resulting in the suspensions of five top Sierra executives. The FBI investigation exposed the company's involvement in a scheme to obtain secret military documents, and in August of 1990, Sierra admitted its illegal efforts to win a government contract and agreed to pay a $1.5 million civil fine. Under the provisions of the federal False Claims Act—sometimes known as the "whistle-blower law"—Grasty was awarded $375,000 of the fine paid by the company. He continued to be unemployed for well over a year after his dismissal and was told by an employment agency that companies are very reluctant to hire people that have been whistle-blowers.

Important questions arise when whistle-blowing has occurred. First, we should ask whether the claims made and the charges leveled were accurate or not. We may also have questions about the intentions and motivations of the whistle-blower. Whistle-blowing is not always undertaken for high-minded moral reasons. An employee may "blow the whistle" as a way of carrying out a personal vendetta against superiors. What conclusions are we to draw when the charges leveled were accurate, but when the action was taken primarily to harm others or an entire organization, rather than to stop wrongdoing?

Whistle-blowing involves serious consequences for any corporation. Taking sensitive information out of corporate channels and giving it to outside agencies and individuals, such as reporters and law enforcement officials, has the effect not only of threatening the faith employees have in the adequacy of the firm's formal and informal lines of communication but also of undermining the trust that exists between employees themselves. One must consider whether the wrongdoing revealed justifies the harm done to a corporation. Did the whistle-blower make sufficient attempts to bring the problem to the attention of superiors and to resolve the matter within the corporation before going outside the corporate walls?

In addition to moral issues concerning individual employees, there is an organizational aspect to whistle-blowing. According to Michael Davis:

> Whistleblowing is always proof of organizational trouble. Employees do not go out of channels unless the channels at least seem inadequate. . . . While managers tend to think of whistleblowers as traitors to the organization, most whistleblowers seem to feel that, on the contrary, it is the organization that has betrayed them.[13]

He outlines three approaches useful to corporations interested in avoiding whistle-blowing. The first approach is to provide regular procedures within the corporation for reporting information which raises questions about the morality of company activities. Those who hold higher positions in the firm's CID Structure are more likely to use such information constructively to prevent wrongdoing if it is received as a part of standard operating procedure. This approach can be supported by a second one which consists of educational programs and training sessions aimed at teaching all members of the firm that raising moral concerns regarding the conduct of business can be an important part of corporate life. People should be encouraged to view such concerns as useful to an organization committed to morally sound corporate policy.

Procedures such as outside social audits provide a third approach. Social auditing, which will be discussed further in a later chapter, is a method for a corporation to obtain an external evaluation of its moral performance. Employees who are reluctant to report their concerns to superiors may be more willing to do so to outside auditors. Whistle-blowing can involve wrenching moral conflicts for an employee as he or she attempts to balance loyalty to the firm with the obligation to reveal wrongdoing. Emphasizing the organizational aspect of such situations and encouraging corporations to take structural approaches to them may help many instances of whistle-blowing to be avoided.

Imagine that you are a Liberty Oil employee and that you are present for the conversation between Shirley Lewis of public relations and Harry Mayer of the corporate legal team. Shirley asks Harry if the captain and crew of the wrecked tanker have been taken into police custody. Harry's answer to her is clearly evasive and can easily be taken to imply, with regard to the crew's location, that Liberty is engaged in illegal or immoral activity to obstruct a full investigation of the spill. As an employee, what is your obligation to find out for sure if your company is involved in wrongdoing? Does the nature of your obligation depend on your position in the firm, that is, whether you are, say, a secretary or an executive? If you do obtain solid information that Liberty is acting illegally or immorally, what should you do then? What obligation do you have in this case to attempt to resolve the situation within the firm, before going to outside agencies or investigators? These are decidedly difficult questions, but they are very similar to those with which many corporate employees are forced to wrestle in the course of doing their jobs.

MORAL WORK ENVIRONMENTS

As the influence of work environments on the moral life of employees becomes more widely recognized, the responsibility of corporations for the quality of these environments will become clearer. While corporations may not have a positive obligation to provide work environments that are morally uplifting, they do have one to avoid environments in which employees must make significant sacrifices in order to do the morally right thing. An indictment against Eastern Airlines will help to understand this latter, morally defective kind of environment.

In 1990, a federal grand jury charged both Eastern and some of its senior maintenance executives with conspiring to systematically falsify maintenance records and use improperly maintained aircraft in its passenger operations over a three-and-one-half-year period. When federal investigators questioned mechanics and supervisors at Eastern about maintenance records and procedures, they discovered widespread indications of systematic violations. The corporation and individual executives were charged with conspiring to institute policies and practices, "including intimidation and coercion, designed to encourage and cause" the falsification of safety records by supervisors and mechanics. According to the U.S. Attorney in charge of the case, employees who did not submit to the intimidation risked losing their jobs.[14]

This is an example of a corporation being responsible for knowingly creating and maintaining a work environment which forced employees to make unfair sacrifices—risking the loss of their jobs—to do the morally right thing by inspecting aircraft properly. Mechanics and supervisors must still bear moral responsibility for their individual actions and omissions, but Eastern Airlines, the corporate agent itself, must bear much of the blame for the situation.

Researchers have identified a phenomenon called "storming," which may help to explain how, under certain circumstances, corporate employees are strongly encouraged to cut corners and take risks affecting the safety of entire operations. Storming "is an accelerated rate of activity which occurs in response to an arbitrary, time-dependent incentive system."[15] One researcher has used the example of imposing a penalty on a deliverer if, for example, a pizza is not delivered within 30 minutes. The deliverer's attempts to meet the deadline by speeding, not halting at stop signs, or otherwise driving unsafely, constitute storming. This phenomenon has been associated with such dissimilar disasters as the nuclear emergency at Three Mile Island, the explosion of the space shuttle *Challenger*, and a tragic mine fire in 1984 in Wilberg, Utah. One reason that storming can cause disaster is that when it is in progress, "accurate, important, negative information is suppressed as managers focus on short-run, narrowly defined goals."[16] This exciting research on storming should be of interest to every corporation concerned with preventing the kinds of disasters that can result from work environments where employees are discouraged or prevented from taking the moral course of action.

Corporate moral agency strongly underscores the responsibility that firms bear for the moral quality of the environments in which millions of employees spend their working lives. In the next chapter, we will examine how corporate moral agency helps us to better understand the important roles of directors and shareholders.

Notes

1. Metzger, Michael. "Organizations and the Law." *American Business Law Journal* 25. (1987): 407, 410.

2. Jackall, Robert. *Moral Mazes: The World of Corporate Managers*. New York: Oxford University Press, 1988. 101.

3. *Ibid.*, 6.

4. Murphy, Patrick. "Creating Ethical Corporate Structures." *Sloan Management Review* 30. (1989): 81.

5. *Ibid.*, 81.

6. *Ibid.*

7. *Ibid.*

8. *Ibid.*, 84.

9. *Ibid.*, 85.

10. *Ibid.*

11. Hodgetts, Richard M., Fred Luthans, and Kenneth R. Thompson, *Social Issues in Business*, 5th ed. New York: Macmillan, 1987. 270.

12. *Richmond* v. *Corson*, 102 L. Ed. 2d at 854 (1989).

13. Davis, Michael. "Avoiding the Tragedy of Whistleblowing." *Business and Professional Ethics Journal* Vol. 8, No. 4 (Winter 1989): 3-19.

14. McKenna, James T. "Eastern, Maintenance Heads Indicted by U.S. Grand Jury." *Aviation Week and Space Technology* 30 July, 1990: 84.

15. Radell, Willard W., Jr. "Storming: The Losing Edge." *Scholars* Vol. 2, No. 1 (Fall 1990): 24.

16. *Ibid.*, 28.

CHAPTER 5

Directors and Shareholders

In our discussion of corporate management, we made several references to both the board of directors and corporate shareholders. In the first part of this chapter we will focus more specifically on the board, and in the second part, move on to a discussion of shareholder issues.[1]

THE DIRECTORS

The unique and changing position of board members in large corporations offers a number of challenges and opportunities. Often, the decisions made by the board involve ethical choices with far-reaching implications. Under the law, the directors stand at the top of the corporate hierarchy and are given the legal authority to direct the affairs of the corporation, although such legal authority does not automatically translate into real power. In many cases, the most powerful individual in the corporation is its chief executive officer or CEO, who may also hold the position of chairman of the board. The director in our story, Robert Krebs, seems unsure of what exactly his role should be and spends more time reacting than acting. Is this the way a director should perform? Directors of corporations express conflicting views regarding the nature of their jobs. Drawing on a recent study of corporate directors, we suggest the ways in which directors view themselves and their positions. Of particular interest to us are the insights of corporate directors into the moral aspects of their work. Directors do seem to feel that part of their job is to ensure ethical corporate choices. Do directors have a special role to play in promoting responsible corporate actions? Robert Krebs often voices concern about whether Liberty Oil is doing the right thing. What particular responsibilities does he have in this regard?

We will first look at the current status of corporate directors, and then return to the concept of corporate moral agency, which we have been developing. Conceiving of the corporation itself as a moral agent can help to illuminate some of the issues facing a board of directors and will indicate how the scope of the directors' moral responsibility can be expanded. We conclude this section on directors with some specific comments on their responsibility to ensure ethically sound, corporate decision-making.

AN EXPANDED ROLE FOR DIRECTORS

In times past, an appointment as a corporate director meant increased prestige, but little more. While many welcomed the honor, few expected to participate in crucial corporate decisions in an active and significant way. Corporate directors today find themselves in a markedly different position, and also find that the modern business environment demands from them a greater commitment of their time and talents. By accepting a position on a corporate board, a person takes on an increasingly complex set of demands and responsibilities, and this is reflected in the comments modern corporate directors make regarding their jobs.

> In the early years, being invited to join a board was a sign of respect. . . some people served on a lot of boards because the duties were minimal. We weren't given much information before a meeting and even attendance wasn't essential. If you went, it was to listen to management describe its plans. But now that the courts hold directors liable if they don't uphold the business judgement rule, directors have begun to ask for information so they can make informed decisions. They have to be more responsible now—they can't go on 18 boards now, because it's too dangerous.

> Directors today don't want colleagues like the old ones who rubber-stamped management's decisions. You don't want to share responsibilities—or liabilities—with people who don't pull their own weight or do their homework.

> Directors are more forward nowadays. There's no more of the good-old-boy club meeting atmosphere, because of the directors' responsibility and liability. They don't assume something is correct simply because the CEO said it. They want proof he's right. I'm on seven boards, and the directors question deeply at every meeting I attend.[2]

This new orientation of directors is resulting in more active corporate boards. Board members are less likely than they once were to "assume something is correct simply because the CEO said it." The greater board activity associated with this new independence is indicative of a shift in power toward corporate directors. Jay W. Lorsch and Elizabeth MacIver recently published a study of corporate directors, *Pawns or Potentates: The Reality of America's Corporate Boards*, in which they suggest that the real power of directors still falls far short of their legal authority. The title of their book captures the problem perfectly. Should directors be "pawns" of the chief executive officer, used only to rubber-stamp the executive's decisions? Or, should directors be corporate "potentates," exercising real power in the affairs of the corporation?

Directors should have greater input into corporate affairs, but their influence must be given a more specific structure and focus. A central part of a director's job, which directors themselves are beginning to acknowledge, is to foster ethical corporate choices. Lorsch and MacIver report that directors identify "a third, less talked-of area of responsibility—assuring that the corporation's affairs are conducted in an ethical, legal, and socially responsible fashion. In essence, directors believe that part of their job is to ensure that managers are doing the right thing."[3]

This general perception of ethical responsibility among corporate directors should be encouraged, but how is it to be implemented? It is laudable to claim that directors have a responsibility to ensure ethical corporate choices, but such assertions are useless unless accompanied by more specific proposals for director involvement in the affairs of the corporation. Later in the chapter we will discuss the implications of a special moral responsibility of directors to ensure the proper functioning of the CID Structure.

At this point, we should emphasize that the situation is complicated by the fact that corporate directors themselves express conflicting views regarding the nature of their jobs. Lorsch and MacIver have examined these conflicting views regarding the issue of the director's proper constituency, and report that the comments of directors range from the belief that the shareholders are their only proper constituency to the notion that directors are responsible to a much broader range of groups, including consumers, employees, and local communities.

Lorsch and MacIver refer to one group of directors as the traditionalists. This group adheres "to a strict belief in the primacy of the shareholder."[4] The directors in this group provide an excellent illustration of how one's view of the board's proper constituency will influence the moral choices a director makes. The traditionalist directors do not evaluate the relative worthiness of the competing goals which contribute to the corporation's long-term viability. Rather, their decision-making is dominated by a single goal: shareholder welfare. Lorsch and MacIver write, "They have no doubts: in the land of the corporation, the shareholder is king."[5]

What this means is that the traditionalist director is able to avoid the ethical conflicts which typically inhere in ethical decision-making. As one such traditionalist director noted, the resolution of any conflicts which do exist must be left to "hope."

The conflict between the company's long-term interest and that of the shareholders happens all the time, but a director is legally obligated to act on the shareholder's behalf, so you just have to hope that the two will balance out if you exercise your best judgment.[6]

Lorsch and MacIver refer to a second group of directors as the rationalizers. The members of this group do see "the conflicts and feel the tensions inherent in their responsibilities."[7] but "they rationalize them away."[8] They hold the view that "what's good for the shareholder will be good for other constituencies, and for the corporation."[9] These directors see the conflict inherent in the decisions they make, but their failure to confront it is evident from their interview comments.

> "Relating the interests of the employees, the shareholders, the management, and so forth, is very difficult. I don't think the shareholders can be evaluated in a vacuum disregarding all of the other parties, but then again you have a legal responsibility to them. I guess I've always felt that if you do the best thing for the employee, in the long run, then, you'll be automatically doing the best thing for the shareholders."

> "I feel that the stockholders are definitely my first priority. I am representing them and consequently I must always have their best interests in mind when I make a decision. If the company—more specifically, the board—is fair to the stockholders, then it generally follows that we'll be fair to the employees and the community."[10]

These directors appear to deny that their positions present them with the need to make difficult moral decisions. They seem to accept that there is a convenient resolution to the conflict of different goals and thus, for them, no ethical dilemmas exist.

Finally, the authors describe a third group of directors as broad constructionists. This group "openly recognizes that their responsibilities encompass more than shareholders."[11] If conflicts exist, "they recognize and deal with them, without assuming that every decision must be made in the shareholders' interests."[12] Even such broad constructionist directors as these do not engage in open moral reflection and dialogue to any significant degree. Due to their belief that their legal responsibility lies solely with the stockholders, they are unable to explicitly discuss their views in the board room. Even though their broader concept of their responsibilities may be consistent with evolving legal standards, they are unlikely to openly acknowledge their views in the organizational setting. Lorsch and MacIver note that directors are reluctant "to discuss their purposes beyond the traditional salute to shareholder interests."[13] Because of this, say the authors, "board discussions . . . often resemble a charade where directors, working toward the corporation's long-term interests, avoid revealing their standards and criteria or their deep belief in the need for a broad perspective."[14]

Two requirements for more effective action by directors are to have greater clarity about the proper constituency of corporate directors, and to acknowledge the real conflicts and tensions which are part of their positions. This will encourage exchange and moral dialogue on these issues, and directors will be in a better position to decide what legal authority, as well as what power within the corporation, they need to do their jobs properly.

DIRECTORS AND THE CORPORATE MORAL AGENT

Legally, directors stand at the top of the corporate hierarchy, but the enlargement of their role in corporate affairs in recent years has not occurred for legal reasons primarily. It has occurred because there has been a change in directors' perceptions of what their role in the corporation should be. The assumption that they have an expanded role in ensuring that corporations make ethically sound decisions is the most significant aspect of this new perception. Although individual directors express conflicting views regarding the nature of their jobs, a trend toward more active corporate boards has clearly been established.

A board of directors is in a particularly auspicious position to exercise a moral oversight function because of its relationship to the decision structure of the corporation. The CID Structure, as we have seen, is the feature of a corporation which enables it to reach decisions and to act. It is truly the "heart" and the "brains" of a corporation, and ensuring that it is intact and functioning properly is an essential part of ensuring responsible corporate behavior. Of the various corporate groups—shareholders, employees, managers, and directors—it is the directors who are in the best position to observe the functioning of the corporation's CID Structure, discover flaws in it, and propose changes. In Chapter 6, we will look more closely at the specific functions that an internal decision structure performs in a corporation, and discuss the kinds of flaws that can lead to wrongdoing, but here we are concerned with the relationship of directors to the structure.

Shareholders, whether individual or institutional, are primarily interested in earning a profit on their investments. The ethical investment movement and shareholder initiatives to promote corporate responsibility are important factors and will be discussed later, but practically speaking, shareholders stand outside the structure of the corporate organization. They are not in a good position to observe the corporate operations or exercise a moral oversight function on a regular basis.

Employees, on the other hand, have closer contact with the day-to-day workings of the firm and are often in a good position to identify structural flaws, particularly in corporate policy. For example, an airline mechanic may realize that his company's requirement that he and his crew meet an exceptionally high quota for daily aircraft safety inspections encourages substandard work. The problem with the employees' position is that in most corporations it does not hold the power to do more than report the problem to management.

Managers have the power to bring about changes, but the corporate hierarchy they fill is itself part of the decision structure. This fact encourages loyalty to the system among managers, and discourages them from openly acknowledging problems.

Directors also have an interest in protecting the corporate status quo, and this is particularly true when a director is also the CEO. Generally speaking though, their distance from the daily operations of a firm allows directors to develop a different perspective from that of managers. Corporate directors are also more likely than managers to be influenced by outside constituencies to which the corporation has responsibilities. When directors have no financial interest in the firm, as is the case with "public directorships," the tendency of the board to take a moral point of view is further enhanced. All of these factors put the directors in the best position among the members of a corporation to monitor its decision structure.

This unique position entails a moral responsibility for directors to discover and repair corporate procedures and policies that produce morally questionable behavior that is greater than the moral responsibility that either shareholders, employees, or managers have. As we argued in Chapter 3, managers also have a duty to maintain an ethically sound CID Structure, but the position of directors in the corporation implies a special responsibility for them. This responsibility involves a duty to make changes in a flawed structure after wrongdoing, as well as a duty to identify such flaws before wrongdoing occurs.

It is important to distinguish between the structure itself and those decisions and actions which it produces to understand this special responsibility. There is a difference between the action of Liberty Oil in flying the captain and crew of the damaged tanker out of California to Mexico and the corporate system which produced this action and through which this action was tacitly approved. Board member Robert Krebs is definitely on the right track when he questions the legality of this action, but if he understood and accepted the special responsibility we are discussing, he would also be concerned with how such an action could have been taken at all, and what defects in Liberty's structure might have made it possible. A corporation is ultimately responsible for its decision-making system just as an individual is ultimately responsible for his or her character, but a director, nevertheless, has a responsibility to monitor, discover defects, and propose changes as needed in the CID Structure.

Corporate moral agency is sometimes misunderstood to be a theory that eliminates the moral responsibilities of individual members of the corporation.

This is not the case. In fact, by helping to establish what the corporation itself is responsible for, it can also help to illuminate individual responsibilities more clearly. The responsibility of directors for CID Structures provides a case in point. If a corporate action causes harm, it is the corporation, not the directors, that is to blame, but in the context of that corporate action, questions of individual blame will arise. Perhaps that action, such as an oil spill or the manufacture of a defective product, could have been prevented had the directors identified flaws in the way decisions were corporately made. These directors may have neglected their monitoring duty, and if so, they may be to blame individually for that neglect. The blameworthiness of the directors is a separate issue from the blameworthiness of the corporate agent itself. Both individual and corporate moral responsibility are parts of a complete picture of corporate life, and establishing the responsibility of the corporation itself can help to more clearly understand the boundaries of the responsibility of the members of the corporation.

THE SHAREHOLDERS

We also consider the shareholders in this chapter. Legally, the shareholders are the owners of the corporation, but as we have suggested above, it is important to understand the changing role of the shareholders in the development of the modern corporation. In large, publicly held corporations, the status of the individual shareholder has shifted from *owner* to *beneficiary*. We will explore the changing relationship of the shareholder to the corporation and analyze the issues confronting both individual shareholders and the corporation itself. Finally, we will consider an increasingly active player in the corporate drama, the institutional shareholder, who now holds large blocks of stock, possesses considerable financial expertise, and whose activities are altering a number of the ethical issues facing business today.

THE DISAGGREGATION OF OWNERSHIP

Many of us are shareholders and we are often told that shareholders are the owners of the corporation. While this is true in some sense, it hides as much as it reveals about the shareholder's actual status. What is far more important to understand is the meaning of ownership in the corporate setting, and what has occurred with the development of the large, modern corporation is a change in the nature of ownership.

Ownership involves a bundle of rights that includes such rights as the right to possess, the right to use, the right to benefit from, and the right to manage. In the corporate setting, this bundle of rights has been broken up, and rights that were formerly in the hands of a single person have been divided and distributed to more than one person or legal entity.

This development in the nature of corporate ownership is often referred to as the disaggregation of ownership. Understanding it requires a look at each of the three stages which characterize it: traditional ownership, corporate ownership, and beneficiary ownership.

Traditional ownership

As traditionally conceived, ownership entails control. The owner of a car, for instance, controls its use, and may take it shopping, get it washed, or even lend it to a friend. This form of ownership may exist in small, closely held corporations, and when the shareholders of such corporations make the day-to-day business decisions, they are acting as *owners* in the traditional sense of the term. They own their business in roughly the same way as a person may own a car.

Corporate ownership

In the case of large, publicly held corporations, the relationship between the individual shareholder and the corporate enterprise is no longer one of traditional ownership. As we saw in Chapter 3, there is a separation of control from ownership, because of widely scattered stock holdings, that allows management—not the shareholders—to effectively control decision-making. The position of the individual shareholder shifts from that of owner to that of *investor*, and compared with a traditional owner, her relationship to the corporation is more distant and nominal. A car is usually part of its owner's daily routine. The owner takes it to work and play, fixes it, polishes it, cleans it, and shows it off to friends. With the corporate investor, a wide range of ownership prerogatives is typically reduced to a single interest: profit.

Beneficiary ownership

Even with the separation of control from ownership, there remains an active aspect to the individual shareholder's relation with the corporation. An investor lacks direct control of the corporation's internal decision-making process, to be sure, but is able to exercise an indirect control in the corporation, externally, through the stock market. While the individual shareholder's legal right to vote in board elections and on extraordinary matters has little direct effect, the economic choice of whether to buy or sell the corporation's stock can have a significant impact on the decision-making of management, and does remain a shareholder's prerogative.

In recent years, even the investor's indirect control through the marketplace has diminished because of the trend toward individuals not owning stock directly but rather indirectly through their participation in insurance or pension plans. This means that the decision-making of large institutional actors, such as banks, is interposed between the individual shareholder and the corporate enterprise. In some instances, such as a mandatory pension, this indirect individual stock ownership is involuntary. Even if individuals are allowed some degree of choice regarding their original participation, the day-to-day decisions to buy or sell the stock of particular companies are largely left to professional financial managers or others. Thus, in these circumstances, the stockholder has lost even the investor's choice of whether to buy or sell the stock of individual companies, and his role shifts from that of investor to that of a *beneficiary* of investments made by other parties.

What we see in the changing status of the individual shareholder is a progressive loss of control over the corporation. In the shift from owner to investor, the shareholder's legal right to vote was replaced by the economic choice of whether to buy or sell the corporation's stock. Now, with the shift from owner to simple beneficiary, even these investment decisions are increasingly made by someone other than the individual shareholder.

Let's imagine such an individual shareholder. Martin Johnson is in his late 20s, recently married, with his first child on the way. An English teacher at the local high school, he also acts as a faculty advisor for the Service Club, a student group which takes on community service projects. He is particularly proud of the group's recent efforts to establish a recycling center in town. He likes his job, is glad that high-school teaching salaries are finally on the rise, and has just joined a pension plan provided for teachers by the state.

Picture Johnson sitting down to breakfast on the day of Liberty's oil spill in California. Drinking his coffee and glancing over the newspaper, he notices the morning headline: LARGE OIL SPILL IN CALIFORNIA. He shakes his head, thinking to himself, "Doesn't anyone in these companies care about the environment?" He takes the newspaper to work, thinking the article is something his students should read.

What Johnson is not aware of is that his state pension fund holds several thousand shares in Liberty Oil. He is not alone in this regard. Most of the beneficiaries of the pension plan have little knowledge of the hundreds of companies which, on any given day, are part of the plan's changing investment portfolio. As a major company with a long-term record of profitability, Liberty Oil represents a good investment for the financial managers of the pension fund, and when Johnson reads his quarterly statements from the plan, he is always pleased to see that his funds are getting a good return.

What is noteworthy is how little Johnson's environmental concerns, manifested in other areas of his life, affect his choices about which stocks to own. This is because he is not really an owner in the way we have traditionally understood that term, nor is he even an investor, for he doesn't actively choose to buy or sell stocks on a day-to-day basis. Indeed, Johnson is not even aware, from day to day, of the stock he owns, because his attention is focused solely on the benefits of his participation in the pension plan.

What obligations, if any, does someone in Johnson's position have? Does he bear any responsibility for Liberty's California oil spill? What, if anything, should he do differently?

THE CHANGING STATUS OF THE SHAREHOLDER AND
CORPORATE MORAL AGENCY

The changing status of the shareholder has bearing on the issue of corporate moral agency. Conceiving of the corporation itself as an agent with moral responsibilities conflicts with the common perception of the shareholder, because that perception is based on a traditional legal notion of the stockholders as the *owners* of the corporation. The legal concept of ownership, appears to be inconsistent with the dignity and status appropriate to a moral agent. Ownership entails a kind of control which is incompatible with the autonomy we normally accord an entity capable of moral choice. If corporations are moral agents, how can they be justifiably "owned" by other agents? As individual stockholders progressively lose control over corporate affairs, corporations themselves increasingly exhibit the autonomy that we associate with moral agency. The relationship of stockholders and corporations is perhaps best viewed as one in which corporations are progressively appropriating the capabilities necessary for full moral agency. David Linowes, of the Business School at the University of Illinois, has used an analogy with the development of an individual from a state of slavery to the achievement of full citizenship to suggest how modern corporations are achieving moral autonomy and accepting greater responsibility for social welfare.[15]

We must take this new autonomy into account when considering the rights and duties of the individual shareholder. Corporate moral agency does not mean that such shareholders are relieved of all ethical responsibility for corporate actions, and in many ways, they can still have an important function in ensuring that corporations behave morally. Like other individuals associated with large organizations, shareholders should realize that they are in a relationship with a number of moral implications. The ideal, of course, is when the shareholder feels that the corporation's goals, standards, and policies are consistent with and supportive of her own values. When this is not the case, the individual shareholder has the obligation to take some action. Individual shareholders can make use of both their *voice* within the corporation and their everpresent option of *exit* from the corporation.[16] Because shareholders are no longer an integral part of the decision-making in large corporations, the opportunities to effectively exercise an individual voice are strictly limited. Within certain guidelines, individual shareholders have the right to place resolutions on the proxy statement sent out by the corporation, and currently, one finds resolutions to such issues as abortion, or investment in South Africa. Individual shareholders also need to be more conscious of their decisions in the stock market. For instance, selling the stock of a corporation which is engaged in a morally objectionable activity is an option which should be considered in many cases, because as a matter of moral principle, it is wrong to fund and benefit from activities which run contrary to one's principles. More and more, individuals are linking their investment strategies with their moral views, and some special investment vehicles, such as socially responsible mutual funds, are expanding the market options open to individuals.

We should also note the difficulties inherent in the concerted action of individual shareholders. Stock ownership is often widely scattered, and communication among individual shareholders is difficult. Beyond this difficulty, many individual shareholders lack the information, expertise and time necessary to make fully informed choices on the complex ethical dilemmas which confront the corporation. Finally, there is the problem, which we mentioned earlier, that for the most part, individual shareholders lack direct exposure to and participation in corporate decision-making. These factors may help to explain why so many individual shareholders are not able to bring moral considerations to bear in their investment activities in any serious way. Due to the trend toward indirect stock ownership through an institutional shareholder, many individual shareholders are not even aware of the particular stocks that they own.

In accepting corporations as moral agents, we are acknowledging an important new dimension of responsibility regarding their actions. Holding the corporation itself morally accountable for its actions, provides a way for the law and ethical theory to capture those corporate choices for which shareholders and other individuals cannot legitimately be held responsible. This additional dimension of responsibility complements the responsibilities of the individual shareholders. It also serves to compensate for the obstacles that hinder the average shareholder's ethical scrutiny of corporate activity, and we are hopeful that it can contribute to morally responsible corporate behavior.

It is significant that this additional dimension of corporate responsibility reinforces the obligation of corporations to act from a broader perspective than that of the demands of shareholder profit. No longer can a corporation avoid blame for its actions by arguing that its actions were compelled by simple allegiance to the interests of the stockholders alone.

THE INSTITUTIONAL SHAREHOLDER

In Chapter 3 we mentioned some of the concerns that arise as institutional shareholders come to have increasing influence over corporate decision-making. Those who manage such institutional holders of stock are under tremendous pressure to maximize profit and to maximize it in the short term. Noted one observer, "[A]nd a[n investment]-fund manager has little choice but to focus on the very shortest term, his own job depends on showing immediate gains, with his performance in most cases judged quarter by quarter."[17]

The manager of any institutional fund holding stock in Liberty would thus have to be concerned about the oil spill. Most probably, Liberty Oil will voluntarily take on at least part of the extensive cleanup costs. Furthermore, there are likely to be a number of lawsuits filed against Liberty both by the government and various individuals claiming injury. All of this will undoubtedly cut into profits, thus lessening Liberty's attractiveness as an investment over the short term. But even from a long-term perspective, there are a number of dangers on the horizon. A public outcry against Liberty can be expected, possibly followed by tighter governmental regulations. How might this loss of public confidence in Liberty along with more intrusive government policies affect the corporation's long-term profitability? Moreover, Liberty must now devote substantial time and resources to dealing with the environmental crisis. This will mean there are fewer company resources available for promoting its long-range planning and development.

Let us imagine such thoughts weighing on the mind of Carol Barkley. A recent MBA graduate, she was thrilled to land a job with a major institutional investor. Now, her first assignment is the evaluation of Liberty Oil as both a short- and long-range investment for her employer. Along with all the issues stemming from the California oil spill, Barkley is aware of the possibility of a takeover of Liberty by Bartles Oil. If the stock of Liberty falls because of the oil spill and Bartles is willing to pay a premium in its takeover bid, there may be some quick money to be made by buying Liberty low and later selling to Bartles. What should Barkley recommend? Should she consider anything else besides making money for the fund?

Pressure from institutional investors for short-term profit, coupled with the very real threat of a corporate takeover, has an effect on corporate management. Management must strive to maximize the value of the corporation's shares, even though in some cases the actions required to do so will not, in the long run, benefit the corporation. Beyond this, there are tremendous social costs to such a short-term profit orientation. Martin Lipton writes, "Whatever the perceived vices of management control, management historically pursued socially beneficial objectives such as expanding the enterprise, improving productivity, and cultivating planning, research, and development. In contrast, the new control persons—the institutional investors—share none of these social goals."[18]

Institutional shareholders also raise the possibility of a trend in another direction. For instance, many colleges and universities have begun to consider the ethical implications of their investments. Prominent among campus issues in the 1980s were educational institutions' investments in companies doing business in South Africa. Pressured by student and community groups, a number of colleges and universities divested at least some of their holdings. Thus, nonprofit institutions are also a factor in the modern investment climate. Institutions of higher learning are becoming increasingly sophisticated in their investment practices, and their choices have a high public visibility. It is encouraging that we can expect the dialogue over their proper role to continue.

Moreover, some institutional holders of stock have been trying to give their individual beneficiaries a greater opportunity to act upon ethical concerns. A major pension fund in the United States is the Teachers Insurance and Annuity Association-College Retirement Equities Fund (TIAA-CREF). Many professors and others in higher education are participants in the fund and rely upon it as a way of saving for their retirement years. TIAA-CREF recently instituted what it calls its Social Choice Account. Investments in this account must meet certain social criteria. For example, the Social Choice Account will not invest in corporations which produce nuclear energy. This specialized account allows participants in TIAA-CREF to express their social concerns while investing for their retirement.

One interesting initiative by institutional shareholders occurred in response to Exxon's 1989 Alaskan oil spill. Instead of simply selling their stock in Exxon, the shareholders exercised their influence and convinced the corporation to add an environmentalist to its board of directors. This initiative and the subsequent action by Exxon received front-page coverage in the *New York Times*. Following is an excerpt of the story:

> . . . The president of the Exxon Corporation, bowing to pressure from pension funds holding about $1 billion in the company's stock, said . . . that he would recommend that an environmentalist be named to Exxon's board.
>
> In a letter to Harrison J. Goldin, the Comptroller of New York City and the trustee of the city's pension funds, Exxon's president, Lee R. Howard, said the board would establish a special committee on environmental matters that would review corporate activities, "including their effects on worker safety and health."

Aftermath of the Spill

> The actions represent Exxon's first concessions to environmentalists and others not directly involved in the cleanup of a huge oil spill that occurred after an Exxon tanker, the Exxon Valdez, ran aground in Prince William Sound off the coast of Alaska, March 24. The ruptured tanker released more than 10 million gallons of crude oil into the sound.
>
> The Exxon move is also a significant development in a trend in which institutional investors like pension funds and foundations are taking a more active role in governing the corporations whose stock they hold. Previously such investors tended to simply sell their holdings when they were displeased with a company's management.

A List of Requests

> The pension fund investors also asked that the company spend more on environmental research and the prevention of spills, and that it consult with employees before drug and alcohol policies were changed. Exxon said in its letter that it was already doing such things and would continue to do so.

Mr. Goldin, who is a candidate for Mayor of New York, said: "This is a rather extraordinary development. It represents a company response to shareholders that is salutary, in the public interest and in the enlightened self-interest of the company."[19]

What is interesting about this case and others like it is that institutional shareholders used their power to voice specific concerns and initiate changes rather than to simply divest themselves of their stock in protest. Institutional activities are becoming increasingly significant because of the diminished opportunities for individual shareholders to effectively exercise power in the corporate setting. What is occurring is the substitution of an institutional voice for the voices of separate individuals. Greater ethical possibilities exist in the power to influence corporate governance than in the power to simply divest oneself of stock in that firm. When institutional stockholders express their preferences through their voice in corporate governance, it allows for participation and flexibility that are often useful in attempting to resolve complex moral issues. In contrast, when a stockholder sells all of his shares, he is simply divorcing himself from the company. Once the stock is gone, the power to influence management and the internal affairs of the corporation is also gone. A stockholder may achieve a clean conscience in this manner, but at the price of exercising an effective voice for moral concerns within the corporation.

NEW POSSIBILITIES FOR SOCIAL ACTION

Mutual funds are often attractive investment vehicles for small individual investors. Mutual funds pool the resources of many investors and use this pool of resources to invest in a diversified group of companies. In addition to allowing the individual to diversify her investment portfolio, they provide the small investor with professional investment management.

There are a number of ethical mutual funds which, in addition to seeking a good financial return, use ethical guidelines in choosing their investments. These ethical mutual funds differ in the particular ethical criteria they use in choosing companies for investment and offer individuals a relatively easy way to integrate their moral principles with their investment activities by allowing participation in the fund which best represents these principles.

Two of the most well-known mutual funds using ethical criteria are the Dreyfus Third Century Fund and the Pax World Fund.[20] In evaluating companies, Third Century looks at the company's performance regarding environmental protection, equal opportunity employment, consumer protection, and occupational health and safety. The Pax World Fund seeks to contribute to world peace through investments in "nonwar-related industries, firms with fair employment practices, companies exercising pollution control, and some international development."[21] Pax also refuses to invest in gambling, liquor, and tobacco industries.

In our discussion of directors and shareholders, we have suggested that treating the corporation as a moral agent implies significant changes in the roles which we traditionally associate with the members of these two groups. It implies a more active and responsible role for directors and suggests that shareholders should no longer be seen as the single or most important constituency to be served by the corporation. In the next chapter, we will examine how corporate moral agency affects our conventional view of the legal and political relationships in which corporations are engaged. Looking at corporations as moral agents not only requires us to adjust our ideas about the roles of managers, directors, stockholders, and employees, it also requires a revision in our ideas about the place of the corporation in the moral community.

Notes

1. This chapter uses and at times modifies copyrighted material from the following sources:

   Nesteruk, Jeffrey. "Corporations, Shareholders, and Moral Choice: A New Perspective on Corporate Social Responsibility." *University of Cincinnati Law Review* 58. (1989): 451.

   Nesteruk, Jeffrey. "Legal Persons and Moral Worlds: Ethical Choices Within the Corporate Environment." *American Business Law Journal* 28. (1991): 75–87.

2. Lorsch, J., and E. MacIver. *Pawns or Potentates: The Reality of America's Corporate Boards.* Boston: Harvard Business School Press, 1989. These remarks and other quoted comments from directors in this section are from this book.

3. *Ibid.,* 70.

4. *Ibid.,* 39.

5. *Ibid.*

6. *Ibid.*

7. *Ibid.,* 40.

8. *Ibid.*

9. *Ibid.*

10. *Ibid.,* 40-41.

11. *Ibid.,* 41.

12. *Ibid.*

13. *Ibid.,* 49.

14. *Ibid.*

15. Linowes, David. "The Corporation as Citizen," in *Vital Speeches of the Day* Vol. 53, No. 24 (Oct. 1, 1987).

16. For the terms "voice" and "exit," see A. Hirshman. *Exit, Voice, and Loyalty.* Cambridge, MA: Harvard University Press, 1970. 101.

17. Drucker, Peter F. "A Crisis of Capitalism." *Wall Street Journal* 30 Sept. 1986: 32; as quoted in Martin Lipton, "Corporate Governance in the Age of Finance Corporatism." *University of Pennsylvania Law Review* 136. (1987): 7.

18. *Ibid.,* Lipton, note 17, 8-9.

19. *New York Times* 12 May 1989: 1, Col. 4.

20. These two funds are described in A. Domini and P. Kinder, *Ethical Investing.* Reading, MA: Addison-Wesley, 1984. 133-135.

21. *Ibid.,* 135. Quotation from Pax World Fund's prospectus.

Political Perspectives, Economic Justice, and Legal Aspects of Corporations

I n this chapter we will examine corporations from a different perspective. We will look at their place in the moral community from the perspective of courts, regulatory agencies, legislatures, and consider the involvement of corporations in the political process.

Our central theme is that corporations are moral agents in their own right and that questions concerning their obligations, responsibilities, or rights are at least as important to examine as questions concerning the obligations, responsibilities or rights of the individual human agents who manage them and work in them.

Corporations are able to take account of the effects of their actions on others and can include moral considerations in their internal decision processes. Today, a large number of corporations are acknowledging their moral agency, and this is being reflected in their behavior. In 1990, the Dayton Hudson Corporation, along with 46 other companies, was boycotted by the Christian Action Council for providing financial support for Planned Parenthood educational programs intended to prevent pregnancy. Dayton Hudson decided to end its 22 years of aid to family planning, but in the wake of this action, it became the target of various groups that strongly support the programs of Planned Parenthood. Several weeks after this decision, it reversed itself and restored its aid to Planned Parenthood. Dayton Hudson has a history of taking its social responsibilities seriously, but there may be disagreement about whether it did the morally right thing in this situation. Was it right or wrong for the company to cut off the funding? What about its decision to reverse that action? The point is that in responding to such a situation, the corporation needed to evaluate external political pressures, consider both financial and moral consequences of alternative courses of action, and reach a decision which conformed to the corporate policy embedded in its CID Structure. In short, the corporation acted as a moral agent.

By placing corporate moral agency at the center of our treatment of corporations and the whole field of business ethics, we hope to shed more light on some traditional issues in the field as well as to address new ones. For example, in considering the relationship of corporations to courts, regulatory agencies, and legislatures, an issue of central importance that arises is the place of corporations in the law. Corporate moral agency provides a new vantage point from which to answer questions such as the following. What are appropriate punishments for corporations? What is their proper legal status? What new approaches to the control of corporate conduct should be developed?

In examining corporations from a political perspective, several important issues regarding their relationship to government in the United States arise. In particular, this chapter will look at the role of corporations as participants in the political process. Of course, corporations do not cast votes as human citizens do, but they can and do influence politics in significant ways. Should corporate political activity be limited? What implications does corporate moral agency have in answering this question?

A recurrent topic in business ethics is economic justice. The state provides a somewhat different system for the distribution of rewards than corporations do, and we will examine the principle of distributive justice associated with corporate life. We will look at the distribution of income and other valued commodities within corporations, at the ways in which decision-making power is divided among the members of a corporation, and discuss the topic of workers' participation. The topic of economic justice goes to the very heart of questions concerning the nature of corporations as social institutions and also has implications for them as moral agents.

We will review tort and regulatory law and try to show that neither area rests on a clear concept of what a corporation is or on what the law aims to achieve with regard to them. We will examine the broad features of the traditional legal approach to corporations, present several criticisms, and suggest a new approach based upon corporations as moral agents.

CORPORATIONS AS POLITICAL PARTICIPANTS

Corporations are powerful participants in the political process in the United States, and although they cannot cast votes, they influence politics far more than most human participants do. Corporations, like other groups and organizations, are regularly involved in activities such as lobbying, grass-roots political advocacy, and electioneering. From the moral point of view, the most important question concerning the political activities of corporations is: are corporations too politically powerful? More specifically, do their political activities threaten attempts by individuals or other organizations to participate meaningfully?

The conventional view of American politics is that the interests of corporations, like the interests of unions, consumer groups, professional associations, and the like, compete with each other for the attention of public decision-makers. In this system of countervailing powers, often referred to as pluralism, no one interest dominates. In fact, it is claimed that the multiplicity of interests evident in the American political arena check and balance each other. Organizations representing the interests of corporations, like competing organizations representing the interests of labor, consumers, or environmentalists, are seen as the means by which citizens in a large mass society can effectively represent and pursue their individual interests. According to this pluralist picture of politics, corporations are not too politically powerful. Pluralists will sometimes concede that corporations have resources, especially financial and technical ones, which are superior to those of competing groups, but they do not think that the political process is systematically tilted to the advantage of corporations.

If we look more closely at the political process in the United States we will see that corporations and their interests are consistently favored and supported by the government. The Constitution itself was written by men who were quite wealthy and sympathetic to others who controlled large concentrations of wealth. Early political elites tended to view those with large amounts of land and other property as somehow more politically virtuous and public-spirited than average-income or poorer Americans. Throughout much of the nineteenth and twentieth centuries, it was widely assumed that what was beneficial to major corporations was also in the national interest. The claim that "what's good for General Motors is good for America" was more than business propaganda, it was a principle of public policy.

Contrary to the pluralist view, all interests and the organizations which represent them are not created equal. A review of the long struggle of organized labor to gain political rights during the late nineteenth and early twentieth centuries or a survey of the tremendous impact that corporate interests have had on public policy in the United States, produces a picture that is different from the pluralist one. The imbalance between the political strength of corporate interests and that of organized labor is reinforced by the attitudes of individual citizens. In times of prosperity, most people tend to credit corporate activity, while in times of economic hardship, the same people, often including many union members themselves, tend to blame organized labor. American government has favored corporate interests, while its relationship with labor has been neutral at best.

There are two reasons for the preferential treatment that corporations receive from the government. First, to a great extent, political elites and business leaders come from the same social backgrounds, share common experiences in education, and have similar values and goals.[1] Quite frequently, people in high political offices also have held high positions in the corporate world. Robert McNamara, secretary of defense under Presidents Kennedy and Johnson was president of Ford Motor Company, and George Schultz, secretary of state in the Reagan administration was president of Bechtel Corporation. These are not exceptions, but instances of a commonly occurring pattern.

Second, the survival and success of the government is inextricably intertwined with the survival and success of major corporations. Government depends upon healthy corporations in an expanding economy to provide full employment, enabling the government to collect taxes and implement programs that will retain the allegiance of the citizenry. The fate of government is far more closely tied to the prosperity and well-being of corporations than it is to the well-being of other social organizations, such as religious groups or labor unions.[2]

United States government at all levels supports corporations by providing them with three important kinds of services: (1) managing the business cycle; (2) providing crucial infrastructural services; and (3) providing social programs aimed at preventing popular discontent from being directed at corporations.

The economy in the United States is not self-regulating. Corporations are provided some protection from inflationary cycles as well as from periods of high unemployment by economic intervention by agencies, such as the Federal Reserve System (FRS) and the Securities and Exchange Commission (SEC). The government also uses budgetary measures, known as fiscal policy, to even out the bumps and dips in the business cycle. By cutting taxes and spending more than it collects, the government can stimulate economic activity. Some agencies, such as the SEC, have functions that concern both the regulation of corporations and the maintenance of growth and economic stability.

The regulatory process usually serves the interests of corporations and helps them to preserve their positions of dominance within various sectors of the economy. Governmental activity that influences or manages the business cycle complements the effects of its regulatory activities by providing corporations with a stable, predictable environment that encourages maximum profitability.

Although corporations frequently take an adversarial approach to regulation, their interests and those of the government are complementary in important ways. Conflicts between corporations and the government often result from differing interpretations of the same interest, not from different interests. Corporations are likely to view their interests primarily in terms of short-term maximization of profit. The government is more likely to aim at preserving economic and political conditions that support profitability in the long run. Regarding some important issues, the distance between governmental and corporate perceptions is decreasing. For example, as corporations have come to realize that continued damage to the environment threatens their future successful operations, they have become less resistant to environmental legislation.

As the U.S. economy continues to evolve from one based on traditional industrial manufacturing to one based on services and high technology, corporate success will depend upon improvements in the tools of production. Advances in technology, convenient and efficient transportation systems, an educated workforce, and other infrastructural services essential to corporations are increasingly being provided by government and are part of a trend which one author calls "the socialization of the costs of production."[3] Through taxes, the public pays the costs of services, such as building and maintaining transportation systems or education, but corporations are allowed to reap the profits that such necessary services help to make possible. The costs of repairing many of the side-effects of corporate activity are also paid for with tax revenues. Much of the cost of protecting and restoring an environment damaged by industrial activity or of treating and researching various occupational illnesses are borne by government. When corporations do help to pay, it is often after they have been offered encouragement to do so with tax credits and subsidies.

Many of the effects of capitalism can be quite disruptive to the lives of ordinary workers. Periods of unemployment occur, local communities change rapidly as their economies respond to new circumstances, and serious occupational illnesses inflict their tolls. Left unameliorated, such circumstances can lead to social discontent which can threaten both governments and corporations. In response to many of the harsher consequences of capitalism, government has provided a host of social programs: workmen's compensation, Social Security, guarantees of collective bargaining, antitrust laws, unemployment insurance, and the like. In fact, many of these programs have resulted from governmental responses to mass discontent with prevailing economic and political conditions. These programs have been able to improve conditions sufficiently to quell discontent without significantly altering the economic arrangements in which corporations operate profitably.[4]

Our original question concerning whether corporations are too politically powerful leads to a second question. Should limitations be put on corporate political activity to protect the participation of individuals? The foregoing discussion of the pervasive governmental support for corporations does not, in itself, suggest an answer to this question, but it provides information which is important to have in attempting to answer it.

Unlike its relationship to other interests and organizations, the relationship of government to corporations is fundamentally supportive. This does not mean that corporations will prevail on every particular issue, but rather that the basic rules of the political game in America have a distinct bias in their favor. This bias may justify society in applying different rules to corporate participation in the political process from those applied to individual participation, or even to the participation of other groups.

The activities of corporate Political Action Committees (PACs) raise issues crucial to understanding the tremendous influence that corporations have in American politics. A PAC is the political arm of a corporation or of a group of corporations in a particular industry, labor union, or other interest group. The primary purpose of PACs is to channel money to political candidates. From the early 1970s to the mid-1980s, total PAC contributions to national campaigns increased almost tenfold, and corporate PACs alone contributed more than $103 million in the 1988 congressional and presidential campaigns.[5] In fact, the real "explosion" in PAC activity has occurred in the corporate sector. The total number of PACs increased from 89 in 1974 to more than 2,000 in 1986, and corporate PACs now outnumber PACs of any other type.[6] Through their corporate PACs, business-related interests accounted for 65 percent of all the money contributed in 1988.[7]

PACs present several dangers to the democratic process, and because of their strength and numbers, corporate PACs in particular, are implicated in this problem.

The first danger concerns the recipients of PAC money. Presidential elections in the United States are publicly financed, so most PAC money goes to candidates running for seats in the Senate and House of Representatives. Because incumbents—i.e., candidates seeking reelection, rather than challengers seeking seats for the first time—have a distinct advantage, the lion's share of PAC money goes to incumbents' campaigns. The already considerable advantage of incumbency is further reinforced by the greater amounts of PAC money and has led to a situation in recent years in which more than nine out of 10 incumbents win reelection to Congress. This situation stands in stark contrast to the reasoning of the constitutional framers who assumed that the membership of Congress would change significantly from term to term, thereby more adequately representing the citizenry and reflecting changes in grass-roots opinions. As legislative seats become increasingly "safe," and thus less subject to turnover, the ability of Congress to properly represent the people may be jeopardized.

A healthy democracy depends on a balance between attention to special interests, such as those of corporations, unions, and professional associations, and attention to the common interests of all the people. James Madison was convinced that both the integrity and the stability of a democracy is endangered when narrow, special interests come to dominate the political arena and exclude common interests. As the costs of congressional campaigns skyrocket and legislators come to depend increasingly on PACs, the special interests which they represent come to dominate politics. "Talking with politicians is a fine thing, but with a little money they hear you better," commented Justin Dart, chairperson of Dart Industries.[8]

This tension between special and common interests is evident in the account of Liberty Oil and the California oil spill. At one point in the conversation between Vice President Mary Rogers and President Quinn, the issue of California's attempts to get Congress to investigate Liberty's shipping procedures arises. Quinn believes that these attempts have little chance of success precisely because the Texas delegation in Congress, and Senator Grafton in particular, have allegiance to the special interests of Liberty Oil. We may assume that the support which Grafton has received from Liberty over the years is an important reason for that allegiance. The relationship of Congress to Liberty Oil has many parallels in American politics. In an environment that is already supportive of corporations, corporate PACs reinforce this bias and ensure that politicans will continue to pay greater attention to the interests of corporations rather than to common interests or most other special interests. Although it is widely acknowledged that cutting the federal deficit and reducing the national debt is in the common interest of all Americans, little progress has been made in this area because interest groups and their PACs, including the literally thousands operated by corporations, have been effective in defeating public policy that would be disadvantageous to the special interests they represent.

PAC activity also endangers individual political participation. As politicians become more dependent on PACs for campaign financing and as organized interests represented by PACs, particularly corporations, come to monopolize access to decision-makers, the voices of individuals are being squeezed out. Corporate PACs primarily target those legislators, regardless of their party, who hold positions of power on the specific congressional committees that write the legislation that directly affects the industry in question. Perhaps one reason why Americans have become cynical about the value of voting as a means of participation is that they see legislators and other public decision-makers giving less and less attention to the concerns of those not formally organized and represented by PACs.

The original national legislation outlining and regulating PACs, the Federal Election Campaign Act, was written by Congress in 1971 and amended in 1974, 1976, and 1979. It was intended to control campaign spending by setting limits and to regulate the influence of interest groups in the election process. In a series of decisions by the U.S. Supreme Court, such limits in the law, except those on money going *directly* to a candidate or to his or her campaign organization, were found to be unconstitutional.[9] These decisions have weakened the legislation considerably.

Protecting the individual citizen's participation in the electoral process was the primary purpose of the Massachusetts statute at issue in the landmark U.S. Supreme Court case of *First National Bank of Boston* v. *Bellotti*, discussed in Chapter 3. In that decision, the Court's majority struck down the attempt of Massachusetts to limit corporate political activity and laid the legal foundation for giving First Amendment rights to corporations. The statute in question did not prohibit corporate lobbying or electioneering. It only prohibited corporations from making contributions or expenditures advocating a position on a question submitted directly to voters in a referendum. Massachusetts was concerned that because of the size and strength of corporations, their involvement in grass-roots political advocacy during a referendum would threaten the deliberation and decision-making of individual citizens.

In addition to examining its effect on corporate political participation, it is tempting to infer a position on the moral status of corporations from the decision in the *Bellotti* case, because a legal foundation is laid for granting them the First Amendment right of free speech. The possession of this right by humans is so closely connected with their status as moral agents that it is tempting to infer from the decision that, in the view of the Court, corporations can also be considered moral agents. Actually, the justices did not specifically address the issue of corporate moral agency in the *Bellotti* case, but, rather, focused on the nature of corporate speech. Part of the value of free speech is that it helps to provide society with the fullest possible dissemination of information and ideas. A majority of justices concluded that limiting corporate political involvement, as Massachusetts had done, threatened full dissemination. On this basis, the Supreme Court decided that the facts warranted extending the legal protection of the First Amendment to corporations.

Are corporations too politically powerful? Should limitations be put on their political activities in order to protect individual participation in government? Any answers to these questions will be extraordinarily complex. It seems, in the interests of preserving democracy, however, that society is justified in restricting corporate political activity to some degree, because there is already a bias in our political system in favor of corporate interests and because the integrity of individual participation is worthy of protection.

Students are encouraged to examine the decision reached by the Supreme Court in the *Bellotti* case. Is the kind of corporate political activity which Massachusetts tried to prohibit really necessary to ensure the fullest possible dissemination of information and ideas in society? What about the value of individual participation which Massachusetts sought to protect? Isn't this value threatened when corporations become too heavily involved in politics, and isn't it a value worthy of serious consideration when deciding which legal rights should either be extended to or withheld from corporations?

In *Austin* v. *Michigan Chamber of Commerce*[10] in 1990, a Michigan law that prohibits corporations from using general treasury funds to support or oppose political candidates was upheld by a majority of the U.S. Supreme Court. This law does permit separate segregated funds to be used if done in a way which accurately reflects the contributors' support for the corporation's political views. Although this decision upheld certain limitations on corporations, it does not necessarily conflict with the decision in the *Bellotti* case, because this case concerns corporate involvement in elections rather than in referendums. Nonetheless, a clear and consistent approach to corporate rights with respect to political activity has yet to be provided by either the Supreme Court or by Congress.

CORPORATIONS AND SOME CONSIDERATIONS OF ECONOMIC JUSTICE

There is tremendous inequality in the distribution of wealth in American society. The 5 percent of the population at the top of the socio-economic scale possesses 20 percent of the national wealth while the 20 percent at the bottom have only 5 percent. Although these statistics remained rather stable for at least a generation, the percentage of the wealth possessed by those at the top has actually increased during the 1980s.[11] Can such a disparity in the distribution of wealth be morally justified?

The question of the justness of the distribution of wealth across an economic system is too complex to be dealt with here. We will look instead at a more manageable version of the problem: the distribution of income within a corporation. As is true in the case of wealth within the economic system, the distribution of income within corporations is highly unequal. In American corporations in particular, the difference between the incomes of high-level managers and those of employees engaged in clerical or production work is considerable. The pay of CEOs in the United States is roughly 93 times that of the average corporate worker. Can the difference between the wages of CEOs and other top corporate managers and those of secretaries, machinists, janitors, and other corporate employees be justified on moral grounds?

The *principle of contribution* is often appealed to in order to justify the distribution of income within corporations. This principle states that the greater an employee's contribution to the success of the corporation, the greater his or her income should be. CEOs are generally considered to make greater contributions to the success and profitability of a firm than vice presidents who, it is assumed, make greater contributions than laborers, secretaries, or other production employees. It also can be argued that CEOs are compensated more than assembly-line workers because suitable ones are more difficult to attract and retain than suitable assembly-line workers. Laws of supply and demand regarding the labor force may provide an explanation for the higher pay of managers, but if one is seeking a moral justification, the principle of contribution seems to provide it.

Are we willing to accept the principle of contribution as justification for the distribution of income in corporations? The difficulties involved in assessing the relative values of individual contributions often make application of this principle problematic. The situation at Liberty Oil provides a case in point. If you remember, Mary Rogers is called to President Quinn's office and praised for her report to the board defending the hike in gasoline prices. She tells Quinn that the report was really a group project and that her staff deserves credit as well. In fact, we learn that although Rogers organized the staff's efforts and assembled the final preparation, most of the work on the report was done by three members of that staff. Who deserves the credit for the contribution that the report represents? Rogers? The whole staff, including Rogers? Or, perhaps, the three staff members who did most of the work? The value of individual contributions cannot be easily assessed in such circumstances.

Cases such as these abound in corporate life. The difficulties in assessing the comparative value of individual contributions are multiplied in cases that involve a series of actions over time by an entire corporation, such as developing a new product line. By including contributions from *outside* of the corporation in his consideration, Robert Dahl comes to the following conclusion:

> Finally consider a larger firm. A firm is inherently a social and political enterprise. It is inherently *social* in the sense that its very existence and functioning depend on contributions made by joint actions, past and cur-

rent, that cannot be attributed to specific persons: the arrow of causation is released by "social forces," history, culture, or other poorly defined agents. Without the protection of a dense network of laws enforced by public governments, the largest American corporation could not exist for a day. Without a labor force the firm would vanish. It would slowly languish if the labor force were not suitably educated. Who then provides for the education of its skilled workers, its white-collar employees, its executives? One of a firm's most critical resources is language. Language comes free, provided by "society" and millennia of evolution. Concepts, ideas, civic orientations like the famous Protestant ethic, the condition of science and technology: these are social. Who has made a larger contribution to the operation of General Electric—its chief executive or Albert Einstein or Michael Faraday or Isaac Newton?[12]

If we look at corporations as moral agents, other problems in judging individual contributions and other questions concerning the distribution of income in corporations arise. Corporations may themselves be responsible for events, and it is the *whole* corporation which is to blame when there is wrongdoing or when harm occurs, or which deserves praise when some desirable goal is reached, such as making a profit, successfully marketing a new product, or providing some benefit for the entire community. As we have stressed throughout, a corporation is not simply an artificial arrangement of individuals among whom responsibility for achievements and failures can be divided—it is itself a responsible agent. Assessing individual contribution in the way which the principle of contribution implies is impossible when we look at corporations themselves as agents, and its use as a basis for income distribution within corporations may be extremely problematic. Corporate moral agency implies a reevaluation of conventional justifications for the extreme differences in income between various members of a corporation.

Power and status are highly correlated with income and are also distributed unequally within corporations. Those who have corporate power, especially managers, have higher incomes and higher status than other employees. Power in the corporate world is measured by the ability to participate in corporate decision-making, and in the typical U.S. firm, it is concentrated in the hands of management. Can this concentration of power in the hands of management be justified?

The fundamental value of democracy is the ability of people to participate in making the collective decisions which affect their lives. To one degree or another, traditional political institutions in the United States are structured, at least ostensibly, to allow for this participation. Corporations also make decisions that have significant, and often profound, effects upon the lives of the members of various constituencies: workers, local communities, consumers, and the general public. In this sense, they are also political institutions. This implies that CID Structures should be reformulated to distribute power more equally and in a manner that represents these constituencies in corporate decision-making.

A number of proposals for democratizing corporations have been offered. They generally include worker participation in corporate decision-making, and suggestions for modifying CID Structures to make that possible. The following is a description of how worker participation operates in several plywood manufacturing firms in Oregon and Washington.

> The organization of the plants varies from one to another, but all reflect the same general process. Employee-shareholders meet annually to elect from their own number a board of directors (which could just as accurately be termed a worker council). The board makes most policy decisions, but its power is checked by the whole group: for example, expenditures over $25,000 must be approved by the entire membership of the company. Similarly, any major decision to invest, build a subsidiary plant, borrow a large sum of money, open a sales contract, or sell a sizable asset must be voted on by all workers. . . .
>
> A president, vice-president, and secretary-treasurer are also elected yearly. In several mills, the president is the worker who received the most votes in the board election. . . .
>
> The board of directors appoints a general manager to coordinate day-to-day affairs. He is the company's expert on business matters and usually comes from outside the firm. The rest of the administrative staff consists of a plant supervisor, sales manager, logs purchaser, accountant, shipping expediter, and their assistants, usually all shareholders.[13]

These firms are worker-owned as well as worker-managed, but the participation of workers in governance can also exist in firms with private stockholders.

There are several arguments for preferring workers' participation to other proposals for corporate democratization, such as shareholder democracy. First, workers spend much of their lives within corporations and are more directly affected on a day-to-day basis by corporate decisions than any other group. In addition, because workers are an *internal* corporate constituency, they are likely to better understand the alternatives open to their firm than members of an *external* constituency, such as the general public. Finally, workers are also members of other important corporate constituencies, such as consumers and the local communities in which their firms operate, and may be expected to represent the interests of these constituencies in the decision-making process.

Workers' participation goes to the very heart of the nature of corporations as *social and political* institutions. The private ownership of corporations, it is often claimed, legitimates management monopoly of decision-making. On the other hand, the values associated with democratic participation in the significant decisions that affect one's life support efforts to distribute the power that is now concentrated in management's hands. Worker participation does not threaten private property, but it does require that the decision process be more open to those constituencies profoundly affected by corporate decisions. Worker participation also reinforces the principle that moral responsibility entails consideration of the effects of one's actions on others, by modifying CID Structures to guarantee this broader participation.

Workers' participation in management also would have implications for the very identity of corporate moral agents. The CID Structure is the "heart" and "brains" of a corporation, and if democratized, we can expect changes in the corporation's behavior. What might be the nature of these changes? Might we expect the behavior of worker-managed corporations to be more or less morally responsible than that of traditional management-controlled firms? Some critics have suggested that workers would be more selfish and short-sighted than managers. Others claim that after workers attain a participatory consciousness, in which they can see the connection between their participation and the consequences of their decisions, the decisions of the corporation will become more responsible. American corporations have experimented with workplace democratization for some time, but in the past several years, along with attempts to increase productivity and meet stiffer global competition, there has been a significant growth in the number of these programs. Currently, about one-half of the thousand largest corporations have at least some employees in situations which allow them participation in a wide variety of decisions concerning such matters as profit goals, budgets, assembly-line design, the purchasing of new equipment, work schedules, and even the hiring and firing of personnel.

Readers are encouraged to speculate on the effects of workers' participation, as well as other alternative arrangements of CID Structures, on the moral performance of corporations.

THE LEGAL ENVIRONMENT OF CORPORATIONS

In the United States, courts, regulatory agencies, and legislatures have the legal responsibilities for public policy regarding corporate conduct. The law pertaining to corporations can be divided into three broad categories. There are: (1) those laws regarding the relationship between corporations and their stockholders; (2) those under which corporations can be sued; and (3) those underlying the large network of regulatory agencies. The first category has been covered in Chapter 5. The second and third will be discussed below.

TORT LAW

A tort is a wrong inflicted on a person or property and primarily covers wrongs which are civil, not criminal, in nature. A tort is a private wrong, and the harm involved is considered to be limited to the person(s) directly affected.

A public wrong, on the other hand, is referred to as a crime and is an offense against society. Crimes, such as kidnapping or rape, cause great harm to individuals, but because crimes such as these are considered to be attacks on society, they have a public aspect, and the state has the responsibility for prosecuting those who commit these crimes. In the case of a tort, legal action in the form of a suit is left up to the injured person. Torts can also be distinguished from crimes by the absence of malicious intent. An action is usually referred to as a tort when the harm was not intended, but was the result of negligence or the failure to take adequate precautions.

Tort law is a part of common law, that body of law created by judicial decision on a case-by-case basis, and is sometimes known as judge-made law. One usually thinks of legislatures making laws and of judges as simply applying and interpreting them. Often, however, what various courts have done in deciding tort cases is tantamount to law-making and has been a major factor in the development of tort law.

The case of *MacPherson* v. *Buick Motor Company*[14] in 1916, familiar to most law students, is a good example of the courts making law. It involves an area in corporate torts known as product liability in which a suit is brought because of some harm caused by a product. A more recent example of product liability involves the pharmaceutical firm of A.H. Robins which manufactured the Dalkon Shield contraceptive device that resulted in serious injuries to thousands of women. Sales of the device ended in 1974, but the product was not recalled until 1984. In 1985, A.H. Robins was forced to reorganize under federal bankruptcy laws because of thousands of suits against it by users of the device. The firm set up a $2.5 billion trust fund to pay claims, but final settlements in the Dalkon Shield cases were not possible until these arrangements for compensation were approved by the U.S. Supreme Court in 1989.

For most of the nineteenth century, corporations were covered under a legal doctrine known as privity of contract. This doctrine, in effect, prevented consumers from suing manufacturers or any party other than the one from which they bought the product. By the time of the *MacPherson* case in the early twentieth century, this doctrine had begun to be dismantled by the courts, and the decision in this case was an important landmark in its demise.

MacPherson, the plaintiff in the case, purchased a new car from a dealer. The spokes on one of its wheels were defective and shortly after the purchase, the wheel collapsed while the car was being driven. Macpherson was injured. He sued Buick, but the company argued, appealing to the doctrine of privity, that because the car had been bought from a dealer and not from Buick, it had no legal obligation to the driver. The court ruled that Buick was liable for defects in its products resulting from negligence, regardless of the number of middlemen between manufacture and final sale.

As a result of this decision and others that followed, tort law has been modified to make it far easier for consumers to sue corporations for injuries from defects in product design, quality, or inspection. Such judicial lawmaking reflects the court's goal of maximizing the ability of consumers to receive financial compensation for their product-related injuries by shifting the burden of legal responsibility from the retailer, often a small enterprise, to the manufacturer, more often than not a large corporation with sizable financial resources. Currently, all parties involved, from the manufacturer of a product to consumers, including wholesalers, retailers, and even advertisers, are potentially liable for the safety and quality of the products and services they handle.

Like product liability, workmen's compensation is an important area of corporate tort law in which the need to provide the means for adequate compensation has led to significant legal changes. In this area, it has been legislatures rather than courts, and changes in statutory rather than common law, that are responsible for the changes.

In the early twentieth century, state legislatures began to enact workmen's compensation statutes that removed on-the-job injuries from the tort law system. Before these statutes, it was quite difficult for workers, suing on a case-by-case basis, to collect for their injuries. After removing these cases from the legal system, state legislatures set up government-sponsored, no-fault insurance funds for which employers are assessed premiums and from which employees receive comparatively prompt payment for their injuries. In accepting payment from the workmen's compensation fund, a worker is banned from bringing a tort action against his employer. The goal of these statutes is to guarantee more effective compensation for the victims of occupational injuries by bypassing the court system.

In both these broad areas of corporate tort law, product liability and workmen's compensation, the effect of modern legal changes has been to establish the compensation of victims as the overriding goal, one which continues to dominate corporate tort law today.

There are three forms of corporate tort: (1) an intentional tort, (2) a tort of negligence, and (3) strict liability in tort.

Intentional torts are those which are purposely inflicted or undertaken, such as fraud, libel, or trespass. Often a corporation sued for an intentional tort will argue that while the actions in question were intentional, the damages caused were not. Suppose that a corporation buried several hundred drums of toxic waste material on a privately owned farm adjacent to one of its plants and that after a number of years the drums leaked into the water supply of the farm resulting in the fatal poisoning of the farmer and his family. The corporation might argue that although it intentionally trespassed in order to bury the waste, it did not intend the deaths that occurred. The court must then ask if any corporation in the same situation as the defendant could reasonably have expected the harm to have occurred. An answer of yes supports holding the corporation legally responsible for the deaths, as well as for trespassing.

Torts of negligence involve harm caused by conduct which is careless and which in some way creates an unreasonable risk. At issue in the *MacPherson* case was a tort of negligence. It was decided that Buick was negligent for breaching acceptable inspection procedures for its automobile wheels and that this created an unreasonable risk of injury. In order to establish a tort of negligence, it is necessary to show that a corporation was at fault and that it breached the duty to take reasonable precautions in its activities. This requirement, that a corporation be at fault or morally to blame in order to be held legally liable, has its roots in the model of moral responsibility that we apply to human agents.

Strict liability in tort has, since the mid-twentieth century, come to dominate judicial policy in the product liability area because it supports the goal of victim compensation. Under strict liability, the injured party does not need to prove that the corporation has been in any way negligent or morally blameworthy. The fault requirement is simply dropped, and it is necessary to show only that the product in question was defective and that it caused the harm. Strict liability has made it easier for consumers to receive compensation, and in numerous decisions throughout the United States, the courts have established it as the dominant doctrine in product liability. Strict liability deviates from the model of moral responsibility applied to human agents, because a human agent is usually not liable to pay compensation unless it can be shown that he or she was blameworthy in some way.

One controversial issue in the area of product liability involves the problems that arise when it is not possible to determine exactly who manufactured the product which caused injury. The synthetic drug, DES, produced by a number of different pharmaceutical firms, was administered to pregnant women to prevent miscarriages. It was later discovered that DES could cause vaginal and cervical cancers in some of these women's daughters who were exposed to it before birth. A number of suits, both individual and class-action, were filed, but because none of the women could prove which of the several manufacturers had produced the particular doses she had been given, the suits at first were dismissed. In 1980 in a landmark decision, a higher court in one state reinstated the suits and decided that in certain circumstances it is not necessary to prove exactly who manufactured a product in order to be compensated. Liability was shared by the several companies which produced DES, and this policy has now been adopted by courts in most states.[15]

Corporate tort law also includes important issues outside the area of product liability. Corporations are now regularly sued for a wide variety of environmental damages and because the interests of many people are usually at stake in such cases, class action suits are frequently used.

As described above, the primary goal in corporate tort law has been to facilitate the compensation of victims. Critics have argued that another equally important goal, deterrence, is seriously neglected. Strict liability allows corporations to be held liable regardless of whether or not they are negligent. They have no special incentive to review their procedures or to give additional attention to the safety of their products or activities under strict liability, because they can still be held liable even if they scrupulously attend to their moral duties. In addition, damages are paid from corporate liability insurance. The huge liability insurance premiums that corporations pay are considered another cost of doing business, ultimately to be passed on to consumers.

In workmen's compensation, state-administered programs also currently allow recovery without proof of negligence and bar an injured worker from bringing suit against his employer. The fund from which workers collect is supported by premiums collected from the employers, although some of the costs end up being borne by government itself. Most critics agree that the statutory amounts awarded for work-related injuries are too low. Many also believe that current arrangements work as effectively to limit corporate liability and prevent suits, which might actually induce the improvement of safe working conditions, as they do to compensate workers. In both product liability and workmen's compensation the law seems unable to effectively deter corporations from activities endangering consumers and workers.

As moral agents, the same model of moral responsibility based on desert which is applied to human agents should also be applied to corporations. According to this model, an agent deserves punishment only if he or she is blameworthy. To punish someone in the absence of any moral fault, for instance in order to pursue some social goal, would violate our deepest convictions regarding moral responsibility. There is an intimate connection between legal liability and punishment and the requirements for holding someone morally responsible. Both entail finding the agent at fault in some way.

Morally speaking, the significant difference between a tort of negligence and strict liability is that in proving the former, a corporation must be shown to have been negligent, whereas under strict liability, this fault requirement is dropped. If, as we have argued, the model of individual human moral responsibility were to be applied to corporate agents, the place of strict liability in corporate law would need to be limited considerably.

Limiting strict liability and returning to a negligence standard of liability would support the law's deterrent effects in two ways. First, by punishing corporations only when they are negligent, there would be an incentive for them to review the safety of their activities and products. If corporations knew that they could avoid liability by scrupulously guarding safety, they would be far more likely to do so. This incentive is lacking under current arrangements which allow punishment without fault. Deterrence might be enhanced by assessing corporations punitive damages, in addition to compensatory damages, which would not be covered by liability insurance.[16] Such a measure would be most appropriate in cases where the harm caused or the breach of safety were particularly serious. In workmen's compensation, the law could be amended to allow for cases in which injured employees could sue their employers to supplement awards received from the public fund. Currently, some states do allow employees to sue employers in addition to recovering under workmen's compensation, and negligence must be proven in order to win such a suit.

A second way that replacing strict liability would support deterrence is by maximizing punishment's expressive function. The expression of social disapproval in response to actual malfeasance is an important function of punishment in a legal system.[17] Corporations have an obligation not to cause harm with the products and services on which the public depends, and those which violate this obligation deserve the type of social disapproval normally associated with legal punishment. In order to protect their reputations, corporations would be more likely to avoid risks involving the safety of consumers or employees.

REGULATORY LAW

The federal legislation which authorizes the regulation of business has produced a large network of regulating agencies. Among the most prominent of these are the following:

Food and Drug Administration (FDA)
Equal Employment Opportunity Commission (EEOC)
Federal Trade Commission (FTC)
Federal Communications Commission (FCC)
Federal Aviation Administration (FAA)
Securities and Exchange Commission (SEC)
Consumer Products Safety Council (CPSC)
Environmental Protection Agency (EPA)
Federal Energy Administration (FEA)
Federal Power Commission (FPC)
Federal Reserve System (FRS)
Interstate Commerce Commission (ICC)
Nuclear Regulatory Commission (NRC)
National Labor Relations Board (NLRB)
Occupational Safety and Health Administration (OSHA).

Congress created the first regulatory agency, the Interstate Commerce Commission, in 1887 and gave it specific authority to regulate the transportation industries and certain other aspects of interstate commerce. During the Progressive Era, from 1900 to the First World War, legislation was passed that created the Federal Trade Commission, the Federal Reserve System, and other regulatory initiatives were also taken by Congress. During the New Deal, Congress created the Food and Drug Administration and the Securities and Exchange Commission, among other regulatory agencies. In the 1960s and 1970s, a powerful consumer and public-interest movement provided much of the push behind the creation of agencies such as the Environmental Protection Agency, the Occupational Health and Safety Administration, and the Nuclear Regulatory Commission.

It is often assumed that the interests of business are threatened by regulation, but many of the regulations have, in fact, served corporate interests. Much of the Progressive Era regulatory legislation assisted corporations in their efforts to maintain positions of market dominance, and many New Deal regulatory programs aided major corporations in recovering economic strength after the Great Depression.[18]

The decade of the 1980s was a period of deregulation. Although usually associated with the Reagan administration, most of the legislative efforts to deregulate, particularly those affecting trucking, airlines, and banks, occurred during the Carter administration. For example, the entire Civil Aeronautics Board was abolished by the end of 1984 after a change in regulatory policy initiated in 1978. This change, which ended all regulation of domestic airline rates and routes, was actually strongly opposed by the airline industry and its unions because they saw it as depriving them of government protection from competition. Despite the movement toward deregulation, regulation is still very much a fact of life for corporations doing business in the United States. Regulatory agencies use a wide variety of techniques to bring corporations in line with the standards they set, including issuing orders of compliance, bringing civil actions, and levying fines and other penalties.

Several criticisms of the current regulatory approach are worth considering. Legal theorist Christopher Stone points out that this approach relies primarily on "harm-based enterprise liability rules."[19] The rules are harm-based because they are not called into play until after harm has occurred or until after a corporation has engaged in some prohibited conduct. They are enterprise-based because the corporation as a whole is the target of fines and other penalties. The conventional wisdom is that by targeting the entire enterprise from the "outside," and by threatening its profits with fines and the like, regulators can force it to conform to the required standards. Under the current system, no attempt is made to directly influence the internal organizational arrangements or procedures of a malfeasant corporation.

Corporate moral agency suggests a different approach which would use the law and the regulatory apparatus to encourage or perhaps mandate those organizational arrangements and procedures likely to bring about responsible behavior. The actions of a corporate agent are based upon decisions reached through a process embodied in its CID Structure. In the final section of this chapter, we will examine new strategies for controlling corporate behavior, which are based on moral agency and which emphasize the importance of changes in CID Structures.

Another criticism of the current regulatory approach focuses on the political context in which regulation takes place. It has been suggested that agencies become unavoidably "captured" by the very corporations they are authorized to regulate. According to this view, the Food and Drug Administration, for example, comes to function in a way which furthers the interests of the pharmaceutical industry, and the Nuclear Regulatory Commission becomes an advocate for the nuclear power industry. There is evidence to support this view, and researchers have argued further that agencies follow a predictable pattern in which they start out conscientiously enforcing relevant standards, but ultimately become sympathetic to the interests of the regulated industries.[20] Corporations are also able to influence the regulatory process in their favor by having their representatives present and involved on a day-to-day basis in the decision-making of those agencies which write the rules that are applied in implementing legislation. The agencies publish the proposals for these rules in the *Federal Register* and by doing so, invite reactions and responses to them from interested groups, such as corporations, before they are formally adopted. Lobbyists representing various industries are also present in the halls of Congress when relevant legislation concerning the scope and jurisdiction of the regulatory agencies is pending and they regularly exercise considerable influence.

This "capture" phenomenon raises several moral questions. Do corporations have an obligation to recognize when they have captured the regulators? Do they have an obligation to recognize when regulatory standards and procedures have become so lax that the safety of consumers is threatened? Do they have an obligation to take actions, independent of the regulators, to protect the health and safety of consumers and workers, even if doing so requires sacrificing some profit?

Such questions are raised by criticism of the Federal Aviation Administration suggesting that the agency has become sympathetic to the airlines it regulates. Critics point to a number of postponements by the FAA, particularly in the mid-1980s, of deadlines for required safety modifications on the planes of several airlines. They charge that these postponements, which were in the airlines' financial interests, unjustifiably endangered air travelers. Does this situation suggest that the FAA is too sympathetic to the industry it is regulating? What obligations do the airlines have to make safety modifications voluntarily, before they are required by law?

The conventional wisdom holds that corporations have no "consciences," have no status in the moral community, and cannot have the kinds of moral obligations we are suggesting. We believe that, as moral agents, more can be expected of them than that they comply minimally, mechanically, and reluctantly with the law.

Should Liberty Oil use three-hulled rather than single-hulled tankers? A three-hulled ship would not have broken up as did the single-hulled one polluting Monterey Bay. Single-hulled tankers are not illegal, but the industry standard calls for three-hulled vessels. Does Liberty Oil have an obligation to go beyond minimal legal compliance in the construction of its tankers? We can also question Liberty's active involvement in getting Congress to weaken the hull-strength requirements. Is this behavior morally wrong, or is it permissible for corporations to use all means necessary to aggressively pursue their interests?

A final problem in the regulatory system is created by what might be called the "attitude of minimal compliance." This attitude, often taken by a corporation and perpetuated by its attorneys, encourages the firm to comply with the law only at a bare minimum and when possible to use political influence to weaken the regulations. This attitude is reminiscent of one that children often have when faced with overbearing and authoritarian parents. It encourages them to devote more time avoiding obedience than conscientiously evaluating the demands made upon them. Stone aptly describes how this attitude is manifested in corporate behavior and reflected in the behavior of the regulatory agencies.

> When the evidence suggests a potential problem such as work-related cancer, governmental agencies, distrustful of what is going on within the corporation's walls, are under pressure to slap together a battery of regulations without adequate information, if only to protect themselves from criticism. For their part, the corporations incline to deny, delay, cover-up, and counterattack.[21]

Perhaps this situation will improve when corporations are acknowledged to be moral agents capable of more than reluctant minimal compliance.

NEW STRATEGIES FOR REGULATING CORPORATE CONDUCT

Our discussion of tort and regulatory law suggests that there is no common legal concept of corporate identity or agreement about the aim of the law regarding corporations. In tort law, corporations are seen as "deep pockets," that is, as good sources of financial compensation. Regulatory agencies often view corporations in much the same way that James Madison viewed political factions: "adverse to the rights of other citizens or to the common and aggregate interests of the community,"[22] and consider them threatening and often unruly organizations which must be closely controlled in order to protect society. The place of corporations in the criminal law is unclear and a matter of ongoing debate. In 1979, Indiana charged the Ford Motor Company with reckless homicide in a case involving defects in the Pinto. Ford was acquitted of the charges, but this landmark case did help to establish a precedent for corporations, separate from their employees, being held responsible as criminal defendants.

Moral agency provides a useful new concept of corporate identity which could serve as a common basis for tort, regulatory, and even criminal law regarding corporations. In the remainder of this chapter, we will see how it might also provide a basis for new strategies for regulating corporate conduct.

As we have seen, it is the possession of an internal decision structure which separates groups, such as corporations, which are moral agents, from groups such as mobs, which are not. An understanding of CID Structures is essential to both explain and control the conduct of corporations.

Kenneth Goodpaster has identified four stages or processes in decision-making.[23] The four: perception, reasoning, coordination, and implementation are useful in describing moral decision-making in particular, and apply to agents of both the human and corporate variety.

> . . . The responsible corporation manifests in its organizational structure, its control systems, its manufacturing and marketing practices and its management development efforts, the four elements that we have seen to be characteristic of responsibility: moral perception, moral reasoning, coordination, and sensitivity to implementation.[24]

A properly functioning CID Structure, capable of performing well at each of these four stages is necessary in order for a corporation to be able to make morally responsible decisions.

Perception is the first stage in decision-making. All corporations (as well as individual human agents) scan their environments and gather various sorts of information before acting. In particular, a morally responsible corporation will attempt to assess the potential impact that alternative courses of action are likely to have on others. When a corporation does not possess departments or units capable of gathering such morally relevant information or when its departments are under-supported or structurally isolated from other parts of the corporation, or when the lines of communication with these departments are defective, the corporation has an identifiable structural flaw which can lead to misconduct. It is quite possible, for example, that the Exxon Corporation failed to adequately assess both the likelihood and the extent of an oil spill, such as that which occurred in Alaska in 1989, and as a result, failed to take steps that might have decreased that likelihood or reduced the severity of the consequences.

Reasoning is the process by which the morally relevant information gathered in the perception stage is evaluated by the corporation in conjunction with its values and norms to reach a decision among alternative courses of action. This process can, and usually does, involve both formal factors, such as corporate ethics codes, and more informal ones, such as those values contained in what is referred to generally as the corporate culture. Goodpaster claims, referring to circumstances surrounding the production of the Ford Pinto, that considerations based on information about significant engineering defects in the vehicle, which could have prevented the Pinto from being put on the market, were excluded from the decision process. This exclusion represents a failure at the reasoning stage. Observing a corporation during a series of decisions allows one to see whether certain norms are formally or informally embodied in the organization and to determine the extent to which the CID Structure facilitates their inclusion in decision-making.

The **coordination** stage consists of a corporation's attempt to chart a course of action consistent with both moral and nonmoral imperatives. Morally responsible corporations find ways to fulfill their moral obligations and at the same time, to meet the nonmoral demands of profit, a reasonable return on investment, and the like. Success at this stage hinges heavily on the skill and creativity of management, and structural flaws affecting coordination often reveal themselves as inadequacies in manager recruitment, training, and supervision. In December 1989, the IBM Corporation announced that it would do away with 10,000 jobs in its U.S. operations by instituting a number of measures which it claimed would allow it to avoid layoffs. The attempt to harmonize these different imperatives—in this case, the nonmoral one to reduce operating expenses and a moral obligation to employees—represents coordination.

Many times, corporations act as if their moral and nonmoral goals were fundamentally opposed and as if one goal could be achieved only at the expense of the other goal. In fact, moral and nonmoral goals are often complementary, and skillful, creative managers chart courses of action for their firms which seek to harmonize these goals. Corporations with flaws in their training programs, such as the failure to promote sensitivity among managers to the potential harmony of moral and nonmoral goals, are those which are likely to perform poorly at the coordination stage of decision-making.

Implementation, which is the final stage in decision-making, involves attention to the means by which a corporate goal is achieved. The most morally commendable goal is only as good as the steps taken to implement it, because good intentions depend upon careful attention to effective means for their realization. Flaws in quality-control mechanisms and in the mechanisms by which corporations monitor and evaluate their performance are among the more important reasons for defective implementation. These flaws can lead to inadequate or mistaken information about the effects of corporate actions on others. If, for example, a corporation enacts a plan to dispose of its industrial wastes, it should have effective mechanisms and procedures in place for carefully choosing implementation methods and for monitoring the plan's overall results on the community. This implies that the corporation will take measures to closely examine the operations and safety records of any subcontractors (such as trucking companies and treatment facilities) involved before hiring them, and to review their performance as the plan is carried out.

These four stages of decision-making—perception, reasoning, coordination, and implementation—form a cycle in which information gained during implementation is part of the material evaluated in the perception stage when the corporation moves on to new decisions. The successful completion of any stage of decision-making by a corporation depends upon the successful completion of the preceding stage.

This four-part scheme is not only useful in understanding how corporations make decisions, it can also be useful in attempts to influence corporate decisions. One proposal is for a system that would warn corporations when their CID Structures are defective in ways which decrease the firm's ability to perform each stage of decision-making well.[25] A corporation, for example, in which formal or informal communication channels do not effectively transmit the morally relevant information gathered in the perception stage to loci in the firm where it can be used in decision-making, has a defective CID Structure.

Corporate actions are made possible by the operation of a CID Structure. Defective or flawed CID Structures are more likely to lead to morally substandard conduct. A warning system would provide notification for corporations when such flaws are discovered. The warning would fully describe the flaw in question, indicate how the flaw could lead to misconduct, and suggest possible structural remedies. This warning would be a moral evaluation, not a punishment. It would not require the corporation to take any particular action, and the firm would be free to respond to it as it saw fit. If a corporation chose to disregard a warning, however, and was later charged with the sort of misconduct it had been warned about, there would then be even stronger grounds for finding it guilty and punishing it. The authority for issuing warnings would rest with the various federal regulatory agencies. The Environmental Protection Agency, for example, would have responsibility for warnings where flaws could lead to environmental harm, and the Federal Trade Commission would have responsibility where flaws might lead to defective products or services. The publication of annotated versions of the warnings, along with the names of the corporations targeted, could enhance the effectiveness of this system by encouraging firms interested in protecting their images to make the changes necessary to alter their behavior.

One advantage of warning corporations about defective CID Structures is that, unlike the harm-based conventional approach to regulating corporations, it attempts to prevent harm before it occurs. The most important feature of this system, though, is that it is based on treating corporations as moral agents.

Corporate moral agency does not dictate which moral principles are correct. It suggests that corporations are organizations capable of appreciating and acting in accordance with moral principles, whatever they may be, and that they are responsible for their actions. By virtue of possessing CID Structures, corporations are moral agents. This fact should be reflected in the law, in the manner in which corporations are viewed by consumers, their employees, other organizations, and most important, in how they view themselves.

If a corporation pursues profit to the exclusion of all other values, it is because the firm has made the decisions associated with this behavior, not because the firm is incapable of pursuing other values as well. Profit maximization is a defining corporate goal, but it is not the only possible goal, and it is not the reason for every action a corporation takes. To claim that corporations act solely to maximize profit is to fail to acknowledge the many Fortune 500 companies that have established public responsibility committees on their boards of directors, or the large, publicly held corporations, including the Norton Company of Massachusetts, Gulf Oil, and Dow Corning, that have advanced further by establishing ethics committees on their boards.[26] Measures such as these may be dismissed as self-serving, public-relations gimmicks, but this would be an incorrect assessment, because acting in a morally responsible manner can often also serve an agent's other important interests. For both corporations and humans, acting morally will frequently be in one's long-range interests. Unless a potential harmony between an agent's moral and nonmoral goals were possible, morality would be an impossible project.

This proposal for warning corporations of flaws in their CID Structures rests on the assumption that corporations are capable of understanding and responding to moral evaluation by making changes aimed at bringing their behavior in line with self-imposed standards. Warnings, as indicated above, are a nonpunitive form of moral evaluation, but when harm has occurred or the law has been broken, actual punishment is in order.

One proposal for corporate punishment which has received considerable attention and which emphasizes the expressive function of punishment referred to earlier, relies on the use of mandatory, adverse publicity campaigns.[27] According to this proposal, a liable corporation would be required by the court to finance and carry out an adverse publicity campaign focusing on its misconduct, the harm it has caused, and the results of its conviction. The scope and content of the campaign would be approved by the court and overseen by an objective party which it appoints.

Corporations are concerned with their images and normally guard them assiduously, because tarnished ones can result in the loss of business, and because they value the respect of the community and their status in it. Accordingly, corporations are not likely to regard mandatory adverse publicity simply as another business expense to be passed on to consumers. For this reason, the use of mandatory adverse publicity campaigns is likely to deter future misconduct.

Adverse publicity punishment involves the interested segments of the community in controlling corporate conduct because it is the pressure of public condemnation which induces shame and encourages reform. The pressure of the condemnation exerted in a particular case will vary with the nature of the offense and with the nature of public priorities at any particular time. If there happens to be especially strong community disapproval of, for instance, environmental violations, the public can use the strength of its condemnation to send a message to the liable corporation and to the entire corporate community.

The strongest feature of adverse publicity punishment is its potential for having reformative effects.[28] It involves moral evaluation, but includes a strong retributive (punitive) element. Public attention is directed to the corporation's conduct in order to elicit condemnation, and the firm is put on notice that it has fallen below some standard of behavior and that its status in the community has been lowered accordingly. If a corporation regards itself as having acted shamefully, such a punishment can be the impetus for a responsive adjustment to regain its status and moral worth. The focus on the image and reputation of a corporation enables adverse publicity to target the whole enterprise, but at the same time, to reach into the organization and direct attention to the CID Structure. Corporations that are serious about restoring their reputations will have a clear incentive to make structural changes aimed at preventing future misconduct.

Another proposal for punishing corporations relies upon court-ordered community service. Under this proposal, a liable corporation is required to make charitable contributions in place of fines. In the famous case of *United States* v. *Allied Chemical Corporation Company*,[29] Allied's $13.24 million fine for pollution was reduced to $5 million after it agreed to contribute approximately $8 million to the Virginia Environmental Endowment. As Brent Fisse has pointed out:

> This approach to sentencing, like that of imposing fines or monetary penalties, merely requires the defendant to write a check and, unlike the position in the case of fines, or monetary penalties, gives the defendant a public relations bonus.[30]

An alternative approach to community service sanctions would require a liable corporation to design and implement some socially useful project. It might, for example, create a small business center and administer frequent workshops where its executives would use their expertise to aid owners of small businesses in the community. Such a project requires a commitment of skills and effort over an extended time and could stimulate attitudes and internal changes that would make the corporation more sensitive to ethical considerations. In order to neutralize the public relations advantage for a corporation, the community service project could be clearly identified as court-ordered.[31]

Strategies, such as a warning system or court-ordered adverse publicity and community service, could all be employed in an integrated approach to regulating corporate conduct. Warnings would be the first stage in the approach, but when harm or wrongdoing occurred, adverse publicity campaigns, community service orders, as well as conventional sanctions, such as fines, would be applied. At this second stage, any adverse publicity might be required to mention warnings that the corporation received prior to conviction, because doing so would enhance public condemnation and help to induce shame. In addition, reference to prior warnings, which contained recommendations for reform, may guide the corporation in making appropriate structural changes.

There will be cases, such as that of a recalcitrant repeat offender, in which more stringent responses are appropriate and so, a third stage in the approach is called for. At this stage, the court would *impose* changes in the liable corporation's CID Structure. Mandatory restructuring orders would express a court's judgment that the convicted corporation is unable or unwilling to voluntarily make the changes necessary to alter its behavior. Consider Liberty Oil. From what you have read, does this firm seem either unable or unwilling to voluntarily make the changes necessary to alter its behavior? If so, what mandatory changes in its CID Structure do you think might be appropriate?

There are several widely discussed options for redesigning CID Structures which have merit and could be imposed from outside the corporation. Two particularly promising ones are *public directorships* and *social audits*.

The idea behind the public directorship is to include members on the corporate board of directors who are neither stockholders nor executives. Various plans have been suggested for giving directorships to persons from groups other than those whose interests are usually represented on corporate boards. For instance, public directors could be representatives of employees, consumers, the immediate community, or the general public.[32] The job of the public director

> . . . would be to ensure that laws were being obeyed, to gather ethically sensitive information from inside and outside the corporate ranks, to serve as a liaison between government and business, and to function as a "superego" for the corporation. The director would receive complaints from employees about ethical abuses . . . and would air relevant grievances with other board members. He or she would periodically check the internal corporate system of information flow to see if it accommodated morally relevant information. The director would also evaluate and oversee the preparation of environmental impact studies, equal opportunity reports, and employee safety evaluations.[33]

In short, the public director would serve as one important channel for the firm to be apprised of important moral considerations and would be responsible for monitoring the corporation at each stage of decision-making.

A CID Structure consists of both a system of differentiated positions and procedures for reaching and ratifying decisions. Proposals for public directorships involve modification of the first of these two elements, while those for social audits involve changes in the second.

A number of approaches have been suggested for conducting corporate social audits, but all attempt, in some fashion, to formally list a firm's moral obligations and evaluate its success in meeting them.[34] It is not possible to attain nearly the level of precision in a social audit that is commonly found in a financial audit, but conducting a social audit can be one useful method by which a corporation can assess its ethical performance. The results of a social audit, which may contain descriptions of voluntary or mandatory community service projects, are presented to stockholders and made available to other interested groups. Conducting a social audit does not guarantee moral behavior, and in some cases it may be little more than a public relations ploy, but it can serve to sensitize corporations to moral considerations and can be an aid to them in meeting their obligations.

Public directorships and social audits are only two of a number of proposals for reformulating CID Structures with which both courts and liable corporations could experiment. Corporations faced with court-ordered mandatory restructuring might be required to prepare their own reform proposals and defend them in terms of the changes in their conduct they want to achieve. They might also be required to comment on any warnings they had received and on the suggestions for reform in them. The court would then review proposals, perhaps in consultation with outside experts, and when approved, issue implementation schedules. By requiring a corporation to prepare its own proposal for restructuring and reform, the court would involve those personnel most familiar with the firm and help to ensure conscientious implementation.

A 1975 case involving the Northrop Corporation provides one example of judicial experimentation with court-imposed restructuring. A suit initiated by a Northrop stockholder and the Center for Law in the Public Interest revealed a 13-year pattern in the corporation of making illegal political contributions and payoffs in the United States and abroad. Among the terms of the agreement reached between Northrop and the plaintiffs was a requirement that the board of directors be enlarged and that four new "outside" directors, subject to judicial approval, be elected. In a further measure, also aimed at preventing similar illegal corporate actions, the agreement mandated strengthening and restructuring the audit committee of the board. The degree to which cases such as this, emphasizing court-imposed restructuring, become models for policy in the future remains to be seen.[35]

Each stage of this approach to regulating corporate conduct—warnings, punishment, and mandatory restructuring—directs attention to the CID Structure and provides content sensitive to the moral status of the corporation and to Stone's recommendation that:

> Instead of treating the corporation's inner processes as a "black box," to be influenced only indirectly through its environment like a trap [referring to conventional sanctions], we need more straightforward "intrusions" into the corporation's decision structure and processes than society has yet undertaken[36]

This approach acknowledges that corporations are moral agents and gives them credit for being capable of reforming themselves. The goal at each stage is to increase the likelihood that a corporation will take the steps and make the changes necessary to act responsibly in the future.

Notes

1. The classic statement of this explanation is in C. Wright Mills, *The Power Elite*. New York: Oxford University Press, 1956. See also Thomas R. Dye, *Who's Running America?* 3rd. ed. Englewood Cliffs, NJ: Prentice-Hall, Inc., 1983.

2. See, in particular, Michael H. Best and William E. Connolly, *The Politicized Economy*. Lexington, MA: D. C. Heath and Company, 1976, especially Chapter 6, 159-187.

3. O'Connor, James. *The Fiscal Crisis of the State*. New York: St. Martin's Press, 1973. Trends involving the socialization of the costs of production are discussed primarily in Chapters 4, 5, 97-149.

4. For an excellent treatment of the role of mass discontent in the formulation of social welfare policy, see Frances Fox Piven and Richard A. Cloward, *Poor People's Movements: Why They Succeed and How They Fail*. New York: Pantheon Books, 1977. See also *Regulating the Poor*. New York: Pantheon Books, 1971, by the same authors.

5. Berke, Richard L. "Study Confirms Interest Groups' Pattern of Giving," *New York Times*, 16 Sept. 1990: 26.

6. See Figure 3 in Susan Welch, John Gruhl, Michael Steinman, and John Comer, *American Government*, 2nd ed. St. Paul: West Publishing Company, 1988. 132.

7. Berke, op. cit., 26.

8. As quoted in James MacGregor Burns, J. W. Peltason, and Thomas E. Cronin, *Government by the People*, 13th ed. Englewood Cliffs, NJ: Prentice-Hall, Inc., 1990. 162.

9. The most important of these decisions is in *Buckley* v. *Valeo*, 424 U.S. at 1 (1976).

10. *Austin* v. *Michigan Chamber of Commerce*. 110 S. Ct. 1391 (1990).

11. Reich, Robert B. "Secession of the Successful." *New York Times Magazine*. 20 Jan. 1991: 42.

12. Dahl, Robert A. *Dilemmas of Pluralist Democracy*. New Haven, CT: Yale University Press, 1982. 183-184.

13. Bernstein, Paul. *Workplace Democratization*. New Brunswick, NJ: Transaction Books, 1976. 15.

14. 217 N.Y. at 382, 111 N.E. at 1050 (Court of Appeals of New York, 1916). Cited in Richard M. Hodgetts, Fred Luthans, and Kenneth R. Thompson, *Social Issues in Business*, 5th ed. New York: Macmillan, 1987. 369.

15. *Sindell* v. *Abbot Laboratories*, 607 p. 2d at 924 (Supreme Court of California, 1980).

16. Punitive damages are those in excess of actual damages that are awarded to a plaintiff in order to punish the wrongdoer.

17. The expressive function of punishment is well described and defended by Joel Feinberg in "The Expressive Function of Punishment," in Feinberg, *Doing and Deserving: Essays in the Theory of Responsibility*. Princeton University Press, 1970. 95-118.

18. This argument is convincingly presented by Gabriel Kolko in *The Triumph of Conservatism*. Chicago: Quadrangle, 1967. See also Edward S. Greenburg, *Capitalism and the American Political Ideal*. Armonk, NY: M. E. Sharpe, 1985.

19. Stone, Christopher. "Corporate Regulation: The Place of Social Responsibility," in B. Fisse and Peter French, eds., *Corrigible Corporations and Unruly Laws*. San Antonio: Trinity University Press, 1985. 15.

20. For a review of this evidence, see *Mark v. Nadel, Corporations and Political Accountability*. Lexington, MA: D. C. Heath and Company, 1976. Chapter 4, 75-104.

21. Stone, in Fisse and French, op. cit., 34.

22. Madison, James. "Federalist #10" in Alexander Hamilton, James Madison, and John Jay, *The Federalist Papers*, Clinton Rossiter, ed. New York: New American Library, 1961. 78.

23. Goodpaster, Kenneth. "The Concept of Corporate Responsibility." *Journal of Business Ethics* Vol. 2, No. 1. (February 1983): 7-14.

24. *Ibid.*, 14.

25. Risser, David T. "Punishing Corporations: A Proposal." *Business and Professional Ethics Journal* Vol. 8, No. 3. (Fall 1989): 83-92.

26. For a discussion of these corporate initiatives, see Theodore V. Purcell, S.J., "Ethics Committees on Boards of Directors? The Norton Experience" in W. Michael Hoffman, Jennifer Mills Moore, and David A. Fedo, eds., *Corporate Government and Institutionalizing Ethics* (Proceedings of the Fifth National Conference on Business Ethics). 193-204.

27. French, Peter A. "Publicity and the Control of Corporate Conduct: Hester Prynne's New Image," in Fisse and French, op. cit., 159-172.

28. *Ibid.*, 161-166.

29. 420 F. Supp. at 122 (1976).

30. Fisse, Brent. "Sanctions Against Corporations: The Limitations of Fines and the Enterprise of Creating Alternatives," in Fisse and French, op. cit., 149.

31. French, Peter A. "Publicity and the Control of Corporate Conduct: Hester Prynne's New Image," in Fisse and French, op. cit., 169. French also suggests that for a community service project to serve the purpose of restoring a corporation's tarnished image, it must be undertaken voluntarily.

32. Christopher Stone outlines procedures for creating two kinds of full-time public directorships: general public directorships and special public directorships. See his discussion in *Where the Law Ends: The Social Control of Corporate Behavior*. New York: Harper and Row, 1975. 152-183.

33. Donaldson, Thomas. *Corporations and Morality*. Englewood Cliffs, NJ: Prentice-Hall, Inc., 1982. 191-192.

34. See Clark C. Abt, *The Social Audit for Management*. New York: AMA-COM, 1977.

35. For a more detailed discussion of this case, see S. Prakash Sethi, *Up Against the Corporate Wall: Modern Corporations and Social Issues of the Eighties*, 4th ed. Englewood Cliffs, NJ: Prentice-Hall, Inc., 1982. 86-98.

36. Stone, *Where the Law Ends: The Social Control of Corporate Behavior*, op. cit., 120.

CHAPTER 7

Corporations in a Global Community

Throughout the preceding chapters, we have emphasized the power and size of modern corporations and the tremendous influence that their actions have on individuals and on the quality of life in entire communities. The protection of individuals and society from the negative effects of powerful institutions has been a central objective in liberal democratic thought at least since the American Revolution.

The political leaders who fought and supported the American Revolution as well as those who helped to write the U.S. Constitution in 1787 were primarily concerned with building protections against the state becoming too powerful and thus threatening individual rights. The separation of the powers of national government into three branches and the elaborate, often inefficient, system of checks and balances among the three branches are both mechanisms used by the framers of the Constitution to keep the power of the government within its proper limits. The leaders who opposed the new Constitution, the Antifederalists, were even more concerned than were constitutional supporters about protecting individual rights against oppressive government. It was largely due to Antifederalist efforts that the Bill of Rights was added to the Constitution shortly after ratification.

Organized religion represented power which many influential people in both the states and the emerging national government feared and sought to limit in the name of protecting the freedom of conscience of individual citizens. Thomas Jefferson's recommendation that a "wall of separation" between church and state be erected, and the First Amendment's prohibition that "Congress shall make no law regarding the establishment of religion" are concrete examples of measures designed to prevent the government from joining forces with religious institutions in ways that would make them too powerful, and in particular, from establishing an official state religion.

The Constitution does not address the subject of corporations because, of course, they played no significant role in American social and economic life when the document was written, and because the democratic thought which informed the activities of political elites at the time concerned itself principally with how best to place limitations on explicitly political, rather than economic, institutions. Today, political decision-making and economic decision-making are interdependent. Placing political institutions and economic institutions into separate categories serves no useful purpose. As democratic thought has developed, the definition of a political institution has been expanded to include any institution whose decisions have profound effects upon the lives of the members of various constituencies.[1] Corporations, according to this expanded definition, are political and therefore are among those institutions that should be of concern to democratic theory. Had corporations dominated the economic landscape in Revolutionary America as they do today, political elites would surely have included them in their practical and theoretical, political writing and activities.

The early American political leader who made the most significant contribution to an understanding of how society might be arranged and governed so that no group or institution would become too powerful was James Madison. In *Federalist Paper #10*, he outlines his vision of a free society in which a wide variety of groups and institutions, which he refers to as "factions," coexist with no one group being dominant or oppressive. In fact, it is the wide variety of different factions which prevents any one from gaining too much power and becoming "tyrannical." Madison suggests that in such a situation, the power of each faction is to be counterbalanced by the power of the others, allowing none to dominate, and thus, protecting the individual. The Madisonian vision is the basis for the view of contemporary political activity, referred to as pluralism, and discussed in the preceding chapter. Economist John Kenneth Galbraith, among others, describes a system of countervailing powers—corporations, labor organizations, consumer groups, and government—in which each is attempting to influence the others and the public in a way that will further its own interests.[2] This interaction of institutional powers, according to those who ascribe to this view, results in a nontyrannical balance. According to the pluralist picture, corporations are not disproportionately powerful, but as we have seen in the last chapter, there are serious reasons for discarding this view in favor of one which acknowledges that the political process in the United States is systematically tilted to their advantage. This advantage, in addition to the tremendous growth in the power and prevalence of multinational corporations, which we will discuss in this chapter, make it incumbent upon us to reevaluate corporations and corporate activity in light of democratic theory's central concern with preventing institutions from becoming too powerful at the expense of individual rights.

The concept of corporate moral agency, which we have developed, can be useful in this task. After taking a look at international corporate activity, we

will discuss the contribution that corporate moral agency can make to democratic theory.

MULTINATIONAL CORPORATIONS

When we move from a national to an international perspective, our point
about the great power of corporations and the profound effects that their decisions can have on various constituencies—sometimes on entire countries—
becomes even stronger. The largest of the many businesses which operate in
the international market are known as multinational corporations. A multinational may be based in the United States or in some other country, but will
have operations in more than one country, a mix of managers, and a distribution of ownership that reflects international diversity. The extent of multinational activity is significant. In 1988, multinationals based in the United States
had $327 billion invested in foreign operations (which represented 17 percent
of total corporate assets) and 6 million employees overseas. From 1985 to
1988, they increased spending for research in foreign operations by a full 40
percent, indicating a far greater rise in spending on research overseas in this
period than at home.[3] As a point of comparison, the operating budgets of a
number of multinationals are larger than the budgets of some Third World
countries. Multinational corporations have tremendous clout, and their
strength, along with the size of their operations, continues to grow.
    "Globalization" is a term used to describe the dominant strategy of U.S.
multinationals taking shape in the last decade. Basically, the advent of globalization means that success is no longer seen by these firms as being strictly
dependent upon the U.S. economy. Increasingly, U.S.-based multinationals are
seeking financing, sites for new manufacturing plants, research facilities, and
employees at all levels, with little or no preference being given to the home
country. In taking a global approach to their affairs, these firms have given up
much of their national identity and are, to some degree, becoming organizational entities independent of loyalties to particular nation-states. This means
that in many important ways, the goals of these firms are now often at odds
with national goals. According to Cyrill Siewert, chief financial officer at
Colgate-Palmolive: "The United States does not have an automatic call on our
resources. . . . There is no mindset that puts this country first."[4] As multinationals build up their holdings abroad, they are able to effectively distance
themselves from issues, such as the balance of trade or domestic scientific
research and development, which are matters of great importance to the U.S.
government. For example, if the United States fails to capture the lead in
developing newer technologies such as high-definition television or semicon-
ductors, it will not directly affect U.S. multinationals. They are becoming truly
global firms, able to incorporate technological advances no matter in what
country they are developed, and consequently, they feel no obligation to foster
their development exclusively or even primarily in the home country.

A divergence of national and corporate goals is also evident regarding employment issues. The government clearly faces public pressure to reduce unemployment in periods of economic slowdown, but multinationals are becoming less and less likely to favor hiring members of the American labor force. The development of a global labor market in which the nationality of prospective employees is no longer an important factor extends to high-paying positions for professionals in such fields as engineering, research, and management. The increasing divergence of the goals of U.S.-based multinationals from national goals raises prickly moral questions. What obligations, if any, do multinationals have to bring corporate policy in line with national goals? If they have such an obligation, in which cases does it apply, and to what degree should corporations be willing to sacrifice their own interests to further national goals?

These questions are illustrated nicely by Liberty Oil's Irish venture. Liberty is seriously considering closing its Galveston plant and relocating some of its operations in Ireland in order to escape the costs associated with OSHA and EPA regulations. Its management is aware that such a relocation would detrimentally affect the Galveston economy, as well as the U.S. national economy to some extent, and is attempting to keep any news of the possible move from the public. There is a question regarding the morality of Liberty's policy of secrecy concerning a decision which has such far-reaching consequences for the community, but there is a larger question which deserves our attention. Does Liberty have a moral obligation to Galveston and its citizens? Should it promote the national economy by maintaining its domestic operations even to the extent of keeping open a plant whose operations it could run more profitably outside the United States?

Globalization is altering what has been a rather symbiotic relationship between corporations and the U.S. government throughout the nineteenth and much of the twentieth centuries. Not only did national public policy during this period reflect and support corporate goals; corporate policy also tended to coincide with national priorities in areas such as balance of trade and employment, as well as foreign policy. The alterations which are occurring in this relationship are likely to favor an increase in corporate rather than in governmental power. For reasons discussed earlier, the national government will continue to have strong incentives to foster successful corporate activity, especially in domestic operations. With the further development of a truly worldwide market composed of global firms, however, there will be less incentive for these corporate giants to tailor their policies to complement the interests of any particular country. This will give them more discretion in decision-making and thus increase their power relative to government.

Even in Japan where the government has traditionally had a high degree of control in important sectors of the economy, such as the financial markets, globalization is having effects. As Japanese-based multinationals increasingly invest and seek financing abroad, the Japanese government has been unable to successfully pursue its longstanding policy of stabilizing stock prices and maintaining the value of the yen. The integration of Japan's huge capital resources into the world market represents one clear area in which the goals of multinationals are diverging from national goals. In the new global free-market economy whose strength is growing, especially since the recent democratic upheavals in Eastern Europe, multinational corporations, not nation-states, are likely to be the principal power brokers. As national success comes to depend more and more on successful economic rather than military policy the political and ethical implications of this divergence of the goals of multinationals from those of their home countries will become increasingly significant.

While corporate activity is increasingly international in scope, the regulation of these activities remains primarily national. For the most part, regulations applicable to multinationals depend on the particular country in which they are operating.

The significance of this fact in human terms was brought dramatically to the attention of the public in 1984 by the toxic chemical leak from a Union Carbide plant in Bhopal, India, that killed more than 1,000 people. It was learned that although the plant conformed to Indian law, it was operating below the safety standards required of a similar Union Carbide plant in West Virginia. Might the leak have been prevented, or could the death toll have been reduced had the firm adhered to the higher U.S. standards at the Bhopal plant? Did Union Carbide have a moral obligation to go beyond the Indian law in order to protect its employees and the surrounding community? Following the disaster in Bhopal, many American corporations did adopt the standards they followed at home for all their subsidiaries.

Another case that raises similar issues involves the sale by U.S.-based corporations of certain pesticides and herbicides, classified as hazardous by domestic regulatory agencies and removed from the American market, in Third World countries, including India. The basic moral question raised by cases of this sort is: in the face of standards, such as those for the safety of products and operations which vary from country to country, what is the obligation of multinational corporations to exercise independent moral judgment? Is it possible for corporations to use domestic laws and regulations as a guide and to voluntarily develop more uniform regulations for operations around the world?

The financial advantage of locating costly facilities in countries where regulatory intervention is minimal is undeniable. The opportunity to cut costs and maximize profits is most tempting. The hope of such a financial gain figures prominently in Liberty Oil's attempts to locate a refinery and storage plant in Ireland. From the moral point of view, how should we judge the firm's proposed project? Liberty would surely be taking advantage of the fact that the Irish government, desperate for jobs, is apparently more willing than the American government to risk environmental damage, but is the project morally acceptable or morally reprehensible? This is a difficult question to answer. We suggested earlier that in many instances, the corporate action which is morally right will also be one that is in its interests as a profit-making entity, but that may not be the case here. Retaining the refinery and storage plant in Galveston, or adhering to the stricter U.S. environmental regulations in Ireland would probably mean a sacrifice of profits. Does the corporation have a moral obligation to make such a sacrifice? If so, what about the legal obligation of the Liberty management to the shareholders? Is there a conflict between the two obligations? We are not offering answers to these questions, but we think that corporations are capable of bringing considerations of the sort discussed above to bear in their decision-making.

THE FOREIGN CORRUPT PRACTICES ACT

Legislation has been passed by Congress which covers some aspects of U.S. corporate operations abroad and has brought a small degree of uniformity to the standards regarding foreign operations. An example of such legislation is the Foreign Corrupt Practices Act (FCPA), which was signed in 1977 and is administered by the Securities and Exchange Commission (SEC). This law was passed following findings in 1976 by the special prosecutor in the Watergate investigation and by a voluntary disclosure program conducted by the SEC which indicated that more than 250 publicly owned U.S. corporations, such as Northrop and Grumman, had made illegal or questionable payments to foreign (and domestic) governments.[5] Before the FCPA, which makes it an offense for any U.S. corporation or its executives to attempt to influence a foreign government or governmental officials through payments or gifts, the SEC had no legal power to prosecute cases of this sort. The FCPA contains two types of provisions: (1) those in the foreign corrupt practices section prohibiting bribes, gifts, etc. and providing penalties of up to $1 million in fines for company officials; and (2) those in the accounting standards section which set out certain internal record-keeping and accounting procedures which must be followed by every firm. This second section provides for penalties of up to $10,000 for companies, and $10,000 and five years of imprisonment for officials of the company.

The FCPA, with its provisions for certain mandatory internal record-keeping and accounting control procedures, is unique. The authors of a business text, commenting on the FCPA, claim: "Although other laws have provided constraints defining ethical conduct, no previous law has been as extensive as this in outlining management's responsibilities to provide a system for detecting illegal, unethical actions."[6] This legislation acknowledges the importance of reaching into a firm and influencing its CID Structure in order to guide its conduct and prevent wrongdoing. It does that by mandating certain internal record-keeping and accounting procedures and by holding managers legally responsible for adopting these procedures.

Since the FCPA was passed, the SEC has attempted to strengthen its application by proposing in 1979 that annual reports include statements as to whether corporations had met the law's objectives for internal accounting control. In 1980, the SEC proposed that independent accountants, hired by the corporations, be required to report on the efficiency of these controls.

Prosecutions under the FCPA have been infrequent, but the law appears to have had significant impact on the behavior of firms engaged in international business. A General Accounting Office report indicates that of 185 firms surveyed, 70 percent reported believing that this law which, as we noted, targets the CID Structure rather than overt corporate behavior, has been effective in reducing questionable foreign payments.

Critics of the FCPA have claimed that it unduly restricts the overseas activities of U.S. corporations by holding them to a standard from which firms based in other countries are exempt. This criticism is supported by the common, albeit incorrect, assumption that acting morally and remaining profitable and competitive are incompatible goals. We believe that the demands of morality and those of profitability are often, if not in most cases, complementary. A firm whose CID Structure is functioning properly, particularly at the coordination stage of decision-making, is able to chart a course of action that fulfills its moral obligations as well as one meeting the nonmoral demands of profitability. It may be both wiser and more profitable in the long term for multinationals to channel the time, energy, and money which would have been devoted to illegal payments to developing the firm's legitimate competitive advantages.

The assumption that acting morally and being profitable are incompatible can be used to justify an attitude on the part of management that moral considerations have no part in a successful business. When this attitude pervades a corporation, the decision-making process can become biased in a way that systematically precludes moral considerations. Notice that this is the attitude demonstrated by most of the members of Liberty Oil's management. The comments of Liberty's managers, the firm's actions concerning the oil spill in Monterey Bay, its lack of environmental concern, its proposed project in Ireland and closing of the Galveston plant, and its domestic political activity certainly suggest that Liberty's behavior in many of its operations reflects questionable moral character. When the profits-above-all-else attitude pervades a corporation's management as completely as it seems to at Liberty Oil, it is unclear exactly what steps can be taken to alter its behavior. It is clear that firms engaged in international activities which manifest this attitude present a particular threat, because variation of law from country to country works to the advantage of corporations that are seeking to avoid their moral responsibilities. Strengthening the oversight functions of Liberty's board of directors, enlarging it to include public directorships, or instituting a social auditing procedure for the firm could help to improve its behavior. It may well be unrealistic to expect voluntary changes to be initiated within Liberty Oil, therefore, mandatory restructuring directed by some outside agency, such as a court, may be the only answer. Whether the initiative comes from inside or from outside the firm, it must involve significant changes at Liberty in order to be successful.

One approach to achieving uniformity in the face of various national laws and regulations is the United Nations proposal to establish a committee which would set reporting and accounting standards for multinational corporations. According to a description of this plan, corporations would be required to:

> . . . provide balance sheets, income statements, and funds statements for the parent company and each subordinate company. Similar financial statements would also be required for every major subsidiary of the MNC (multinational corporation) that is doing business in any particular part of the world. Geographical and product-line information. . . would be required from both groups. Additionally, details on accounting policies and company ownership would be required.[7]

Accounting standards and disclosure policy are only two of several areas of multinational activity in which uniformity could be achieved, but the U.N.'s initiative is a good beginning. It underscores the point that only through some international forum, such as the United Nations, can regulations for a global economy be developed. The activities of the European community to achieve common policies regarding trade, immigration, and currency for member nations is an example on a regional level of how uniform regulations can be developed through international cooperation.

ENVIRONMENTAL QUALITY: THE GROWTH OF AN ISSUE

Environmental quality is the issue which is most likely to encourage international cooperation for the development of common global policies and regulations. In fact, this will probably be the single most important issue facing corporations, regardless of home country, in the twenty-first century. Several of the reasons for this are clear.

First, the damage occurring to the environment is not confined within national borders. For example, acid rain caused by U.S. factories destroys forests in Canada. A damaged nuclear reactor in the Soviet Union can produce radioactive fallout that affects Scandinavian countries, and the dumping of industrial wastes into the oceans has repercussions for all countries.

Second, in the last 20 years the growth of the movement by consumers, particularly in the United States and Europe, to demand greater corporate attention to environmental concerns has been tremendous. What has been labeled the "green" movement, including groups as varied as Greenpeace, the Sierra Club, World Wide Fund for Nature, and the Green Party in West Germany, is becoming better organized and is using more sophisticated techniques to advance its goals. It is becoming a worldwide movement that is having considerable effect upon public policy in various countries, as well as upon corporate policy.

A third reason for the increasing importance of environmental issues is less clear, but equally significant and involves developments such as *perestroika* in the Soviet Union, the democratization of Eastern Europe, and the ending of the Cold War. For the entire post-World War II period, the ideological confrontation between the United States with its military and economic allies, and the Soviet Union with its allies, prevented important issues, such as the environment, from emerging. During the Cold War, there was interest in whether industrial development was taking place according to the ideological tenets of the free market or those of communism. This obscured attention to the fact that the environment was being polluted by industries operating in both political frameworks. A strong emphasis on industrial output, regardless of environmental consequences, was directly linked to the political struggle between the East and West blocs. In a world largely divided into two armed camps, the issue of economic development in the Third World revolved around the question of whether that development was following the U.S. or the Soviet model, and not whether it was taking place in a manner which preserved the environment.

In the politically repressive communist regimes of Eastern Europe and the Soviet Union, the environmental movement remained almost completely submerged, while the environmental damage done in these countries by way of maximizing output was even greater than in the West. In their rush to compete with the West, these countries have virtually destroyed the quality of the environments in some areas. In East Germany, according to the country's own environmental minister, 41 percent of the forests are either dead or diseased and 10 percent of its people drink water that does not meet public health standards. In northern Czechoslovakia, air pollution shortens life expectancy by three to four years, and in Hungary it is estimated that one death in 17 is due to the pollution of the air.[8] These same countries are now moving toward achieving multiparty democracies where there is greater protection for individual political liberties. In this new atmosphere of openness, environmental groups are quickly strengthening their organizations and making their voices heard in the political arena.

The political liberalization in previously communist countries has also provided a boost for environmental groups in established democracies. With the end of the Cold War, the political agenda, which in the United States particularly had been dominated by the issue of the free market versus communism, is evolving to include nonideological issues. Environmental quality, which was already a very important issue in the West, will become a major issue as this evolution takes place. Economic affairs are becoming increasingly global, and as the operations of multinational corporations continue to expand and to extend into previously communist countries, environmental quality will be a major world issue as well. This should provide the impetus for organizations, such as the United Nations or the European Economic Community, to propose uniform environmental standards and regulations.

All of these developments may appear to threaten corporate interests, but they actually present corporations with an opportunity to exercise independent moral judgment in developing their own responses to the issue of environmental quality. In fact, many American and European corporations have voluntarily adopted procedures for "environmental auditing." An environmental audit, a specialized kind of social audit, is usually conducted for the firm by outside consultants. The auditing process enables corporations to be sure that they are complying with relevant regulations, but it can also help them go beyond strict compliance to test the environmental friendliness of their products and activities. The International Chamber of Commerce currently has a committee studying the possibility of establishing a common code of practice for environmental auditing. Important questions have been raised as to whether such audits should be made compulsory and whether public disclosure of the results should be required. Environmental auditing is good business because it guarantees compliance with antipollution legislation and helps a firm protect its public image. It also demonstrates that corporations can take the initiative and act responsibly to address issues, such as environmental quality, which have important moral implications.

THE CONTRIBUTION OF CORPORATE MORAL AGENCY TO DEMOCRATIC THEORY

Part of this chapter has been devoted to examining several important issues regarding the activities of multinational corporations. In the global, free-market economy which is rapidly taking shape, these activities will affect the citizens of all countries, and corporations, not nation-states, will be the primary loci of power. We have already seen from the discussion in the preceding chapter that, compared with other groups, corporations are the most powerful organizational participants in the American political process. Given the tremendous power of corporations, both nationally and internationally, it is crucial to examine ways in which individuals, as well as the larger community, might be protected from abuses of their power. Attempting to protect others against the negative effects of powerful institutions has been, as we indicated, a central concern of democratic theory at least since the American Revolution.

There are several reasons why the notion of moral agency will lend itself significantly to attempts within a democratic framework to prevent abuses of corporate power.

First, moral agency can help to remedy the absence of uniformity in regulations and standards regarding international corporate activity. Corporations can exercise independent moral judgment to develop self-imposed standards of conduct, and when there is a community of corporations exercising such judgment, common standards of conduct, particularly regarding important issues, will develop. This evolving community standard can transcend disparate and sometimes conflicting laws and provide a common moral guide for corporate action. The evolution of a community standard for corporate conduct can be facilitated in an expanding international economic arena where the absence of common codes encourages moral innovation and independence. This is not to discount the value and importance of attempts by governments and international organizations to develop common standards which are legally binding. This process could, in fact, be significantly augmented by the responsible participation of the corporations themselves. Meaningful participation in this process can only be achieved when corporations discard the "attitude of minimal compliance" with the law and accept themselves as moral agents responsible for their decisions as well as for the self-imposed standards by which decisions are made.

Robert Krebs asks Nevels: "How then do we and Liberty Oil survive . . . and thrive in that community? You're the corporate counsel. What's the law of the jungle?" This question is based on a hidden assumption that Liberty Oil is not a moral agent and that the "law" referred to is something to be imposed from somewhere outside of the corporation itself. On the contrary, Liberty as an organization is fully capable of participating in the development of the principles, both moral and legal, which govern its behavior and as a moral agent, has an obligation to do so. Most corporations are not as unscrupulous as Liberty appears to be, but many have not acknowledged their citizenship in the moral community, with its attendant advantages and responsibilities.

A second reason why moral agency can make a valuable contribution to democratic attempts to control abuses of corporate power is its emphasis on voluntary corporate action. The traditional answer to controlling corporations is greater regulation and intervention by the government. Although governmental action may be desirable in some cases, such as putting certain limitations on corporate PACs, it presents economic and political disadvantages which the moral agency approach avoids. Advocates of deregulation have argued that extensive government regulation reduces corporate competitiveness and contributes to higher prices for goods and services. There is truth to this claim, but the deregulationists also believe that certain features outside of the corporation that are inherent in the free market itself and referred to collectively as the "invisible hand," will serve to prevent abuses, protect consumers, and make much regulation unnecessary. The weakness of this belief can be shown by looking at any one of several examples, including the current scandal involving the savings-and-loan industry, which demonstrate that the free market is not self-regulating. Some degree of government regulation will always be necessary and desirable, but moral agency places part of the burden of regulating business activities on the corporations themselves and allows the role of the government to be minimized.

The political disadvantages of governmental regulation of the economy have been outlined by Milton Friedman, whose argument is based on the Madisonian vision of powerful institutions in society checking and balancing each other.[9] Friedman believes that when the government's role in the economy becomes too extensive, the distinction between the public and private sectors begins to erode. When this happens, he believes that private corporate power no longer acts as a check on the power of the public sector, i.e., government, and individual liberties are put in jeopardy. He points to the political repression characteristic of communist regimes and to their governments, which make all important economic decisions, to underscore his argument. By allowing for a less direct role for government in controlling corporate conduct, corporate moral agency avoids the political disadvantages of heavy regulation, as well as the economic ones. In the past several years, governments in Europe and the United States have become interested in legislation, which like our theory of corporate moral agency, places the emphasis on voluntary corporate action. Specifically, such legislation is based on providing incentives for firms to voluntarily meet regulatory goals. One approach, now in effect in Sweden and likely to follow in other countries, makes use of a tax levied on various emissions, such as sulfur, carbon dioxide, and nitrous oxide. Corporations are able to reduce these emissions in the way that they choose, and are encouraged to do so because this also enables them to reduce operating expenses.

One approach, which is part of the clean-air legislation recently passed by the U.S. Congress, allows corporations to accumulate credits by reducing the output of certain emissions. These credits can be used by the firm to lower operating expenses, saved for future use, or even sold to other firms.

Another proposal which emphasizes voluntary action by corporations involves possible self-regulation of business activities. Programs have been advocated which would use corporate legal counsel to ensure compliance with regulations, rather than challenge them, which is now the case.[10] The current system, which is distinctly adversarial and litigious, is costly and often ineffective. Corporate compliance programs, on the other hand, would emphasize constructive interaction between corporations and regulatory agencies. The success of such compliance programs would require a high level of commitment by management and the use of internal audits to guarantee the quality of program implementation. On the side of government, the regulatory agencies would need to promulgate the law adequately to make sure that it is more clearly understood by corporations.

Traditional harm-based regulatory legislation provides for punishment after a violation has occurred, but these new approaches encourage corporations to change their behavior voluntarily before harm is caused and to participate in the process by which their activities are regulated.

Finally, moral agency implies a benefit for individual human agents. As our lives become increasingly intertwined with and influenced by the activities of large organizations, especially corporations, there is a growing feeling by people that a clear sense of individual achievement and responsibility is being lost. Were this sense to be lost completely, the exercise of individual rights would become less valuable, regardless of how well-protected the rights themselves are. As we have seen, moral agency entails the responsibility of corporations for their actions and provides a basis for distinguishing the praise and the blame which belong to the corporation from that which belong to individual members of the firm. It is never a simple task to separate individual from corporate responsibility, as the case of Liberty's oil spill in Monterey Bay has shown us, but such distinctions can be made and are necessary if a realistic sense of individual achievement and responsibility is to be maintained in a society and a world increasingly dominated by large corporations.

Notes

1. See especially Peter Bachrach. *A Theory of Democratic Elitism.* Boston: Little, Brown and Co., 1967. 102-107; and Robert Dahl, *A Preface to Economic Democracy.* Berkeley, CA: University of California Press, 1985. Chapter 4.

2. Galbraith, John Kenneth. *American Capitalism.* Boston: Houghton Mifflin, 1952. 120-123.

3. Samuelson, Robert J. "Globalization: It's Become More Than a Catchword." *International Herald Tribune* 29 Aug. 1989.

4. As quoted in Louis Uchitelle, "Firms Loosen U.S. Ties in Global Market Quest." *International Herald Tribune* 22 May 1989.

5. For further discussion of the FCPA, see Richard M. Hodgetts, Fred Luthans, and Kenneth R. Thompson, *Social Issues in Business*, 5th ed. New York: Macmillan, 1987. 110-113.

6. *Ibid.*, 112-113.

7. *Ibid.*, 250.

8. These statistics reported in "Stalin's Legacy of Filth," editorial. *New York Times* 7 Feb. 1990.

9. Friedman, Milton. *Capitalism and Freedom.* Chicago: University of Chicago Press, 1962. See especially Chapters 1, 2.

10. For a full description of such programs, see Jay Sigler and Joseph Murphy, *Interactive Corporate Compliance.* Westport, CT: Greenwood Press, 1988.

APPENDIX

A–1   ORGANIZATIONAL FLOW CHART: LIBERTY OIL COMPANY

A–2   ORGANIZATIONAL FLOW CHART: IBM

B   UNITED STATES SUPREME COURT DECISIONS

B–1   *COUNTY OF SANTA CLARA V. SOUTHERN PACIFIC RAILROAD*

B–2   *HALE V. HENKEL*

B–3   *FIRST NATIONAL BANK OF BOSTON V. BELLOTTI*

C–1   CORPORATION CREDOS

C–2   CORPORATE CODES OF ETHICS

C–3   CORPORATE ETHICS COMMITTEES

C–4   ETHICAL GUIDELINES IN PROFESSIONS

D–1   CIVIL RIGHTS ACT OF 1964: TITLE VII

D–2   AFFIRMATIVE ACTION: LEGAL AND MORAL STATUS

E–1   CORPORATE RESPONSIBILITY IN SOUTH AFRICA: THE SULLIVAN
      PRINCIPLES

E–2   REQUIREMENTS: PRINCIPLES 1, 2, AND 3

E–3   QUALITATIVE CRITERIA FOR PRINCIPLES 4, 5, 6, AND 7

E–4   THE SULLIVAN PRINCIPLES REASSESSED

F   CORPORATE MERGERS AND TAKEOVERS: THE NORTON CASE

G   EVALUATION OF CORPORATE SOCIAL RESPONSIBILITY

H–1   MULTINATIONAL CORPORATIONS AND THIRD WORLD NATIONS:
      THE NESTLE CASE

H–2   CONSTITUTION OF THE WORLD HEALTH ORGANIZATION

I   PROPOSED DRAFT OF A UNITED NATIONS CODE OF CONDUCT FOR
      MULTINATIONAL CORPORATIONS

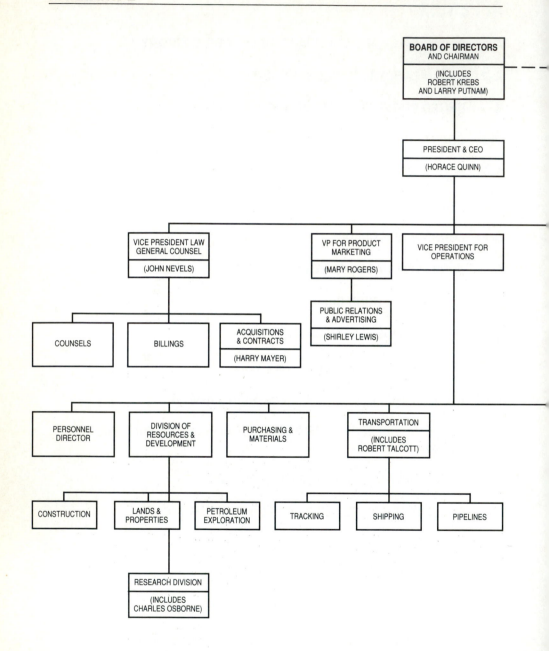

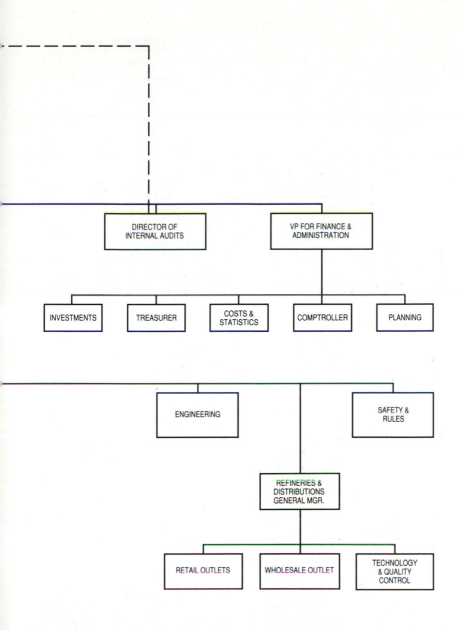

REPORTING RELATIONSHIPS ARE
INDICATED BY LETTERS A, B, C, D.

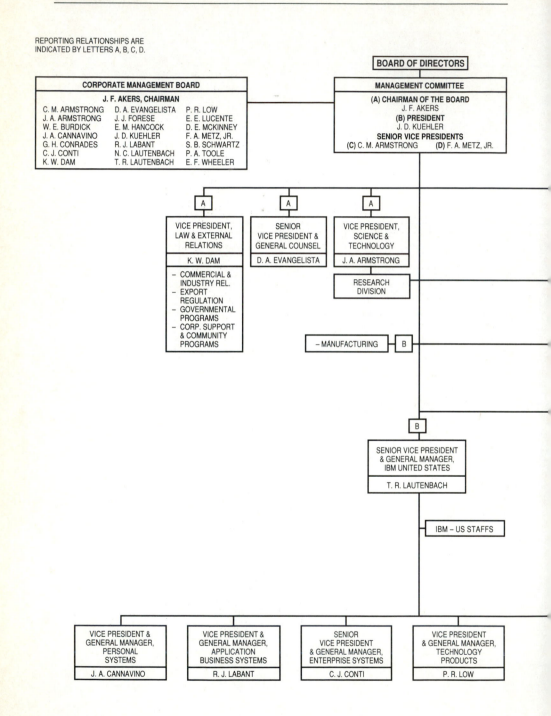

BOARD OF DIRECTORS

CORPORATE MANAGEMENT BOARD

J. F. AKERS, CHAIRMAN

C. M. ARMSTRONG	D. A. EVANGELISTA	P. R. LOW
J. A. ARMSTRONG	J. J. FORESE	E. E. LUCENTE
W. E. BURDICK	E. M. HANCOCK	D. E. MCKINNEY
J. A. CANNAVINO	J. D. KUEHLER	F. A. METZ, JR.
G. H. CONRADES	R. J. LABANT	S. B. SCHWARTZ
C. J. CONTI	N. C. LAUTENBACH	P. A. TOOLE
K. W. DAM	T. R. LAUTENBACH	E. F. WHEELER

MANAGEMENT COMMITTEE

(A) CHAIRMAN OF THE BOARD
J. F. AKERS
(B) PRESIDENT
J. D. KUEHLER
SENIOR VICE PRESIDENTS
(C) C. M. ARMSTRONG   **(D)** F. A. METZ, JR.

A

VICE PRESIDENT, LAW & EXTERNAL RELATIONS

K. W. DAM

– COMMERCIAL & INDUSTRY REL.
– EXPORT REGULATION
– GOVERNMENTAL PROGRAMS
– CORP. SUPPORT & COMMUNITY PROGRAMS

A

SENIOR VICE PRESIDENT & GENERAL COUNSEL

D. A. EVANGELISTA

A

VICE PRESIDENT, SCIENCE & TECHNOLOGY

J. A. ARMSTRONG

RESEARCH DIVISION

– MANUFACTURING   B

B

SENIOR VICE PRESIDENT & GENERAL MANAGER, IBM UNITED STATES

T. R. LAUTENBACH

IBM – US STAFFS

VICE PRESIDENT & GENERAL MANAGER, PERSONAL SYSTEMS

J. A. CANNAVINO

VICE PRESIDENT & GENERAL MANAGER, APPLICATION BUSINESS SYSTEMS

R. J. LABANT

SENIOR VICE PRESIDENT & GENERAL MANAGER, ENTERPRISE SYSTEMS

C. J. CONTI

VICE PRESIDENT & GENERAL MANAGER, TECHNOLOGY PRODUCTS

P. R. LOW

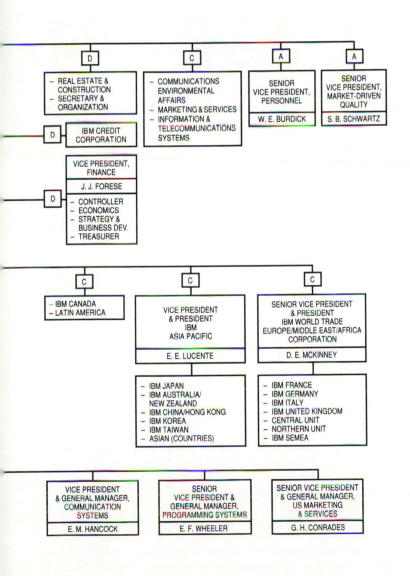

D
- REAL ESTATE & CONSTRUCTION
- SECRETARY & ORGANIZATION

D | IBM CREDIT CORPORATION

D
VICE PRESIDENT, FINANCE
J. J. FORESE
- CONTROLLER
- ECONOMICS
- STRATEGY & BUSINESS DEV.
- TREASURER

C
- COMMUNICATIONS ENVIRONMENTAL AFFAIRS
- MARKETING & SERVICES
- INFORMATION & TELECOMMUNICATIONS SYSTEMS

A
SENIOR VICE PRESIDENT, PERSONNEL
W. E. BURDICK

A
SENIOR VICE PRESIDENT, MARKET-DRIVEN QUALITY
S. B. SCHWARTZ

C
- IBM CANADA
- LATIN AMERICA

C
VICE PRESIDENT & PRESIDENT IBM ASIA PACIFIC
E. E. LUCENTE
- IBM JAPAN
- IBM AUSTRALIA/ NEW ZEALAND
- IBM CHINA/HONG KONG
- IBM KOREA
- IBM TAIWAN
- ASIAN (COUNTRIES)

C
SENIOR VICE PRESIDENT & PRESIDENT IBM WORLD TRADE EUROPE/MIDDLE EAST/AFRICA CORPORATION
D. E. MCKINNEY
- IBM FRANCE
- IBM GERMANY
- IBM ITALY
- IBM UNITED KINGDOM
- CENTRAL UNIT
- NORTHERN UNIT
- IBM SEMEA

VICE PRESIDENT & GENERAL MANAGER, COMMUNICATION SYSTEMS
E. M. HANCOCK

SENIOR VICE PRESIDENT & GENERAL MANAGER, PROGRAMMING SYSTEMS
E. F. WHEELER

SENIOR VICE PRESIDENT & GENERAL MANAGER, US MARKETING & SERVICES
G. H. CONRADES

APPENDIX B

Selected passages from U.S. Supreme Court Decisions: Corporations as Persons Under the Law.

APPENDIX B-1

County of Santa Clara v. Southern Pacific Railroad Company
118 U.S. at 394 (1886)

In this 1886 case, it was successfully argued that the Fourteenth Amendment, granting equal rights of protection under the law, extended to corporations. The U.S. Supreme Court found the County of Santa Clara in error when it excessively taxed the Southern Pacific Railroad for land granted by the government.

Chief Justice Waite: The Court does not wish to hear argument on the question whether the provision in the Fourteenth Amendment to the Constitution, which forbids a State to deny to any person within its jurisdiction the equal protection of the laws, applies to these Corporations. We are all of opinion that it does.

On the 17th of December, 1877, the said Southern Pacific Railroad Company and other railroad corporations, then existing under the laws of California, were legally consolidated, and a new corporation thereby formed, under the name of the Southern Pacific Railroad Company, the present defendant in error, 59.30 miles of whose road is in Santa Clara County and 17.93 miles in Fresno County.

In the year 1852 California, by legislative enactment, granted a right of way through that State to the United States for the purpose of constructing a railroad from the Atlantic to the Pacific Ocean, declaring that the interests of California, as well as the whole Union, "require the immediate action of the Government of the United States, for the construction of a national thoroughfare, connecting the navigable waters of the Atlantic and Pacific Oceans, for the purpose of the national safety, in the event of war, and to promote the highest commercial interests of the Republic." Stat. Cal. 1852, p. 150.

The Constitution of California, adopted in 1879, exempts from taxation growing crops, property used exclusively for public schools, and such as may belong to the United States, or to that State, or to any of her county or municipal corporations, and declares that the Legislature "may provide, except in the case of credits secured by mortgage or trust deed, for a reduction from credits of debts due to bonafide residents" of the State. It is provided in the first section of Article XIII that, with these exceptions,

"All property in the State, not exempt under the laws of the United States, shall be taxed in proportion to its value, to be ascertained as provided by law. The word 'property,' as used in this article and section, is hereby declared to include moneys, credits, bonds, stocks, dues, franchises, and all other matters and things, real, personal and mixed, capable of private ownership."

The fourth section of the same article provides: "A mortgage, deed of trust, contract, or other obligation by which a debt is secured, shall, for the purposes of assessment and taxation, be deemed and treated as an interest in the property affected thereby. Except as to railroad and other quasi public corporations, in case of debts so secured, the value of the property affected by such mortgage, deed of trust, contract, or obligation, less the value of such security, shall be assessed and taxed to the owner of the property, and the value of such security shall be assessed and taxed to the owner of the property, and the value of such security shall be assessed and taxed to the owner thereof, in the county, city, or district in which the property affected thereby is situated.

"The state board of equalization, in making the supposed assessment of said roadway of defendant, did knowingly and designedly include in the valuation of said roadway the value of fences erected upon the line between said roadway and the land of coterminous proprietors. Said fences were valued at $300 per mile."

The special grounds of defense by each of the defendants were:

1. That its road is a part of a continuous postal and military route, constructed and maintained under the authority of the United States, by means in part obtained from the General Government; that the Company having, with the consent of the State, become subject to the requirements, conditions, and provisions of the Acts of Congress, it thereby ceased to be merely a state corporation, and became one of the agencies or instrumentalities employed by the General Government to execute its constitutional powers; and that the franchise to operate a postal and military route, for the transportation of troops, munitions of war, public stores, and the mails, being derived from the United States, cannot, without their consent, be subjected to state taxation.

2. That the provisions of the Constitution and laws of California, in respect to the assessment for taxation of the property of railway corporations operating railroads in more than one county, are in violation of the Fourteenth Amendment of the Constitution, in so far as they require the assessment of their property at its full money value, without making deduction, as in the case of railroads operation in one county, and of other corporations, and of natural persons, for the value of the mortgages covering the property assessed; thus imposing upon the defendant unequal burdens, and to that extent denying to it the equal protection of the laws.

The argument on behalf of the defendant is: that the state board knowingly and designedly included in its assessment of "the franchise, roadway, roadbed, rails, and rolling stock" of each Company, the value of the fences erected upon the line between its roadway and the land of coterminous proprietors, that the fences did not constitute a part of such roadway, and therefore could only be assessed for taxation by the proper officer of the several counties in which they were situated; and that an entire assessment which includes property not assessable by the state board against the party assessed is void and, therefore, insufficient to support an action, at least, when—and such is claimed to be the case here—it does not appear, with reasonable certainty, from the fact of the assessment or otherwise, what part of the aggregate valuation represents the property so illegally included therein.

If these positions are tenable, there will be no occasion to consider the grave questions of constitutional law upon which the case was determined below; for in that event, the judgment can be affirmed upon the ground that the assessment cannot properly be the basis of a judgment against the defendant.

. . . It seems to the court that the fences in question are not, within the meaning of the local law, a part of the roadway for purposes of taxation, but are "improvements" assessable by the local authorities of the proper county, and therefore, were improperly included by the state board in its valuation of the property of the defendants.

It follows that there is no occasion to determine under what circumstances the plaintiffs would be entitled to judgment against a delinquent taxpayer for penalties, interest, or attorney's fees; for if the plaintiffs are not entitled to judgment for the taxes arising out of the assessments in question, no liability for penalties, interest, or attorney's fees, could result from a refusal or failure to pay such taxes.

Judgment affirmed.

APPENDIX B-2

Hale v. *Henkel*
201 U.S. at 43 (1905)

The Supreme Court ruled in this case that a corporation cannot claim the Fifth Amendment against self-incrimination. Hale, an employee of the MacAndrews & Forbes Company, failed to answer any questions "regarding the business of the Company, its officers, the location of its office, or its agreement or agreements with other companies. . . . He also declined to produce papers and documents called for in the subpoena." Although Hale could invoke the privilege of the Fifth Amendment for himself; Court ruled that he could not claim protection on behalf of the corporation.

The proceeding originated in a subpoena *duces tecum*, issued April 28, 1905, commanding Hale to appear before the grand jury at a time and place named, to "testify and give evidence in a certain action now pending . . . in the Circuit Court of the United States of America and the American Tobacco Company and MacAndrews & Forbes Company on the part of the United States, and that you bring with you and produce at the time and place aforesaid:"

1. All understandings, agreements, arrangements, or contracts, whether evidenced by correspondence, memoranda, formal agreements, or other writings, between MacAndrews & Forbes Company and six other firms and corporations named, from the date of the organization of the said MacAndrews & Forbes Company.

2. All correspondence by letter or telegram between MacAndrews & Forbes Company and six other firms and corporations.

3. All reports made or accounts rendered by these six companies or corporations to the principal company.

4. Any agreements or contracts or arrangements, however evidenced, between MacAndrews & Forbes Company and the Amsterdam Supply Company or the American Tobacco Company or the Continental Company or the Consolidated Tobacco Company.

5. All letters received by the MacAndrews & Forbes Company since the date of its organization from thirteen other companies named, located in different parts of the United States and also copies of all correspondence with such companies.

The order of May 5 requiring appellant to produce the papers called for in the subpoena *duces tecum* was void under the Fourth Amendment. Its enforcement would amount to the ancient seizure and search which continued by usage in England until the decision of Lord Camden in *Entick* v. *Carrington*, 19 How. St. Tr. 1029. See also *Boyd* v. *United States*, 116 U.S. at 616, 626; Hartranft's Appeal, 85 Pa. St. 433; *Ex parte Brown*, 72 Missouri, 83; *In re Lester*, 77 Georgia, 143; *In re Morer*, 101 N.W. Rep. 588.

The writ must also particularly describe the papers desired. Ex parte Brown, supra; *Sandford* v. *Nichols*, 13 Massachusetts, 286.

A corporation is entitled to the same immunities as an individual. It cannot be compelled to incriminate itself. *Wigmore on Evidence*, 2259; *Logan* v. *Penna. R.R. Co.*, 132 Pa. St. 403; *Santa Clara County* v. *Railroad Company*, 118 U.S. at 394; *King of Siciles* v. *Willcox*, 7 St. Tr. (N.S.) 1049.

By the express provisions of the Sherman Act, corporations are deemed to be persons: Section 8. A corporation can only be examined through its officers, directors or agents. In the present case the Government undertook deliberately by that method to compel the corporation to submit to examination, not as a witness, but by forcing one of its officers and directors to produce its books and papers for the sole purpose of ascertaining whether or not the corporation had committed a crime under the Sherman Act.

The rule that the protection of the Fourth and Fifth Amendments is the personal privilege of the witness and cannot be claimed for the benefit of another has no possible application to the case of an officer, director or agent of a corporation who seeks to secure to the corporation its constitutional rights and immunities; for these rights can only be asserted through its officers, directors and agents.

In this view the witness is not seeking to invoke the privilege of another, but the corporation itself invokes its own privilege in the only manner and by the only means it can employ for that purpose.

If, under these circumstances, it could be said that the corporation was a witness, and, therefore, entitled to the immunity afforded by the statute, this might, perhaps, meet our present contention. But the position of the Government is that the corporation is not protected by the statute. Its avowed purpose is to use the papers as the basis of an indictment against the corporation. See *Davies* v. *Lincoln National Bank*, 4 N.Y. Suppl. 373; *Rex* v. *Purnell*, Wilson, 239; *In re Morse*, 101 N.W. Rep. 588.

The protection of the Fourth and Fifth Amendments is based alone upon the personal privilege of the witness. The objections urged by the witness cannot be relied upon for the benefit of the corporation of which he is an officer, and if the privilege cannot be asserted in behalf of a corporation under the Fifth Amendment it is plain that it may not be so availed of under the Fourth Amendment.

Where the question of criminality is not involved, an officer of a corporation having the books of the company in his custody is bound to produce them in obedience to a subpoena *duces tecum*. *Wertheim* v. *Continental R'y & Trust Co.*, 15 Fed. Rep. 718. The same rule applies, even though the production of the evidence may tend to incriminate the corporation; one of its officers may not assert in its behalf the privilege secured to persons by the Fifth Amendment of the Constitution. See *United States* v. *Amedy*, 11 Wheat. 412; *Beaston* v. *The Farmers' Bank of Delaware*, 12 Pet. 134. That word in the Fifth Amendment does not include corporations, as the mischief intended to be reached did not apply to corporations.

While sporadic cases look in a different direction, there have been many decisions, both in this country and in England, in which the courts have refused to permit the privilege to be asserted by an officer or employe in behalf of a corporation of which he is the representative. *New York Life Ins. Co.* v. *People*, 195 Illinois, 430; *In re Moser*, 101 N.W. Rep. 591; *In re Peasley*, 44 Fed. Rep. 271; *Gibbons* v. *Waterloo Bridge*, 5 Price, 491; *Rex* v. *Purnell*, Wilson, 239.

Mr. Justice Brown, after making the foregoing statement, delivered the opinion of the court.

> 1. The appellant justifies his action in refusing to answer the questions propounded to him, 1st, upon the ground that there was not specific "charge" pending before the grand jury against any particular person; 2d, that the answers would tend to criminate him.

The first objection requires a definition of the word "charge" as used in this connection, which it is not easy to furnish. An accused person is usually charged with crime by a complaint made before a committing magistrate, which has fully performed its office when the party is committed or held to bail, and it is quite unnecessary to the finding of an indictment by a grand jury; or by an information of the district attorney, which is of no legal value in prosecutions for felony; or by a presentment usually made, as in this case, for an offense committed in the presence of the jury; or by an indictment which, as often as not, is drawn after the grand jury has acted upon the testimony. If another kind of charge be contemplated, when and by whom must it be preferred? Must it be in writing, and if so, in what form? Or may it be oral? The suggestion of the witness that he should be furnished with a copy of such charge, if applicable to him is applicable to other witnesses summoned before the grand jury. Indeed, it is a novelty in criminal procedure with which we are wholly unacquainted, and one which might involve a betrayal of the secrets of the grand jury room.

> 2. Appellant also invokes the protection of the Fifth Amendment to the Constitution, which declares that no person "shall be compelled in any criminal case to be a witness against himself," and in reply to various questions put to him he declined to answer, on the ground that he would thereby incriminate himself.

The interdiction of the Fifth Amendment operates only where a witness is asked to incriminate himself, in other words, to give testimony which may possibly expose him to a criminal charge. But if the criminality has already been taken away, the Amendment ceases to apply. The criminality provided against is a present, not a past criminality, which lingers only as a memory and involves no present danger of prosecution. . . .

If, whenever an officer or employe of a corporation were summoned before a grand jury as a witness, he could refuse to produce the books and documents of such corporation, upon the ground that they would incriminate the corporation itself, it would result in the failure of a large number of cases where the illegal combination was determinable only upon the examination of such papers. Conceding that the witness was an officer of the corporation under investigation, and that he was entitled to assert the rights of the corporation with respect to the production of its books and papers, we are of the opinion that there is a clear distinction in this particular between an individual and a corporation, and that the latter has no right to refuse to submit its books and papers for an examination at the suit of the State. The individual may stand upon his constitutional rights as a citizen. He is entitled to carry on his private business in his own way. His power to contract is unlimited. He owes no duty to the State or to his neighbors to divulge his business, or to open his doors to an investigation, so far as it may tend to criminate him. He owes no such duty to the State, since he receives nothing therefrom, beyond the protection of his life and property. His rights are such as existed by the law of the land long antecedent to the organization of the State, and can only be taken from him by due process of law, and in accordance with the Constitution. Among his rights are a refusal to incriminate himself, and the immunity of himself and his property from arrest or seizure except under a warrant of the law. He owes nothing to the public so long as he does not trespass upon their rights.

Upon the other hand, the corporation is a creature of the State. It is presumed to be incorporated for the benefit of the public. It receives certain special privileges and franchises, and holds them subject to the laws of the State and the limitations of its charter. Its powers are limited by law. It can make no contract not authorized by its charter. Its rights to act as a corporation are only preserved to it so long as it obeys the laws of its creation. There is a reserved right in the legislature to investigate its contracts and find out whether it has exceeded its powers. It would be a strange anomaly to hold that a State, having chartered a corporation to make use of certain franchises, could not in the exercise of its sovereignty inquire how these franchises had been employed, and whether they had been abused, and demand the production of the corporate books and papers for that purpose. The defense amounts to this: That an officer of a corporation, which is charged with a criminal violation of the statute, may plead the criminality of such corporation as a refusal to produce its books. To state this proposition is to answer it. While an individual may lawfully refuse to answer incriminating questions unless protected by an immunity statute, it does not follow that a corporation, vested with special privileges and franchises, may refuse to show its hand when charged with an abuse of such privileges.

. . . we do not wish to be understood as holding that a corporation is not entitled to immunity, under the Fourth Amendment, against unreasonable searches and seizures. A corporation is, after all, but an association of individuals under an assumed name and with a distinct legal entity. In organizing itself as a collective body, it waives no constitutional immunities appropriate to such body. Its property cannot be taken without compensation. It can only be proceeded against by due process of law, and is protected, under the Fourteenth Amendment, against unlawful discrimination. *Gulf &c. Railroad Company* v. *Ellis*, 165 U.S. at 150, 154, and cases cited.

But this objection to the subpoena does not go to the validity of the order remanding the petitioner, which is, therefore,

Affirmed.

Mr. Justice Harlan, concurring.

It was not his [Hale] privilege to stand between the corporation and the Government in the investigation before the grand jury. In my opinion, a corporation—"an artificial being, invisible, intangible and existing only in contemplation of law"—cannot claim the immunity given by the Fourth Amendment; for, it is not a part of the "People," within the meaning of that Amendment. Nor is it embraced by the word "persons" in the Amendment. If a contrary view obtains, the power of the Government by its representatives to look into the books, records and papers of a corporation of its own creation, to ascertain whether that Corporation has obeyed or is defying the law, will be greatly curtailed, if not destroyed.

. . . . In my judgment when a grand jury seeking, in the discharge of its public duties, to ascertain whether a corporation has violated the law in any particular, requires the production of the books, papers and records of such corporation, no officer of that corporation can rightfully refuse, when ordered to do so by the court, to produce such books, papers and records in his official custody, upon the ground simply that the order was, as to the corporation, an unreasonable search and seizure with the meaning of the Fourth Amendment.

Mr. Justice McKenna, also concurring.

There are certainly strong reasons for the contention that if corporations cannot plead the immunity of the Fifth Amendment, they cannot plead the immunity of the Fourth Amendment. The protection of both Amendments, it can be contended, is against the compulsory production of evidence to be used in criminal trials. Such warrants are used to aid of public prosecutions (Cooley Constitutional Lim. 6th ed. 364), and in *Boyd v. United States*, 116 U.S. at 616, a relation between the Fourth Amendment and the Fifth Amendment was declared.

. . . [I]f the Amendments are the complements of each other, directed against the different ways by which a man's immunity from giving evidence against himself may be violated, it would seem a strong, if not an inevitable conclusion, that if corporations have not such they can no more claim the protection of the Fourth Amendment than they can of the Fifth.

Mr. Justice Brewer, with whom the Chief Justice concurred, dissenting.

. . . The immunities and protection of Articles 4, 5 and 14 of the Amendments to the Federal Constitution are available to a corporation so far as in the nature of things they are applicable. Its property may not be taken for public use without just compensation. It cannot be subjected to unreasonable searches and seizures. It cannot be deprived of life or property without due process of law.

It may be well to compare the words of description in Articles 4 and 5 with those in Article 14:

"Article 4. The right of the people to be protected in their persons, houses, papers, and effects, against unreasonable searches and seizures, shall not be violated, and no warrants shall issue, but upon probable cause, supported by oath or affirmation, and particularly describing the place to be searched, and the persons or things to be seized."

"Article 5. No person . . . shall be compelled in any criminal case to be a witness against himself, nor to be deprived of life, liberty, or property, without due process of law; nor shall private property be taken for public use, without just compensation."

"Article 14 . . . Nor shall any State deprive any person of life, liberty, or property, without due process of law; nor deny to any person within its jurisdiction the equal protection of the laws."

See also *Pembina Mining Company v. Pennsylvania*, 125 U.S. at 181; *Missouri Pacific Railway Company v. Mackey*, 127 U.S. at 205; *Minneapolis & St. Louis Railway Company v. Beckwith*, 129 U.S. at 26; *Charlotte &c. Railroad v. Gibbes*, 142 U.S. at 386; *Monongahela Navigation Company v. United States*, 148 U.S. at 312; *Gulf, Colorado & Santa Fe Ry v. Ellis*, 165 U.S. at 150, 154. . . .

These decisions were under the Fourteenth Amendment, but if the word "person" in that Amendment includes corporations, it also includes corporations when used in the Fourth and Fifth Amendments.

By the Fourth Amendment the "people" are guaranteed protection against unreasonable searches and seizures. "Citizens" is a descriptive word; no broader, to say the least, than "people."

As repeatedly held, a corporation is a citizen of a State for purposes of jurisdiction of Federal courts, and, as a citizen, it may locate mining claims under the laws of the United States, *McKinley* v. *Wheeler*, 130 U.S. at 630, and is entitled to the benefit of the Indian Depredation Acts. *United States* v. *Northwestern Express Company*, 164 U.S. at 686. Indeed, it is essentially but an association of individuals, to which is given certain rights and privileges, and in which is vested the legal title. The beneficial ownership is in the individuals, the corporation being simply an instrumentality by which the powers granted to these associated individuals may be exercised. As said by Chief Justice Marshall in *Providence Bank* v. *Billings*, 4 Pet. 514, 562: "The great object of an incorporation is to bestow the character and properties of individuality on a collective and changing body of men."

. . . The fact that a state corporation may engage in business which is within the general regulating power of the National Government does not give to Congress any right of visitation or any power to dispense with the immunities and protection of the Fourth and Fifth Amendments. The National Government has jurisdiction over crimes committed within its special territorial limits. Can it dispense in such cases with these immunities and protections? No more can it do so in respect to the acts and conduct of individuals coming within its regulating power. . . .

APPENDIX B–3

First National Bank of Boston v. *Bellotti*
435 U.S. at 765, 98 S. Ct. at 1407, 55 L. Ed. 2d at 707 (1978)

This case concerned a Massachussetts law that prohibited corporations from contributing their expenses to influence votes.

In upholding the constitutionality of the statute, the Massachusetts Supreme Judicial Court stated "that only when a general political issue materially affects a corporation's business property or assets may that corporation claim First Amendment protection for its speech or other activities entitling it to communicate its position on that issue to the general public." 359 N.E. 2d at 1262, 1290. The appellants, two national banking associations and three business corporations, believe that the adoption of a graduated personal income tax would materially affect their business specifically in the words of the Massachusetts Supreme Judicial Court, by "discouraging highly qualified executives and highly skilled professional personnel from settling, working or remaining in Massachusetts; promoting a tax climate which would be considered unfavorable by business corporations, thereby discouraging them from settling in Massachusetts with 'resultant adverse effects' on the plaintiff banks' loans, deposits, and other services; and tending to shrink the disposable income of individuals available for the purchase of the consumer products manufactured by at least one of the plaintiff corporations." 359 N.E. 2d at 1266.

The United States Supreme Court struck down this law in a five-to-four decision. The court held that the statute was an unconstitutional infringement on free speech. This decision emphasizes that the First Amendment guarantee of right of free speech extends to corporations.

. . . If the speakers here were not corporations, no one would suggest that the State could silence their proposed speech. It is the type of speech indispensable to decision-making in a democracy, and this is no less true because the speech comes from a corporation rather than an individual. The inherent worth of the speech in terms of its capacity for informing the public does not depend upon the identity of its source, whether corporation, association, union, or individual. 98 S. Ct at 1416.

Mr. Justice Powell writing for the majority continued:

III

In the realm of protected speech, the legislature is constitutionally disqualified from dictating the subjects about which persons may speak and the speakers who may address a public issue. *Police Dept. of Chicago* v. *Mosley*, 408 U.S. at 92, 96, 92 S. Ct. 22986, at 2290, 33 L. Ed. 2d at 212 (1972). If a legislature may direct business corporations to "stick to business," it also may limit other corporations—religious, charitable, or civic—to their respective "business" when addressing the public. Such power in government to channel the expression of views is unacceptable under the First Amendment. Especially where, as here, the legislature's suppression of speech suggests an attempt to give one side of a debatable public question an advantage in expressing its views to the people, the First Amendment is plainly offended. Yet the State contends that its action is necessitated by governmental interests of the highest order. We next consider these asserted interests.

IV

The constitutionality of (the Massachusett's statute's) prohibition of the "exposition of ideas" by corporations turns on whether it can survive the exacting scrutiny necessitated by a state-imposed restriction of freedom of speech. Especially where, as here, a prohibition is directed at speech itself, and the speech is intimately related to the process of governing, "the State may prevail only upon showing a subordinating interest which is compelling," *Bates* v. *City of Little Rock*, 361 U.S. at 516, 524; 80 S. Ct. at 412, 417; 4 L. Ed. 2d at 480 (1960); "and the burden is on the Government to show the existence of such an interest." *Elrod* v. *Burns*, 427 U.S. at 347, 362; 96 S. Ct. at 2673; 49 L. Ed. 2d at 547 (1976).

. . . [The] [a]ppellee nevertheless advances two principal justifications for the prohibition of corporate speech. The first is the State's interest in sustaining the active role of the individual citizen in the electoral process and thereby preventing diminution of the citizen's confidence in government. The second is the interest in protecting rights of shareholders whose views differ from those expressed by management on behalf of the corporation. However weighty these interests may be in the context of partisan candidate elections, they either are not implicated in this case or are not served at all, or in other than a random manner, by the prohibition in the statute.

A

Preserving the integrity of the electoral process, preventing corruption, and "sustain[ing] the active, alert responsibility of the individual citizen in a democracy for the wise conduct of government" are interests of the highest importance. Preservation of the individual citizen's confidence in government is equally important.

. . . According to appellee, corporations are wealthy and powerful, and their views may drown out other points of view. If appellee's arguments were supported by record or legislative findings that corporate advocacy threatened imminently to undermine democratic processes, thereby denigrating rather than serving First Amendment interests, these arguments would merit our consideration. Cf. *Red Lion Broadcasting Co.* v. *FCC*, 395 U.S. at 367; 89 S. Ct. at 1794; 23 L. Ed. 2d at 371 (1969). But there has been no showing that the relative voice of corporations has been overwhelming or even significant in influencing referenda in Massachusetts, or that there has been any threat to the confidence of the citizenry in government.

. . . Nor are appellee's arguments inherently persuasive or supported by the precedents of this Court. Referenda are held on issues, not candidates for public office. The risk of corruption perceived in cases involving candidate elections simply is not present in a popular vote on a public issue. To be sure, corporate advertising may influence the outcome of the vote; this would be its purpose. But the fact that advocacy may persuade the electorate is hardly a reason to suppress it: The Constitution "protects expression which is eloquent no less than that which is unconvincing." *Kingsley Int'l Pictures Corp.* v. *Regents*, 360 U.S. at 689, 79 S. Ct. at 1365. We noted only recently that "the concept that government may restrict the speech of some elements of our society in order to enhance the relative voice of others is wholly foreign to the First Amendment." *Buckley*, 424 U.S. at 48-49, 96 S. Ct. at 649.

B

Finally, appellee argues that the statute protects corporate shareholders, an interest that is both legitimate and traditionally within the province of state law. *Cort* v. *Ash*, 422 U.S. at 66, 82-84; 95 S. Ct. at 2080, 2089-2091; 45 L. Ed. 2d at 26 (1975). The statute is said to serve this interest by preventing the use of corporate resources in furtherance of views with which some shareholders may disagree. This purpose is belied, however, by the provisions of the statute, which are both underinclusive and overinclusive.

The underinclusiveness of the statute is self-evident. Corporate expenditures with respect to a referendum are prohibited, while corporate activity with respect to the passage or defeat of legislation is permitted, see n. 31, supra, even though corporations may engage in lobbying more often than they take positions on ballot questions submitted to the voters. Nor does the statute prohibit a corporation from expressing its views, by the expenditure of corporate funds, on any public issue until it becomes the subject of a referendum, though the displeasure of disapproving shareholders is unlikely to be any less.

The fact that a particular kind of ballot question has been singled out for special treatment undermines the likelihood of a genuine state interest in protecting shareholders. It suggests instead that the legislature may have been concerned with silencing corporations on a particular subject. Indeed, appellee has conceded that "the legislative and judicial history of the statute indicates . . . that the second crime was "tailor-made" to prohibit corporate campaign contributions to oppose a graduated income tax amendment. Brief for Appellee 6.

The overinclusiveness of the statute is demonstrated by the fact that it would prohibit a corporation from supporting or opposing a referendum proposal even if its shareholders unanimously authorized the contribution or expenditure. Ultimately shareholders may decide, through the procedures of corporate democracy, whether their corporation should engage in debate on public issues. Acting through their power to elect the board of directors or to insist upon protective provisions in the corporation's charter, shareholders normally are presumed competent to protect their own interests. In addition to intracorporate remedies, minority shareholders generally have access to the judicial remedy of a derivative suit to challenge corporate disbursements alleged to have been made for improper corporate purposes or merely to further the personal interests of management.

Assuming, arguendo, that protection of shareholders is a "compelling" interest under the circumstances of this case, we find "no substantially relevant correlation between the governmental interest asserted and the State's effort" to prohibit appellants from speaking. *Shelton* v. *Tucker*, 364 U.S. at 485; 81 S. Ct. at 250.

V

Because that portion of the statute challenged by appellants prohibits protected speech in a manner unjustified by a compelling state interest, it must be invalidated. The judgment of the Supreme Judicial Court is reversed.

Mr. Justice White, with whom Mr. Justice Brennan and Mr. Justice Marshall join, dissenting.

I

There is now little doubt that corporate communications come within the scope of the First Amendment. This, however, is merely the starting point of analysis, because an examination of the First Amendment values that corporate expression furthers and the threat to the functioning of a free society it is capable of posing reveals that it is not fungible with communications emanating from individuals and is subject to restrictions which individual expression is not. Indeed, what some have considered to be the principal function of the First Amendment, the use of communication as a means of self-expression, self-realization, and self-fulfillment, is not at all furthered by corporate speech. It is clear that the communications of profitmaking corporations are not "an integral part of the development of ideas, of mental exploration and of the affirmation of self." They do not represent a manifestation of individual freedom or choice. Undoubtedly, as this Court has recognized, see *NAACP* v. *Button*, 371 U.S. at 415; 83 S. Ct. at 328; 9 L. Ed. 2d at 405 (1963), there are some corporations formed for the express purpose of advancing certain ideological causes shared by all their members, or, as in the case of the press, of disseminating information and ideas. Under such circumstances, association in a corporate form may be viewed as merely a means of achieving effective self-expression. But this is hardly the case generally with corporations operated for the purpose of making profits. Shareholders in such entities do not share a common set of political or social views, and they certainly have not invested their money for the purpose of advancing political or social causes or in an enterprise engaged in the business of disseminating news and opinion. In fact, as discussed infra, the government has a strong interest in assuring that investment decisions are not predicated upon agreement or disagreement with the activities of corporations in the political arena.

Of course, it may be assumed that corporate investors are united by a desire to make money, for the value of their investment to increase. Since even communications which have no purpose other than that of enriching the communicator have some First Amendment protection, activities such as advertising and other communications integrally related to the operation of the corporation's business may be viewed as a means of furthering the desires of individual shareholders. This unanimity of purpose breaks down, however, when corporations make expenditures or undertake activities designed to influence the opinion or votes of the general public on political and social issues that have no material connection with or effect upon their business, property, or assets. Although it is arguable that corporations make such expenditures because their managers believe that it is in the corporations' economic interest to do so, there is no basis whatsoever for concluding that these views are expressive of the heterogeneous beliefs of their shareholders whose convictions on many political issues are undoubtedly shaped by considerations other than a desire to endorse any electoral or ideological cause which would tend to increase the value of a particular corporate investment. . . .

It bears emphasis here that the Massachusetts statute forbids the expenditure of corporate funds in connection with referenda but in no way forbids the board of directors of a corporation from formulating and making public what it represents as the views of the corporation even though the subject addressed has no material effect whatsoever on the business of the corporation. These views could be publicized at the individual expense of the officers, directors, stockholders, or anyone else interested in circulating the corporate view on matters irrelevent to its business.

The governmental interest in regulating corporate political communications, especially those relating to electoral matters, also raises considerations which differ significantly from those governing the regulation of individual speech. Corporations are artificial entities created by law for the purpose of furthering certain economic goals. In order to facilitate the achievement of such ends, special rules relating to such matters as limited liability, perpetual life, and the accumulation, distribution, and taxation of assets are normally applied to them. States have provided corporations with such attributes in order to increase their economic viability and thus strengthen the economy generally. It has long been recognized however, that the special status of corporations has placed them in a position to control vast amounts of economic power which may, if not regulated, dominate not only the economy but also the very heart of our democracy, the electoral process. Although *Buckley* v. *Valeo*, 424 U.S. at 1; 96 S. Ct. at 612; 46 L. Ed. 2d at 659 (1976), provides support for the position that the desire to equalize the financial resources available to candidates does not justify the limitation upon the expression of support which a restriction upon individual contributions entails, the interest of Massachusetts and the many other States which have restricted corporate political activity is quite different. It is not one of equalizing the resources of opposing positions, but rather of preventing institutions which have been permitted to amass wealth as a result of special advantages extended by the State for certain economic purposes from using that wealth to acquire an unfair advantage in the political process, especially where, as here, the issue involved has no material connection with the business of the corporation. The State need not permit its own creation to consume it. Massachusetts could permissibly conclude that not to impose limits upon the political activities of corporations would have placed it in a position of departing from neutrality and indirectly assisting the propagation of corporate views because of the advantages its laws give to the corporate acquisition of funds to finance such activities. Such expenditures may be viewed as seriously threatening the role of the First Amendment as a guarantor of a free marketplace of ideas. Ordinarily, the expenditure of funds to promote political causes may be assumed to bear some relation to the fervency with which they are held. Corporate political expression, however, is not only divorced from the convictions of individual corporate shareholders, but also, because of the ease with which corporations are permitted to accumulate capital, bears no relation to the conviction with which the ideas expressed are held by the communicator.

I would affirm the judgment of the Supreme Judicial Court for the Commonwealth of Massachusetts.

Mr. Justice Rehnquist, dissenting.

This Court decided at an early date, with neither argument nor discussion, that a business coporation is a "person" entitled to the protection of the Equal Protection Clause of the Fourteenth Amendment. *Santa Clara County* v. *Southern Pacific R. Co.*, 118 U.S. at 394, 396; 6 S. Ct. at 1132; 30 L. Ed. at 118 (1886). Likewise, it soon became accepted that the property of a corporation was protected under the Due Process Clause of that same Amendment. See, e.g., *Smyth* v. *Ames*, 169 U.S. at 466, 522; 18 S. Ct. at 418, 424; 42 L. Ed. at 819 (1898). Nevertheless, we concluded so thereafter that the liberty protected by that Amendment "is the liberty of natural, not artificial persons." *Northwestern Nat. Life Ins. Co.* v. *Riggs*, 203 U.S. at 243, 255; 27 S. Ct. at 126, 129; 51 L. Ed. at 168 (1906). Before today, our only considered and explicit departures from that holding have been that a corporation engaged in the business of publishing or broadcasting enjoys the same liberty of the press as in enjoyed by natural persons, *Grosjean* v. *American Press Co.*, 297 U.S. at 233, 244; 56 S. Ct. at 444, 446; 80 L. Ed. at 660 (1936), and that a nonprofit membership corporation organized for the purpose of "achieving . . . equality of treatment by all government, federal, state and local, for the members of the Negro community" enjoys certain liberties of political expression. *NAACP* v. *Button*, 371 U.S. at 415, 429; 83 S. Ct. at 328, 336; 9 L. Ed. 2d at 405 (1963).

The question presented today, whether business corporations have a constitutionally protected liberty to engage in political activities, has never been squarely addressed by a previous decision of this Court. However, the General Court of the Commonwealth of Massachusetts, the Congress of the United States, and the legislatures of 30 other States of this Republic have considered the matter, and have concluded that restrictions upon the political activity of business corporations are both politically desirable and constitutionally permissible. The judgment of such a broad consensus of governmental bodies expressed over a period of many decades is entitled to considerable deference from this Court. I think it quite probable that their judgment may be properly reconciled with our controlling precedents, but I am certain that under my views of the limited application of the First Amendment to the States, which I share with the two immediately preceding occupants of my seat on the Court, but not with my present colleagues, the judgment of the Supreme Judicial Court of Massachusetts should be affirmed.

Early in our history, Mr. Chief Justice Marshall described the status of a corporation in the eyes of federal law:

> A corporation is an artificial being, invisible, intangible, and existing only in contemplation of law. Being the mere creature of law, it possesses only those properties which the charter of creation confers upon it, either expressly, or as incidental to its very existence. There are such as are supposed best calculated to effect the object for which it was created. *Dartmouth College* v. *Woodward*, 4 Wheat 518, 636, 4 L. Ed. at 629 (1819).

The appellants herein either were created by the Commonwealth or were admitted into the Commonwealth only for the limited purposes described in their charters and regulated by state law. Since it cannot be disputed that the mere creation of a corporation does not invest it with all the liberties enjoyed by natural persons, *United States* v.

White, 322 U.S. at 694, 698-701; 64 S. Ct. at 1248, 1251-1252; 88 L. Ed. at 1542 (1944) (corporations do not enjoy the privilege against self-incrimination), our inquiry must seek to determine which constitutional protections are "incidental to its very existence." *Dartmouth College,* supra, 4 Wheat. at 636.

There can be little doubt that when a State creates a corporation with the power to acquire and utilize property, it necessarily and implicitly guarantees that the corporation will not be deprived of that property absent due process of law. Likewise, when a State charters a corporation for the purpose of publishing a newspaper, it necessarily assumes that the corporation is entitled to the liberty of the press essential to conduct of its business. Grosjean so held, and our subsequent cases have so assumed. Until recently, it was not thought that any persons, natural and artificial, had any protected right to engage in commercial speech. See *Virginia State Board of Pharmacy* v. *Virginia Citizens Consumer Council,* 425 U.S. at 748, 761-770; 96 S. Ct. at 1817, 1825-1829; 48 L. Ed. 2d at 346 (1976). Although the Court has never explicitly recognized a corporation's right of commercial speech, such a right might be considered necessarily incidental to the business of a commercial corporation.

It cannot be so readily concluded that the right of political expression is equally necessary to carry out the functions of a corporation organized for commercial purposes. A State grants to a business corporation the blessings perpetual life and limited liability to enhance its efficiency as an economic entity. It might reasonably be concluded that those properties, so beneficial in the economic sphere, pose special dangers in the political sphere. Furthermore, it might be argued that liberties of political expression are not at all necessary to effectuate the purposes for which States permit commercial corporations to exist. . . .

I can see no basis for concluding that the liberty of a corporation to engage in political activity with regard to matters having no material effect on its business is necessarily incidental to the purposes for which the Commonwealth permitted these corporations to be organized or admitted within its boundaries. Nor can I disagree with the Supreme Judicial Court's factual finding that no such effect has been shown by these appellants. Because the statute as construed provides at least as much protection as the Fourteenth Amendment requires, I believe it is constitutionally valid.

It is true, as the Court points out, that recent decisions of this Court have emphasized the interest of the public in receiving the information offered by the speaker seeking protection. The free flow of information is in no way diminished by the Commonwealth's decision to permit the operation of business corporations with limited rights of political expression. All natural persons, who owe their existence to a higher sovereign than the Commonwealth, remain as free as before to engage in political activity. Cf. *Maher* v. *Roe,* 432 U.S. at 464; 97 S. Ct. at 2376, 2382; 53 L. Ed. 2d at 484 (1977).

I would affirm the judgment of the Supreme Judicial Court.

CORPORATION CREDOS

1. Procter & Gamble

We will employ, throughout the Company, the best people we can find without regard to race or gender or any other differences unrelated to performance. We will promote on the same basis.

We recognize the vital importance of continuing employment because of its ultimate tie with the strength and success of our business.

We will build our organization from within. Those persons with ability and performance records will be given the opportunity to move ahead in the Company.

We will pay our employees fairly, with careful attention to the compensation of each individual. Our benefit programs will be designed to provide our employees with adequate protection in time of need.

We will encourage and reward individual innovation, personal initiative and leadership, and willingness to manage risk.

We will encourage teamwork across disciplines, divisions, and geography to get the most effective integration of the ideas and efforts of our people.

We will maximize the development of individuals through training and coaching on what they are doing well and how they can do better. We will evaluate Procter & Gamble managers on their record in developing their subordinates.

We will maintain and build our corporate tradition which is rooted in the principles of personal integrity: doing what's right for the long-term; respect for the individual; and being the best in what we do.

2. 3M

The first is the promotion of entrepreneurship and insistence upon freedom in the work place to pursue innovative ideas. Policies, practices and organizational structure have been flexible and characterized by mutual trust and cooperation.

Second is the adherence to uncompromising honesty and integrity. This is manifested in the commitment to the highest standards of ethics throughout the organization and in all aspects of 3M's operations.

Third is the preservation of individual identity in an organizational structure which embraces widely diverse businesses and operates in different political and economic systems throughout the world. From this endeavor there have developed an identifiable 3M spirit and a sense of belonging to the 3M family.

3. The Norton Company

Uncompromising ethical behavior.

We will uphold the highest ethical standards and act in a socially responsible manner toward all those whose lives we touch.

Quality in everything we do.
We will be relentless in our pursuit of total quality.

Focus on customers.
Our overriding commitment is to serve our customers. We will meet and exceed their expectations.

Commitment to continuous improvement.
We will make continuous improvement a way of life. We believe there is nothing we do that cannot be improved.

Discovering opportunities in change.
We believe the future is change. We will embrace new opportunities with a sense of urgency.

Teamwork.
We will respect and encourage each other as we work together—across functions, business and cultures—to make Norton an exceptional company.

APPENDIX C–2

CORPORATE CODES OF ETHICS

1. Dow Corning*

A. Dow Corning's Responsibilities to Employees:

All relations with employees will be guided by out belief that the dignity of the individual is primary.

Opportunity without bias will be afforded each employee in relation to demonstrated ability, initiative and potential.

Management practices will be consistent with our intent to provide continuing employment for all productive employees.

Qualified citizens of countries where we do business will be hired and trained for available positions consistent with their capabilities.

We will strive to create and maintain a work environment that fosters honesty, personal growth, teamwork, open communications and dedication to our vision and values.

We will provide a safe, clean and pleasant work environment that at minimum meets all applicable laws and regulations.

The privacy of an individual's records will be respected; employees may, however, review their own personnel records upon request.

B. Responsibilities of Dow Corning Employees

Employees will treat Dow Corning proprietary information as a valued asset and diligently protect it from loss or negligent disclosure.

*This is a selective list of Dow Corning's Codes.

Employees will respect our commitment to protect the confidentiality of information entrusted to us by customers, suppliers and others in our business dealings.

The proprietary information of others will be obtained only through the use of legal and ethical methods.

Employees will not engage in activities that either jeopardize or conflict with the company's interests. Recognizing and avoiding conflicts of interest is the responsibility of each employee. When a potential conflict of interest exists, the employee is obligated to bring the situation to the attention of Dow Corning management for resolution.

Employees will use or authorize company resources only for legitimate business purposes.

The cost of goods or services purchased for Dow Corning must be reasonable and in line with competitive standards.

Employees will not engage in bribery, price fixing, kickbacks, collusion or any related practice which might be, or give the appearance of being, illegal or unethical.

Employees will avoid contacts with competitors, suppliers, government agencies and other parties that are or appear to be engaging in unfair competition or the restriction of free trade.

Business interactions with our competitors will be limited to those necessary for buyer-seller agreements, licensing agreements, or matters of general interest to industry or society. All such interactions will be documented.

C. Relations with Customers, Distributors, Suppliers

We are committed to providing products and services that meet the requirements of our customers. We will provide information and support necessary to effectively use our products.

Business integrity is a criterion for selecting and retaining those who represent Dow Corning. Dow Corning will regularly encourage its distributors, agents, and other representatives to conduct their business on our behalf in a legal and ethical manner.

D. Social Responsibilities, Conservation, Environment, and Product Stewardship

We will be responsible for the impact of Dow Corning's technology upon the environment.

We will minimize the generation of waste materials from our operations to the extent economically and technically feasible. Reduction at the source and recycling will be vigorously pursued in all facilities. Non-recyclable waste will be disposed of in accordance with applicable standards.

New facilities will be designed and existing will be modified as necessary to optimize the efficient use of natural resources and to conserve energy.

We will continually strive to assure that our products and services are safe, efficacious and accurately represented in our selling and promotional activities.

Characteristics of Dow Corning raw materials, intermediates and products—including toxicity and potential hazards—will be made known to those who produce, package, transport, purchase, use and dispose of them.

The impact of Dow Corning operations and facilities on the communities where they are located—including hazards and the means employed to safeguard against them—will be made known to those who may be affected, including employees, contractors, local authorities and members of the community.

We will build and maintain positive relationships with communities where we have a presence. Our efforts will focus on education, civic, cultural and health and safety programs.

2. Phillips Petroleum

A. Comply with laws and regulations.

    i. All activities of the company shall be conducted in compliance with all applicable laws, regulations and judicial decrees of the United States (federal, state, and local) and of other countries where the company transacts business.

    ii. No employee should knowingly violate any law or regulation as a company representative.

    iii. Each employee must adhere to and comply with the overriding moral and ethical standards of society in the conduct of business.

B. Comply with Anti-trust and Trade Regulation

    i. The anti-trust laws and regulations shall be observed at all times by all employees of the company . . . price-fixing or bid-rigging acts or arrangements with competitors to divide or allocate markets or customers or exclude others from the market are prohibited.

C. Comply with election campaign law by prohibiting contributions in connection with electing political officials.

D. Except where permitted by law, all payments, gifts, or entertainment to government officials and other government personnel of the United States is prohibited. This restriction extends to other domestic jurisdictions, or to any foreign official. Any exchange of gifts which exceeds customary courtesies extended in accordance with accepted ethical business practices, regardless of motive, is prohibited.

E. There will be proper recording of assets, liabilities, and transactions. Policies are adopted to guide compliance with this code.

F. Conflicts of interest involving bribes, kickbacks or any compensation for work performed with other firms while conducting business for Phillips is not permitted. Any gift or entertainment which could be considered as creating obligations or influence a business decision is beyond the reasonable limit (of courtesy) and must be refused.

G. Employees are prohibited to release any information considered "inside" that may influence anyone to buy or sell the company's securities.

H. All personnel of the company who act as company representatives on the Boards of Directors of subsidiaries and affiliates must cast votes that exert the influence of these codes.

I. Officers and key employees will be required to execute periodic written reports and assurances (under oath if necessary) regarding their compliance with the principles of the code and their knowledge of those who do not employ those principles in their work for Phillips.

APPENDIX C–3

CORPORATE ETHICS COMMITTEES

1. Dow Corning

Dow Corning instituted an ethics program in the mid '70s in an attempt to integrate personal morals in the work place. It established its Business Conduct Committee (BCC) consisting of four experienced managers chosen by the company's CEO, charged with the following tasks:

> to learn more about how the company really operates outside this country;
>
> to draft guidelines that would be the basis for legal and ethical business behavior around the world;
>
> to develop a workable process for monitoring and reporting the company's business practices; and
>
> to recommend ways to correct questionable practices as they become known.[1]

The two means of implementing this charge are the code of conduct and "face-to-face" audits. The code covers a wide range of conduct; from internal responsibilities among employees to the relationships the corporation has with foreign countries. (See Appendix H–2.) The "face-to-face" audit personalizes the code. The Business Conduct Committee visits 18 to 20 Dow Corning sites around the world, working with local managers to identify problems and resolve them.[2] Over several years, employees' ethical concerns become central to business decisions. The audits encourage ethical issues to become visible and out in front . . . which makes it virtually impossible for employees to consciously make an unethical decision."[3]

2. The Norton Company*

The Norton Company Policy on Business Ethics begins with a reminder that business is not only an economic enterprise but "more importantly, an institution of people. As such, a business has moral standards and ethical responsibilities. . . ."[4] The guidelines in its policy are directed to those areas of corporate life that challenge the morality of the organization. Several are highlighted here:

Entertainment, Gifts, Favors, and Gratuities

They cannot be construed as intended to corrupt the judgment of the recipient so as to secure unfair preferential treatment.

---

*These are selections from extensive guidelines on areas of corporate conduct at Norton.

They are of such limited value that they could have no significant impact on the total financial operations of the company concerned or on the total income of the recipient.

Public disclosure would not be embarrassing to Norton or the recipient.

Financial Integrity

No undisclosed or unrecorded fund or asset of the Corporation or any subsidiary shall be maintained or established for any purpose.

No false or artificial entries shall be made on the books or records of the Corporation or its subsidiaries for any reason.

No payment on behalf of the Corporation shall be made or approved with the understanding that it will or might be used for something other than the stated purpose.

Use of Confidential Information

It is Company policy that we must not profit from confidential information obtained by us during the course of our duties on behalf of the Company. This policy and the law forbid, for example, the purchase or sale of Company securities by us, or by any others who learn the information from us, on the basis of information not generally available to the public. Company policy also forbids trading in securities of any other company about which we have learned confidential information in the course of our duties.

Relations with Employees

We affirm the principle of equal employment opportunity without regard to race, religion, national origin, sex, age, physical handicap or personal affiliation, and we practice and promote such policies in all locations as permissible under the law.

It is our intent that we be compensated in wages, salaries, and other benefits, in relation to our responsibilities, to our performance, to our service, and to the prevailing standards of the communities where we are located.

It is our practice to deal fairly and equitably with each employee, and, where unions exist, to negotiate openly with them through their elected or appointed representatives.

Relations with Shareholders

The Company is responsible for producing a fair return on the invested dollars of its shareholders.

The Company has an equal commitment to shareholders' equity. We must not only keep it secure, but we must manage our many businesses so as to keep the Company growing.

Relations with the Public

A company's role is to serve the needs of people. In the societies where we operate, businesses, as well as public and other private institutions, exist only through customer acceptance of their products and services, and public acceptance of their conduct. This implies several intangible but important obligations which we intend to live up to:

We recognize that a corporation has more than an economic existence these days. For example, Norton is part of many communities, and it is important that the Company behave as a good citizen in each of these locations.

When Norton operations have an adverse impact on the physical environment, we will continually strive to minimize any harmful effects so as to preserve the quality of the environment and conserve energy and natural resources.

We live in a political world, one that today tends to look with suspicion upon big business, its motives and its behavior. In this regard, it is important that Norton conduct itself so as to reflect well upon the business community as a whole, responding to reasonable public inquiries in a straightforward manner promptly, and providing the financial communities with accurate and timely performance data.

To assure that Norton's commitment to ethical conduct is practiced, managers have an "open-door" policy on questions of moral conflict. In addition, there are several programs that integrate the ethics policy into managing the business. These steps are as follows:

A Corporate Ethics Committee serves as the final authority with regard to our policy on business conduct and is responsible for specifying procedures to implement this follow-through program. This committee consists of the Chief Executive Officer and other designated members of management and the Board of Directors.

At least once a year, managers will review the Policy on Business Ethics with their employees to ensure that the policy is fully understood.

Managers will investigate any suspicion that unethical or illegal activities are taking place, or call upon the Director of Auditing for assistance.

Each corporate officer, divisional general manager, managing director, and corporate department head will sign a letter every year to be sent to the Chief Executive Officer on behalf of the Corporate Ethics Committee affirming a knowledge and understanding of Norton's Policy on Business Ethics and stating that within the past year:

He or she has reviewed the policy with subordinates.

He or she has investigated all cases of suspicious conduct.

He or she has reported significant violations of the policy to the Corporate Ethics Committee.

The Director of Auditing of the Company, and the Company's independent public accountants, will report immediately to the Corporate Ethics Committee any violations or suspected violations of this Policy on Business Ethics which come to their attention as a result of carrying out normal audits of the Company's accounts.

APPENDIX C–4

ETHICAL GUIDELINES IN THE PROFESSIONS

Principles of Medical Ethics of the American Medical Association

Preamble

These principles are intended to aid physicians individually and collectively in maintaining a high level of ethical conduct. They are not laws but standards by which a physician may determine the propriety of his conduct in his relationship with patients, with colleagues, with members of allied professions, and with the public.

Section 1

The principal objective of the medical profession is to render service to humanity with full respect for the dignity of man. Physicians should merit the confidence of patients entrusted to their care, rendering to each a full measure of service and devotion.

Section 2

Physicians should strive continually to improve their medical knowledge and skill, and should make available to their patients and colleagues the benefits of their professional attainments.

Section 3

A physician should practice a method of healing founded on a scientific basis; and he should not voluntarily associate professionally with anyone who violates this principle.

Section 4

The medical profession should safeguard the public and itself against physicians deficient in moral character or professional competence. Physicians should observe all laws, uphold the dignity and honor of the profession and accept its self-imposed disciplines. They should expose, without hesitation, illegal or unethical conduct of fellow members of the profession.

Section 5

A physician may choose whom he will serve. In an emergency, however, he should render service to the best of his ability. Having undertaken the care of a patient, he may not neglect him; and unless the patient has been discharged, he may discontinue his services only after giving adequate notice. He should not solicit patients.

Section 6

A physician should not dispose of his services under terms or conditions which tend to interfere with or impair the free and complete exercise of his medical judgment and skill, or tend to cause a deterioration of the quality of medical care.

Section 7

In the practice of medicine a physician should limit the source of his professional income to medical services actually rendered by him, or under his supervision, to his patients. His fee should be commensurate with the services rendered and the patient's ability to pay. He should neither pay nor receive a commission for referral of patients. Drugs, remedies, or appliances may be dispensed or supplied by the physician, provided it is in the best interests of the patient.

Section 8

A physician should seek consultation upon request; in doubtful or difficult cases, or whenever it appears that the quality of medical service may be enhanced thereby.

Section 9

A physician may not reveal the confidences entrusted to him in the course of medical attendance, or the deficiencies he may observe in the character of patients, unless he is required to do so by law, or unless it becomes necessary in order to protect the welfare of the individual or of the community.

Section 10

The honored ideals of the medical profession imply that the responsibilities of the physician extend not only to the individual, but also to society where these responsibilities deserve his interest and participation in activities which have the purpose of improving both the health and the well-being of the individual and the community.

Code of Ethics For Engineers

Preamble

Engineering is an important and learned profession. The members of the profession recognize that their work has a direct and vital impact on the quality of life for all people. Accordingly, the services provided by engineers require honesty, impartiality, fairness and equity, and must be dedicated to the protection of the public health, safety and welfare. In the practice of their profession, engineers must perform under a standard of professional behavior which requires adherence to the highest principles of ethical conduct on behalf of the public, clients, employers and the profession.

I. FUNDAMENTAL CANONS

Engineers, in the fulfillment of their professional duties, shall:

1. Hold paramount the safety, health and welfare of the public in the performance of their professional duties.
2. Perform services only in areas of their competence.
3. Issue public statements only in an objective and truthful manner.
4. Act in professional matters for each employer or client as faithful agents or trustees.
5. Avoid deceptive acts in the solicitation of professional employment.

II. RULES OF PRACTICE

1. Engineers shall hold paramount the safety, health, and welfare of the public in the performance of their professional duties.
2. Engineers shall perform services only in the areas of their competence.
3. Engineers shall issue public statements only in an objective and truthful manner.
4. Engineers shall act in professional matters for each employer or client as faithful agents or trustees.
5. Engineers shall avoid deceptive acts in the solicitation of professional employment.

III. PROFESSIONAL OBLIGATIONS

1. Engineers shall be guided in all their professional relations by the highest standards of integrity.
2. Engineers shall at all times strive to serve the public interest.
3. Engineers shall avoid all conduct or practice which is likely to discredit the profession or deceive the public.

4. Engineers shall not disclose confidential information concerning the business affairs or technical processes of any present or former client or employer without his consent.

5. Engineers shall not be influenced in their professional duties by conflicting interests.

6. Engineers shall uphold the principle of appropriate and adequate compensation for those engaged in engineering work.

7. Engineers shall not attempt to obtain employment or advancement or professional engagements by untruthfully criticizing other engineers, or by other improper or questionable methods.

8. Engineers shall not attempt to injure, maliciously or falsely, directly or indirectly, the professional reputation, prospects, practice, or employment of other engineers, nor untruthfully criticize other engineers' work. Engineers who believe others are guilty of unethical or illegal practices shall present such information to the proper authority for action.

9. Engineers shall accept responsibility for their professional activities; provided, however, that engineers may seek indemnification for professional services arising out of their practice for other than gross negligence, where the engineer's interests cannot otherwise be protected.

10. Engineers shall give credit for engineering work to those to whom credit is due, and will recognize the proprietary interests of others.

11. Engineers shall cooperate in extending the effectiveness of the profession by interchanging information and experience with other engineers and students, and will endeavor to provide opportunity for the professional development and advancement of engineers under their supervision.

Model Rules of Professional Conduct

The following are selected from the Model Rules of Professional Conduct of the American Bar Association:

A lawyer shall provide competent representation to a client. Competent representation requires the legal knowledge, skill, thoroughness, and preparation reasonably necessary for the representation.

A lawyer shall act with reasonable diligence and promptness in representing a client.

A lawyer has a duty to communicate information to the client.

(a) A lawyer shall keep a client reasonably informed about the status of a matter and promptly comply with reasonable requests for information.

(b) A lawyer shall explain a matter to the extent reasonably necessary to permit the client to make informed decisions regarding the representation.

A lawyer has a duty to maintain confidentiality.

(a) A lawyer shall not reveal information relating to representation of a client unless the client consents after consultation, except for disclosures that are impliedly authorized in order to carry out the representation, and except as stated in paragraph (b).

(b) A lawyer may reveal such information to the extent the lawyer reasonably believes necessary:

   (1) to prevent the client from committing a criminal or fraudulent act that the lawyer reasonably believes is likely to result in death or substantial bodily harm, or in substantial injury to the financial interests or property of another;

   (2) to rectify the consequences of a client's criminal or fraudulent act in the furtherance of which the lawyer's services had been used;

   (3) to establish a claim or defense on behalf of the lawyer in a controversy between the lawyer and the client, or to establish a defense to a criminal charge, civil claim or disciplinary complaint against the lawyer based upon conduct in which the client was involved; or

   (4) to comply with other law.

A lawyer has a duty to avoid a conflict of interest.

(a) A lawyer shall not represent a client if the representation of that client will be directly adverse to another client, unless:

   (1) the lawyer reasonably believes the representation will not adversely affect the relationship with the other client; and

   (2) each client consents after consultation.

(b) A lawyer shall not represent a client if the representation of that client may be materially limited by the lawyer's responsibilities to another client or to a third person, or by the lawyer's own interests, unless:

   (1) the lawyer reasonably believes the representation will not be adversely affected; and

   (2) the client consents after consultation. When representation of multiple clients in a single matter is undertaken, the consultation shall include explanation of the implications of the common representation and the advantages and risks involved.

A lawyer can choose to terminate a client.

(a) Except as stated in paragraph (c), a lawyer shall not represent a client or, where representation has commenced, shall withdraw from the representation of a client if:

   (1) the representation will result in violation of the rules of professional conduct or other law;

   (2) the lawyer's physical or mental condition materially impairs the lawyer's ability to represent the client; or

   (3) the lawyer is discharged.

(b) Except as stated in paragraph (c), a lawyer may withdraw from representing a client if withdrawal can be accomplished without material adverse effect on the interest of the client, or if:

   (1) the client persists in a course of action involving the lawyer's services that the lawyer reasonably believes is criminal or fraudulent;

   (2) the client fails substantially to fulfill an obligation to the lawyer regarding the lawyer's services and has been given reasonable warning that the lawyer will withdraw unless the obligation is fulfilled;

   (3) the representation will result in an unreasonable financial burden on the lawyer or has been rendered unreasonably difficult by the client; or

(4) other good cause for withdrawal exists.

(c) When ordered to do so by a tribunal, a lawyer shall continue representation notwithstanding good cause for terminating the representation.

(d) Upon termination of representation, a lawyer shall take steps to the extent reasonably practicable to protect a client's interests, such as giving reasonable notice to the client, allowing time for employment of other counsel, surrendering papers and property to which the client is entitled and refunding any advance payment of fee that has not been earned. The lawyer may retain papers relating to the client to the extent permitted by other law.

In representing a client, a lawyer shall exercise independent professional judgment and render candid advice. In rendering advice, a lawyer may refer not only to law but to other considerations such as moral, economic, social, and political factors, that may be relevant to the client's situation.

A lawyer shall not bring or defend a proceeding, or assert or controvert an issue therein, unless there is a basis for doing so that is not frivolous, which includes a good faith argument for an extension, modification or reversal of existing law. A lawyer for the defendant in a criminal proceeding, or the respondent in a proceeding that could result in incarceration, may nevertheless so defend the proceeding as to require that every element of the case be established.

A lawyer has a duty to be impartial.

A lawyer shall not:

(a) seek to influence a judge, juror, prospective juror or other official by means prohibited by law;

(b) communicate ex parte with such a person except as permitted by law; or

(c) engage in conduct intended to disrupt a tribunal.

Notes:

1. *Ethics: Resource Center Report,* Winter, 1986 Vol. Nov 1, p. 4.
2. *Ibid.,* p. 5.
3. *Ibid.,* p. 5.
4. "The Norton Policy on Business Ethics: The Norton Company of Worchester, MA, p. 1, 1990.

Civil Rights Act of 1964: Title VII

Discrimination Because of Race, Color, Religion, Sex, or National Origin

Sec. 703. (a) It shall be an unlawful employment practice for an employer:

(1) to fail or refuse to hire or to discharge any individual, or otherwise to discriminate against any individual with respect to his compensation, terms, conditions, or privileges of employment, because of such individual's race, color, religion, sex, or national origin; or

(2) to limit, segregate, or classify his employees in any way which would deprive or tend to deprive any individual of employment opportunities or otherwise adversely affect his status as an employee, because of such individual's race, color, religion, sex, or national origin.

(b) It shall be an unlawful employment practice for an employment agency to fail or refuse to refer for employment, or otherwise to discriminate against, any individual because of his race, color, religion, sex, or national origin, or to classify or refer for employment any individual on the basis of his race, color, religion, sex, or national origin.

(c) It shall be unlawful employment practice for a labor organization:

(1) to exclude or to expel from its membership, or otherwise to discriminate against, any individual because of his race, color, religion, sex, or national origin;

(2) to limit, segregate, or classify its membership, or to classify or fail to refuse to refer for employment any individual, in any way which would deprive or tend to deprive any individual of employment opportunities, or would limit such employment opportunities or otherwise adversely affect his status as an employee or as an applicant for employment, because of such individual's race, color, religion, sex, or national origin; or

(3) to cause or attempt to cause an employer to discriminate against an individual in violation of this section.[1]

APPENDIX D–2

Affirmative Action: Legal and Moral Status

The Supreme Court's decisions on affirmative action over the past 15 years do not reflect a consensus.

Two court decisions, however, indicate progress toward a standard to determine the changing subjects of affirmative action. *The United States* v. *Paradise and Johnson* v. *Transportation Agency* were decided by the Supreme Court a month apart in 1987.

In the *Paradise* case the Supreme Court decided in favor of a race-based preference for promotion. The Alabama State Police ignored several decrees that required them to improve racial representation in their ranks. Over a 12-year period, discriminatory practices remained unaltered. An involuntary affirmative action plan was ordered by the Court. It required promotion of one black for each white employee. The Court held that at least 50 percent of the promotions to corporal should be awarded to black troopers, if qualified candidates are available. In addition to this first guideline, the Court stated that "if the rank was less than 25 percent black and if they had not developed and implemented a promotion plan without adverse impact for the relevant rank, then blacks could be promoted to an equal representation." They also ordered the department within 30 days to submit a schedule for the development of promotion procedures for all ranks above entry-level.[2]

Justice Powell's separate concurring decision for use of involuntary affirmative action plans is important. He cites five factors that the Court considers in determining whether an affirmative action plan is appropriately tailored for the given circumstance:

1. the offering of alternative remedies

2. the planned duration of the remedy

3. the relationship between the percentage of minority group members in the relevant population or workforce

4. the availability of waiver provisions if a hiring plan could not be met

5. the effect of the remedy upon innocent third parties.[3]

The *Johnson* case challenged the compliance of a voluntary affirmative action plan with Title VII. In this case there were two candidates for a position, differing only by gender. Qualifications were in all relevant respects comparable. The woman was awarded the position based on her sex. The court, in finding in favor of the woman candidate, ruled that:

1. the underutilization of representative group members with a need skill could justify sex/race preference;

2. race or sex should not be the "sole" criterion in making a choice between candidates;

3. where goals can be used instead of quotas, flexibility is encouraged in the program.

These two decisions emphasize that the affirmative action plan adopted by an organization must be appropriate to its location and industry. The *Johnson* case demonstrated that "public employers must justify adoption and implementation of a voluntary affirmative action plan under the Equal Protection Clause" (of the Fourth Amendment).[4] In *Paradise* it was established that race preferences can be used to remedy past racial discriminations.

Notes

1. United States Code Vol. 1, p. 304, July 2, 1964.

2. 585 U.S. Supp 77.

3. p. 515 732 F Supp. 497 (Del. 1990).

4. McDowell, Douglas S. Affirmative Action: The Johnson Decision 1987. National Foundation for the Study of Employment Policy, Washington, DC. 1987.

APPENDIX E*

In order to encourage social responsibility in corporations conducting business in South Africa, the Reverend Leon Sullivan proposed a set of principles. Initially referred to as the Sullivan Principles these are now known as the Statement of Principles for South Africa. Consenting companies make a commitment, as part of their corporate plan, to eliminate apartheid. Companies then have signatory status that commits them to an annual evaluation on their progress toward equalizing conditions in South Africa.

APPENDIX E–1

Corporate Responsibility in South Africa: The Sullivan Principles

Principle 1—Nonsegregation of the races in all eating, comfort, locker room, and work facilities

Principle 2—Equal and fair employment practices for all employees

Principle 3—Equal pay for all employees doing equal or comparable work for the same period of time

Principle 4—Initiation and development of training programs that will prepare blacks, coloureds, and Asians in substantial numbers for supervisory, administrative, clerical, and technical jobs

Principle 5—Increasing the number of blacks, coloureds, and Asians in management and supervisory positions

Principle 6—Improving the quality of employees' lives outside the work environment in such areas as housing, transportation, schooling, recreation, and health facilities

Principle 7—Working to eliminate laws and customs that impede social, economic, and political justice

APPENDIX E–2

Requirements: Principles 1, 2, and 3

1. **Freedom of Association**
   The company supports the elimination of discrimination against the rights of blacks to form or belong to government-registered or unregistered unions; it acknowledges the right of black workers to form their own unions, or to be represented by trade unions where unions already exist.

2. **Benefits**
   All benefits available to whites are also available to other races, and the benefits for blacks, coloureds and Asians are at least equal to those for whites. In health care, the benefits must be technically equal, although the institutions providing the services may be administered separately.

*This material formerly was called "Fourth Amplification."

3. **Equal Pay**
   The company pays all employees equally for doing equal or comparable work for the same length of time.

4. **Minimum Pay**
   The company has an entry, base-pay level for all employees that is at least 30 percent greater than either:

   > The University of South Africa's (UNISA) Minimum Living Level (MLL) for a family of five, or

   > The University of Port Elizabeth's Household Subsistence Level (HSL) for a family of six.

   Companies operating in defined rural areas must pay at least the MLL or HSL and achieve the 30 percent premium within five years of their signing the Statement of Principles.

5. **Communication of Principles**
   The company ensures that all employees see the Statement of Principles in a language that they understand and become aware that the company is a Signatory.

6. **Communication of Rating**
   The company agrees to make its rating category in the Fourteenth Report known to all employees and to review the rating with representative groups of employees.

7. **Review**
   The company agrees to review the implementation of the Principles with representative groups of employees several times each year.

8. **Desegregation**
   All Signatories' facilities are available to all races.

9. **Uniform Medical Aid**
   If a company has a mandatory medical aid plan (health insurance) it must be mandatory for everyone. If a company has a non-mandatory plan, every employee must have the right to join.

10. **Review by Accounting Firm**
    All long-form reports provided by publicly held Signatories must be reviewed by an outside accounting firm(s) to verify the accuracy of the information provided in select numeric questions of the report.

    The requirement's primary purpose is to strengthen the overall credibility of the Principles' reporting effort by having outside entities verify the accuracy of select portions of the questionnaire information.

    Four items of information are required to be verified in the Fourteenth Report:

    > Total payroll;

    > Total employment;

    > Percent by which the lowest paid employee's pay exceeds the MLL/HSL; and

    > Total expenditures made for education, community development and social justice programs.

Accountants are not expected to make judgments about: (1) issues such as the extent of desegregation or equality of benefits; or (2) narrative information provided by Signatories on other qualitative issues.

APPENDIX E–3

Qualitative Criteria for Principles 4, 5, 6, and 7

Action Area	Criteria	Illustrative Programs
Education for Non-Employees	Number of bursaries and grants	Primary, secondary, technical, and university programs that benefit blacks, coloureds, and Asians
	Man day contributions	
	Breadth of employee involvement	South Africans
	Creativity and range of programs	Adopt-A-School Program
		Non-skilled training
	Extent to which Signatory has been able to encourage additional government support for schools it has adopted	Encouraging white schools to admit blacks, coloureds, and Asians
		Creation of parent/teacher associations
	Significance and impact of efforts	
Training and Advancement	Number of people trained	Apprenticeship programs
	Number of training days	Supervisory and managerial training
	Creativity and range of programs	Training for white supervisors to understand and support the Signatory's efforts to provide blacks, coloureds, and Asians advancement opportunities
	Number of blacks, coloureds, and Asians supervising whites and others	
Community Development	Man day contributions	Black, coloured, and Asian business assistance (purchases of goods and services, consulting services, etc.)
	Breadth of employee involvement	
	Creativity and range of programs	Deposits made to banks owned by blacks, coloureds, and Asians
	Significance and impact of efforts	
	Support and use of black, coloured, and Asian businesses	Housing assistance to purchase homes, obtain 99-year leases, or improve conditions of hostels for employees living away from home
	Housing assistance	
	Youth programs	Urban rights assistance

Social Justice	Man day contributions	Lobbying the South African government
	Breadth of employee involvement	Model projects
	Creativity and range of programs	Legal assistance
	Hierarchical distribution of employee efforts	Advocacy/communication
		Strengthening judicial independence
	Significance and impact of efforts	Development of black, coloured, and Asian leadership
	Coordination with blacks, coloureds, and Asians inside and outside the company	Supporting detainees and their families

APPENDIX E–4

The Sullivan Principles Reassessed

The Sullivan Principles are not without critics. Jennifer Davis, in an address[1] to the United Nations in April 1990, argued that apartheid rests on social conditions that the principles do not address. These are:

1. A total monopoly of land ownership;

2. A comprehensive system of control over the movement of all black people, and particularly black workers, in order that the State can channel labour as and when it is required in all sectors of the economy;

3. A political system which excludes blacks from participation in the central state and strips them of their South African citizenship, to be barricaded in the bantustans if they are without employment;

4. A highly repressive security system with virtually unchecked powers.[2]

According to Davis, the principles when fully implemented would employ 40,000 or only 0.01 percent of the black population of South Africa. "The highly capital-intensive character of almost all United States operations in South Africa means that they expand through technological improvement and not by expanding employment."[3]

Prestigious United States corporations which receive the highest rankings in the monitoring of the implementation of the Sullivan Principles contribute to the functioning and maintenance of apartheid in other ways, too. Both Ford ("making progress") and General Motors ("making good progress") supply motor vehicles to the apartheid police and military. For years the spectacle of Ford and General Motors trucks crammed full with pass offenders has been one of the common sights of apartheid South Africa. The extensive raids carried out against at least four neighboring countries by the South African army would have been impossible without Ford and General Motors products. Likewise, Goodyear ("making good progress") and Firestone ("making progress") sell tires to South African government agencies, while Caltex (Texaco), Mobil and Exxon ("making good progress") supply petroleum products that fuel South Africa's illegal occupation of Namibia and its aggression against its neighbors, and send the military and police armoured personnel carriers into the townships to shoot down protesters. . . . [4]

IBM and Control Data technology is used by the strategic South African parastatals which provide all electricity (ESCOM) and most steel (ISCOR) in South Africa. Honeywell has as its major South African clients, SASOL and ISCOR. A Control Data Cyber 170/750 computer with the potential capacity to break United States nuclear codes was sold to the State Council on Scientific and Industrial Research. It was revealed in 1979 that Control Data knowingly violated United States Commerce Department regulations by supplying certain parts to the South African police. But the Sullivan Principles reassure us that the company is "making good progress." Sperry computers are used by the parastatal that oversees SASOL, Pretoria's Atomic Energy Board, and a subsidiary of the State-owned armaments manufacturer, ARMSCOR. All of these computer companies are ranked amongst the highest categories in the monitoring reports on the implementation of the Sullivan Principles. [5]

Notes

1. Davis, Jennifer. "American Committee on Africa: Codes of conduct—aid and comfort for apartheid." Presented at United Nations Public Hearings, Vol. II, Spring 1990. 418.

2. *Ibid.*, 422.

3. *Ibid.*, 423.

4. *Ibid.*, 422.

5. *Ibid.*, 423.

Corporate Mergers and Takeovers: The Norton Case

In March 1990 a British conglomerate, BTR, PLC staged a hostile takeover of the Norton Company of Worcester, Massachusetts. The Norton Company, a maker of abrasives and ceramics, was experiencing a loss of sales during the 1980s. It had a positive global profile, employing 16,000 people worldwide. BTR thought that without their leadership, Norton's stock value would continue to fall. Eventually this would lead to a loss of employment and revenue in Worcester. BTR proposed a price of $75 per share or $1.64 billion dollars for the Norton Company. After the board of directors rejected this bid as inadequate, several defenses against the takeover were initiated by Norton. Each of these defense strategies offers insight into the complex maneuvering of a target corporation.

Fearful that BTR would have enough shares tendered by the annual shareholders' meeting to gain control of its board, Norton's first action was to push the meeting back two months. The later date for the meeting provided time for Norton to consider "third parties which have expressed interest in exploring possible strategic, minority investments in Norton."[1] These parties would increase the value of Norton's product without forcing a buy-out. Second, the Norton board created a poison-pill plan. They approved amendments to its shareholder rights plan that "dilute the holdings of any shareholder who acquires more than 10 percent of common stock by allowing the other shareholders to acquire new Norton stock at half price."[2] This move had the effect of diluting the holdings of the would-be takeover corporation.

Their third, and most effective, defense was one not commonly observed in takeover wars; government intervention. The Governor of Massachusetts, "Michael Dukakis signed into law a bill that tightens the state's anti-takeover laws by making it harder for raiders to win control of a company through a proxy fight."[3] This bill was passed with the intent to provide Norton more time and options. It kept BTR from quickly dominating Norton. More specifically, "(it) prohibits companies incorporated in the state from electing more than a third of their board members each year."[4]

Although the addition to the Massachusetts anti-takeover laws would limit BTR representation on the board, BTR was relentless. The president of BTR, John C. Cahill vowed that his few representatives would "make life miserable for board members."[5]

Norton further expressed its fears about the hostile takeover in Washington. "Norton's specialized skills in advanced technology—many with defense applications —should not pass into foreign hands," the company counseled. More than 100 legislators agreed, sending President Bush a letter urging that "a hard look be taken before a sale is allowed."[6] Congress was, in effect, requesting that the Exon-Florio Amendment be used to stop BTR's bid. The Exon-Florio Amendment permits presidential intervention in the sale of a company when there is imminent foreign threat to U.S. security. Before the president acted, however, Norton accepted another company's offer. Sain-Gobain, a French corporation, offered Norton $90 a share.

Notes

1. *Wall Street Journal* 30 March 1990.
2. *New York Times* 19 April 1990: D2, Col. 1.

3. *Washington Post* 2 May 1990: G3, Col. 1.

4. *Ibid.,* D2, Col 2.

5. *Ibid.,* D2, Col 2.

6. *Washington Post* 2 May 1990: G3, Col 1.

Evaluation of Corporate Social Responsibility

One tool that some corporations use for assessing their efforts to be socially responsible is the social audit.[1] Since the classifications of outgoing expenditure in social activities is not directly related to the substance of the product, but rather to the quality of its production, a social audit requires a novel appraising device. The evaluation tool presented below is one that an eastern corporation used to determine its progress in social responsibility issues. The worksheet is designed to cover all areas in which the company had programs. In each of these a continuum is drawn showing degrees of progress in responding to a particular social issue.

0	20	40	60	80	100
Little effort to hire the hard-core unemployed.	Some effort to hire the hard-core unemployed; occasionally employment ads directed at this objective.	Fairly active campaign to hire the hard-core unemployed; advertising and personal recruiting used.	Very active efforts designed toward hiring the hard-core unemployed, including close cooperation with local community employment.	Vigorous program designed to both hire and maintain the hard-core unemployed. Some members of the staff work on this program on a full-time basis.	

0	20	40	60	80	100
Most ecological efforts are directed toward fighting implementation of current ecological legislation.	Some attempts to fight present legislation; minimum attempts to clean up operations.	General adherence to ecological legislation; operations meet all legislative requirements.	In addition to meeting all ecological requirements, some attention is focused on working with legislative groups in providing information useful in drafting future laws or modifying current ones.	All ecological legislative requirements are met; company is working closely with legislative groups to provide substantive input for any future legislation.	

0	20	40	60	80	100
Advertising is designed only to sell the product.	Advertising staff to eliminate any misleading comments or implications.	Advertising is reviewed by nonadvertising personnel in an effort to eliminate any misleading information.	Advertising is tested in a local market to work out any "bugs" before being transmitted to the general public.	Advertising is as complete and factual as possible; all charges of misleading advertising by the public are reviewed and acted upon within the earliest possible time period.	

Notes

1. This social evaluation tool was adapted from *Social Issues in Business* by Richard M. Hodgetts, Fred Luthans, and Kenneth Thompson. New York: Macmillan, 1980. 508-509.

Multinational Corporations and Third World Nations: The Nestlé Case

In the early 1970s the infant-formula industry was criticized for its marketing strategies in Third World countries. Although several companies were involved (Abbott Laboratories, Wyeth Laboratories, Borden, and Bristol-Myers) the focus was on Nestlé because it controlled 50 percent of the market. Nestlé has an established reputation for high-quality products and genuine concern for customer satisfaction. This image was in stark contrast to the accusation that they were deliberately marketing a harmful product in the Third World.

Included in Nestlé's promotional techniques for the formula were ads that graphically demonstrated how breast-fed infants are inferior next to those that are formula-fed. Pictures of undernourished, and malcontented breast-fed infants were displayed adjacent to smiling, full-faced formula-fed babies. The sales campaign appealed to the maternal instincts of women. They were offered free samples of the formula, which they often mixed with impure water because the importance of using boiled water was not stressed. As the child was weaned onto the formula, the mothers ceased lactating, leaving, in effect, no option but the formula for nourishment. One Nestlé advertisement read, "When mother's milk is not enough, baby needs a special milk . . . Lactogen Full Protein."

The free samples were dispensed by "mothercraft nurses," women hired by Nestlé, who dressed in hospital nursing uniforms and instructed potential customers on the use and nutritional benefits of the product. Hospitals, however, did not endorse the product.

Doug Clement, Coordinator of the National Infant Formula Action Coalition, claims that 25 percent of the formula-fed babies had to be treated for gastroenteritis. "In 13 Latin American countries in 1972, a study conducted by the Pan American Health Organization found that whereas diarrheal diseases were responsible for roughly 52 percent of the deaths of bottle-fed infants, they accounted for only 32 percent of the deaths of breast-fed infants."[1] Also in 1972 the Protein Calorie Advisory Group (PCAG) of the United Nations, comprised of health professionals, scholars, researchers, and government officials, emphasized the value of "breast feeding under socio-economic conditions that prevail in many developing countries." Among their conclusions was a mandate for infant-formula industries to modify their marketing techniques. Bottle-feeding in the PCAG's report was portrayed as nutritionally inferior to breast-feeding, but some members of PCAG argued that the United Nations mandate was not strong enough to prevent disease and malnutrition, resulting from bottle-formula feeding.

The Interfaith Center on Corporate Responsibility (ICCR) spearheaded a seven-year boycott of Nestlé products. Nestlé was brought to trial in 1974 for negligence in selling a product that contributed to the death of many infants. No causal link was established between its sales of baby formula and the deaths of infants. The court, however, admonished Nestlé with regard to its manipulative marketing of baby formula.

In 1981 the member states of the World Health Organization developed an International Code of Marketing of Breast-Milk Substitutes. Their code is designed to bring an end to the questionable advertising campaign conducted by Nestlé and other

MNCs. The WHO code, some have argued, curtails economic benefits to lesser developed countries. In a well-documented book entitled *Out of the Mouths of Babes*, the scientific and moral justifications of WHO came under scrutiny. Author Fred D. Miller provides several examples that suggest that there is no causal link between bottle-feeding and increases in infant mortality.

Miller's study cautions that breast-feeding is not a panacea for infant mortality in the Third World. The health conditions of many mothers in the Third World militate against the survival of the infant whether or not the child is fed the formula. Often, the mother's milk is not in sufficient supply to meet the infant's dietary demands or it is a disease carrier. Miller's study shows that the cause of infant deaths in the Third World nations is complex; to attribute it solely to bottle-feeding is to oversimplify the problem.

The *Washington Post* reported in November 1982 that "the data linking formula marketing and infant mortality turns out to be sketchy at best. . . . Nor is there hard evidence of a major decline in breast-feeding among poor women in most underdeveloped countries."[2]

APPENDIX H–2

Constitution of the World Health Organization

The States Parties to this Constitution declare, in conformity with the Charter of the United Nations, that the following principles are basic to the happiness, harmonious relations and security of all people:

> Health is a state of complete physical, mental and social well-being and not merely the absence of disease or infirmity.

> The enjoyment of the highest attainable standard of health is one of the fundamental rights of every human being without distinction of race, religion, political belief, economic or social condition.

> The health of all peoples is fundamental to the attainment of peace and security and is dependent upon the fullest cooperation of individuals and States.

> The achievement of any State in the promotion and protection of health is of value to all.

> Unequal development in different countries in the promotion of health and control of disease is a common danger.

> Healthy development of the child is of basic importance; the ability to live harmoniously in a changing total environment is essential to such development.

> The extension to all peoples of the benefits of medical, psychological and related knowledge is essential to the fullest attainment of health.

> Informed opinion and active cooperation on the part of the public are of the utmost importance in the improvement of the health of the people.

> Governments have a responsibility for the health of their peoples which can be fulfilled only by the provision of adequate health and social measures.

> Accepting these principles, and for the purpose of cooperation among themselves

and with others to promote and protect the health of all peoples, the Contracting Parties agree to the present Constitution and hereby establish the World Health Organization as a specialized agency within the terms of Article 57 of the Charter of the United Nations.

Notes

1. Clement, Doug. "Infant Formula Malnutrition: Threat to the Third World," in Maureen Ford and Lisa Newton. *Taking Sides*. Guilford, CT: The Dushkin Publishing Group, Inc., 1990. 152.
2. *Washington Post* 5 Nov. 1982: A14, Col. 1.

Proposed Draft of a United Nations Code of Conduct for Multinational Corporations

Preamble

The General Assembly,

Recalling Economic and Social Council resolutions 1908 (ILVII) of 2 August 1974 and 1913 (LVII) of 5 December 1974, establishing a Commission on Transnational Corporations and the United Nations Centre on Transnational Corporations with the mandate, as their highest priority of work, of concluding a Code of Conduct on Transnational Corporations,

Convinced that a universally accepted, comprehensive, and effective Code of Conduct on Transnational Corporations is an essential element in the strengthening of international economic and social cooperation and, in particular, in achieving one of the main objectives in that cooperation, namely, to minimize the negative effects of the activities of these corporations,

Decides to adopt the following Code of Conduct for Transnational Corporations:

Definitions and Scope of Application

(a) This Code is universally applicable to enterprises, irrespective of their country of origin and their ownership, including private, public or mixed, comprising entities in two or more countries, regardless of the legal form and fields of activity of these entities, which operate under a system of decision-making, permitting coherent policies and a common strategy through one or more decision-making centres, in which the entities are so linked, by ownership or otherwise, that one or more of them may be able to exercise a significant influence over the activities of others and, in particular, to share knowledge, resources and responsibilities with the others. Such enterprises are referred to in this Code as transnational corporations.

(b) The term "entities" in the Code refers to both parent entities—that is, entities which are the main source of influence over others—and other entities, unless otherwise specified in the Code.

(c) The term "transnational corporation" in the Code refers to the enterprise as a whole or its various entities.

(d) The term "home country" means the country in which the parent entity is located. The term "host country" means a country other than the home country in which an entity other than the parent entity is located.

(e) The term "country in which a transnational corporation operates" refers to a home or host country in which an entity of a transnational corporation conducts operations.

For the application of this Code, it is irrelevant whether or not enterprises as described in paragraph 1(a) above are referred to in any country as transnational corporations.

The Code is universally applicable in all States, regardless of their political and economic systems or their level of development.

The provisions of the Code addressed to transnational corporations reflect good practice for all enterprises. Subject to the provisions of paragraph 52, wherever the provisions of the Code are relevant to both, transnational corporations and domestic enterprises shall be subject to the same expectations with regard to their conduct.

Subject to the relevant constitutions, charters or other fundamental laws of the regional groups of States concerned, any reference in this Code of States, countries or Governments, also includes regional groupings of States, to the extent that the provisions of this Code relate to matters within these groupings' own competence, with respect to such competence.

Activities of Multinational Corporations

A. **General cooperation with Governments for the review or renegotiation of such contract or agreement.**

Adherence to socio-cultural objectives and values

Transnational corporations should respect the social and cultural objectives, values, and traditions of the countries in which they operate. While economic and technological development is normally accompanied by social change, transnational corporations should avoid practices, products, or services which cause detrimental effects on cultural patterns and socio-cultural objectives as determined by Governments. For this purpose, transnational corporations should respond positively to requests for consultations from Governments concerned.

Respect for human rights and fundamental freedoms

Transnational corporations shall respect human rights and fundamental freedoms in the countries in which they operate. In their social and industrial relations, transnational corporations shall not discriminate on the basis of race, colour, sex, religion, language, social, national and ethnic origin, or political or other opinion. Transnational corporations shall conform to government policies designed to extend equality of opportunity and treatment.

Non-collaboration by transnational corporations with racist minority regimes in Southern Africa

In accordance with the efforts of the international community towards the elimination of apartheid in South Africa and its continued illegal occupation of Namibia,

    (a) Transnational corporations shall refrain from operations and activities supporting and sustaining the racist minority regime of South Africa maintaining the system of apartheid and the illegal occupation of Namibia;

    (b) Transnational corporations shall engage in appropriate activities within their competence with a view to eliminating racial discrimination and all other aspects of the system of apartheid;

    (c) Transnational corporations shall comply strictly with obligations resulting from Security Council decisions and shall fully respect those resulting from all relevant United Nations resolutions;

    (d) With regard to investment in Namibia, transnational corporations shall comply strictly with obligations resulting from Security Council resolution 283

(1970) and other relevant Security Council decisions and shall fully respect those resulting from all relevant United Nations resolutions.

Non-interference in internal affairs of host countries

Transnational corporations shall not interfere in the internal affairs of host countries, without prejudice to their participation in activities that are permitted by the laws, regulations or established administrative practices of host countries.

Transnational corporations shall not engage in activities of a political nature which are not permitted by the laws and established policies and administrative practices of the countries in which they operate.

Abstention from corrupt practices

(a) Transnational corporations shall refrain, in their transactions, from the offering, promising or giving of any payment, gift, or other advantage to or for the benefit of a public official as consideration for performing or refraining from the performance of his duties in connection with those transactions.

(b) Transnational corporations shall maintain accurate records of any payments made by them to any public official or intermediary. They shall make available these records to the competent authorities of the countries in which they operate, upon request, for investigations and proceedings concerning those payments.

B. Economic, financial, and social

Ownership and control

Transnational corporations should make every effort so to allocate their decision-making powers among their entities as to enable them to contribute to the economic and social development of the countries in which they operate.

Transnational corporations should cooperate with Governments and nationals of the countries in which they operate in the implementation of national objectives for local equity participation and for the effective exercise of control by local partners as determined by equity, contractual terms in non-equity arrangements, or the laws of such countries.

Transnational corporations should carry out their personnel policies in accordance with the national policies of each of the countries in which they operate which give priority to the employment and promotion of its nationals at all levels of management and direction of the affairs of each entity so as to enhance the effective participation of its nationals in the decision-making process.

Employment conditions and industrial relations

For the purposes of this Code, the principles set out in the Tripartite Declaration of Principles concerning Multinational Enterprises and Social Policy, adopted by the Governing Body of the International Labour Office, should apply in the field of employment, training, conditions of work and life, and industrial relations.

Consumer protection

Transnational corporations shall carry out their operations, in particular production and marketing, in accordance with national laws, regulations, administrative practices and policies concerning consumer protection of the countries in which they operate. Transnational corporations shall also perform their activities with due regard to relevant international standards, so that they do not cause injury to the health or endanger the safety of consumers or bring about variations in the quality of products in each market which would have detrimental effects on consumers.

Transnational corporations shall, in respect of the products and services which they produce or market or propose to produce or market in any country, supply to the competent authorities of that country on request or on a regular basis, as specified by these authorities, all relevant information concerning:

> Characteristics of these products or services which may be injurious to the health and safety of consumers, including experimental uses and related aspects;

> Prohibitions, restrictions, warnings and other public regulatory measures imposed in other countries on grounds of health and safety protection on these products or services.

Transnational corporations should disclose to the public in the countries in which they operate all appropriate information on the contents and, to the extent known, on possible hazardous effects of the products they produce or market in the countries concerned by means of proper labeling, informative and accurate advertising, or other appropriate methods. Packaging of their products should be safe, and the contents of the product should not be misrepresented.

Transnational corporations should be responsive to requests from Governments of the countries in which they operate and be prepared to cooperate with international organizations in their efforts to develop and promote national and international standards for the protection of the health and safety of consumers and to meet the basic needs of consumers.

Environmental protection

Transnational corporations shall carry out their activities in accordance with national laws, regulations, established administrative practices and policies relating to the preservation of the environment of the countries in which they operate and with due regard to relevant international standards. Transnational corporations should, in performing their activities, take steps to protect the environment and, where damaged, to rehabilitate it, and should make efforts to develop and apply adequate technologies for this purpose.

Transnational corporations shall, in respect of the products, processes and services they have introduced or propose to introduce in any country, supply to the competent authorities of that country on request or on a regular basis, as specified by these authorities, all relevant information concerning:

> Characteristics of these products, processes, and other activities including experimental uses and related aspects which may harm the environment and the measures and costs necessary to avoid or at least to mitigate their harmful effects;

> Prohibitions, restrictions, warnings, and other public regulatory measures imposed in other countries on grounds of protection of the environment on these products, processes, and services.

Transnational corporations should be responsive to requests from Governments of the countries in which they operate and be prepared where appropriate to cooperate with international organizations in their efforts to develop and promote national and international standards for the protection of the environment.

Acknowledgments

For permission to reprint copyrighted material, the publisher is grateful to:

Code of Ethics—Reprinted by permission of Dow Corning Corporation.

Fisse/French—"Corporate Regulation: The Place of Social Responsibility." Reprinted by permission of Trinity University Press.

IBM Organizational Chart. By permission of International Business Machines Corporation.

Arthur D. Little—"Fourteenth Report on the Signatory Companies to the Statement of Principles for South Africa." Reprinted by permission of Arthur D. Little, Inc.

Lorsch/MacIver—"Pawns or Potentates: The Reality of America's Boards." From Jay W. Lorsch (with Elizabeth MacIver), PAWNS OR POTENTATES: THE REALITY OF AMERICA'S CORPORATE BOARDS. Boston: Harvard Business School Press, 1989.

Luthans/Hodgetts—SOCIAL ISSUES IN BUSINESS 3/E. Reprinted by permission of Macmillan Publishing Company from SOCIAL ISSUES IN BUSINESS 3/E by Fred Luthans and Richard M. Hodgetts. Copyright © 1980 by Macmillan Publishing Company.

Murphy—"Implementing Business Ethics." Reprinted from "Creating Ethical Corporate Structures" by Patrick Murphy, *Sloan Management Review*, (Winter 1989), p. 81-87, by permission of the publisher. Copyright 1989 by the Sloan Management Review Association. All rights reserved.

Murphy—"Implementing Business Ethics"; *Journal of Business Ethics*, Vol. VII, 1988, p. 907-915. Reprinted by permission of Kluwer Academic Publishers.

Nesteruk—"Corporations, Shareholders, and Moral Choice." Reprinted by permission of *University of Cincinnati Law Review*.

Smithburg—"An Ethical Approach to Tough Decisions in Today's Competitive Environment." Reprinted by permission of the Center for Ethics and Corporate Policy.

Wald—"Exxon Head Seeks Environmentalist to Serve on Board" Copyright 1989 by The New York Times Company. Reprinted by permission.

Wright—"Human Values in Health Care." Wright, HUMAN VALUES IN HEALTH CARE: THE PRACTICE OF ETHICS, copyright 1987, pages 284-286, 287. Reprinted by permission of McGraw-Hill, Inc.

Proposed draft of United Nations Code of Conduct for Multinational Corporations—Reprinted by permission of the United Nations.

Index

Affirmative action, 57–59, 154
Agent for shareholders, 40–43
American Bar Association, 151–153
American Medical Association, 148–150
Aristotle, 14
Austin v. Michigan Chamber of Commerce, 87
Autonomous professionals, 40–43

Berle and Means, 27–28
Black box theory, 31–32
Business judgment rule, 21, 28
Buzby, G.C., 21, 22

Changing shareholder roles, 70–72
Civil Rights Act of 1964, 57, 154
Code of Conduct of Transnational Corporations, 168–172
Constitution (of the United States), 82, 110–111
Corporate
  codes, 56, 143–146
  conduct, 101–106
  credos, 54, 142–143
  ethics programs, 55, 146–148
  First Amendment Rights, 46–48, 86–87, 135–141
  intentionality, 16–17, 20
  Internal Decision Structures (CID Structures), 17, 18, 19, 20, 21, 44–45, 68–70
  legal model, 14, 26–27
  liability, 35–36
  mergers, 161–162
  non-programmed decisions, 23
  organizational flow charts, 125–126
  policies, 17, 20, 21, 22

political action committees, 84–86, 135–141
political participation, 81–87, 135–141
  reasons, 19
  regulatory law, 96–99
  relationship to government, 82–84
  tort law, 92–96
  work environment, 50–53
Corporations
  as legal fiction, 14, 45–46
  as property, 43

Dahl, Robert, 88–89
Davis, Michael, 60
Dayton Hudson Corporation, 80
Democratic theory, 110–112, 119–122
Deregulation, 97
Discrimination, 154
Dow Corning, 143–145, 146

Eastern Airlines, 61–62
Environmental quality, 117–119
Ethical mutual funds, 77–78
Ethics
  engineering, 150–151
  legal, 151–153
  medical, 148–150

Federal Election Campaign Act, 86
Fiduciary duty, 28
Finance corporatism, 40
Fifth Amendment, 130, 132, 134, 135
First National Bank of Boston v. Bellotti, 46–48, 86–87, 135–141
Foreign Corrupt Practices Act, 115–116
Fourteenth Amendment, 128–133
Fourth Amendment, 131, 133, 134, 135, 155

Globalization, 112–114

Institutional shareholders, 40, 74–77
Interventionism, 32

Japan, 113–114

Lipton, Martin, 75
Lorsch, Jay W., 66–68

MacIver, Elizabeth, 66–68
MacPherson v. Buick Motor Company,
    92–93, 94
Madison, James, 85, 99, 111
Minnesota Mining and Manufacturing
    Company (3M), 142
Mobs, 14
Moral community membership, 14
Multinational corporations, 112–115,
    165–172
Murphy, Patrick E., 53–56

Nestlé, 165
Normative realm, 25–26
Norton Company, 142–143, 146–148,
    161

Outside directorships, 106

Phillips Petroleum, 145–146
Pluralism, 82, 111
Principle of contribution, 88
Procter and Gamble, 142–143
Public directorships, 40–43, 105–106
Punishment (of corporations), 103–106

Reagan administration, 58, 97
Richmond v. Corson, 58
Rules and roles, 29–30

Shareholder democracy, 27
Sherman Act, 131
Smithburg, William D., 41–43
Social audit, 61, 105, 163–164
Stone, Christopher, 32–34, 37–38, 97,
    99, 106
Storming, 62
Sullivan Principles, 156–160

Ultra vires, 28
U.S. v. Allied Chemical Corporation,
    104

Workers' participation, 89–91
World Health Organization (WHO),
    165, 166–167
Whistle-blowing, 59–61